NO-COLLAR

ALSO BY ANDREW ROSS

The Celebration Chronicles:
Life, Liberty, and the Pursuit of Property Value in Disney's New Town

Real Love:
In Pursuit of Cultural Justice

The Chicago Gangster Theory of Life:
Nature's Debt to Society

Strange Weather:
Culture, Science, and Technology in the Age of Limits

No Respect:
Intellectuals and Popular Culture

The Failure of Modernism:
Symptoms of American Poetry

No Sweat: Fashion, Free Trade, and
the Rights of Garment Workers (Editor)

Science Wars (Editor)

Microphone Fiends:
Youth Music and Youth Culture (Coeditor with T. Rose)

Technoculture (Coeditor with C. Penley)

Universal Abandon? (Editor)

NO-COLLAR

The Humane Workplace
and Its Hidden Costs

Andrew Ross

A Member of the Perseus Books Group

Library of Congress Cataloging-in-Publication Data
Ross, Andrew, 1956–
   No-collar : the humane workplace and its hidden costs /
Andrew Ross.
      p.   cm.
   Includes bibliographical references and index.
   ISBN 0-465-07144-9
   1. Organizational change—United States.   2. Downsizing
of organizations—United States.   3. Employee loyalty—
United States.   4. Work environment—United States.
5. Quality of work life—United States.   6. Job satisfaction—
United States.   I. Title.
HD58.8 .R674   2003
306.3'6—dc21

                                                        2002010702

03 04 05 / 10 9 8 7 6 5 4 3 2 1

CONTENTS

ACKNOWLEDGMENTS

The core of *No-Collar* draws on my study of two new media companies. Both gave me full access to their workplace and their employees. For my time at Razorfish, where I spent sixteen months, I am particularly grateful to Corinna Snyder, Adam Lichstein, Alex Snell, Shel Kimen, Stephen Turbek, Camille Habacher, and Oz Lubling. For my six months with 360hiphop, I am especially grateful to Mark Hines, Selwyn Hinds, Sheena Lester, and Jon Caramanica. Hundreds of employees at these companies and others in the new media industry gave me generous amounts of interview time. Their stories and opinions are the basis of my account of their workplaces. Many of their names have been altered to safeguard their privacy.

Other sources of ideas, advice, and kindness include Steve Bodzin, Marisa Bowe, Ted Byfield, Heather Champ, Steve Cisler, Mark Dery, Maggie Gray, Derek Fray, Rachel Greene, Doug Henwood, Geert Lovink, Emily Martin, Toby Miller, Alondra Nelson, Leo Panitch, Ronald Ross, Vivien Selbo, Tiziana Terranova, Mark Tribe, McKenzie Wark, and my colleagues and students at NYU's American Studies Program.

A Guggenheim Fellowship allowed me to take time off and finish the book, but I could not have done so without research help from Alison Redick, Michael Palm, Lisa Knauer, Christina Hanhardt, and Luke Harrison. The Graduate School of Arts and Sciences at New York University also provided some assistance for research.

Liz Maguire, my editor at Basic Books, and Jennifer Swearingen, my copyeditor, shepherded the manuscript with great care. Elyse Cheney, my agent, was a tireless and thoughtful advocate of the project as a whole.

My partner, Maggie Gray, was the book's best friend and my best dream.

Our daughter Zola was born four days after this book was completed, just as if she were the next chapter. In reality, she is the living proof of sweetness and light.

Jobs in Candyland: An Introduction

It is not work that men object to, but the element of drudgery. We must drive out drudgery, whenever we find it. We shall never be wholly civilized until we remove the treadmill from the daily job.

—HENRY FORD, *MY LIFE AND WORK*

GOOD JOBS DON'T FALL FROM THE SKY. NOR, IF THEY DID, WOULD we know what to make of them. Like the aliens who visited us in Cold War science fiction films, they might well be regarded as threats to our way of life. A good job is neither a product of nature nor an extraterrestrial life-form. It is one of the most highly crafted of human inventions, and at times, it seems as if all of history's hardest knocks and sweetest yearnings have gone into its making. Think of all the lives given up or ground down in the long struggle against slavery and indenture and then, once labor was free, how much more strife was needed simply to secure decent, safe conditions for factory workers. Then consider how close to the bone of drudgery the chores of white-collar routine had to be stripped before management gurus decided that office work needed a human touch. In fact, for most people, the right to enjoy humane work has been more difficult to attain than the right to vote, even though they are given equal billing in the United Nations' Universal Declaration of Human Rights.[1]

But what is the point of our never-ending search for work that is both satisfying and well rewarded? After all, for the vast majority, the gospel of work has always been viewed as a wily scheme, cooked up to motivate us to do unpleasant tasks. "If work really were such a good thing, then the rich would surely have found a way to keep it for themselves." Who could dispute the force of that pithy Haitian proverb? Yet we also know how important it has been for people to view their toil as worthy in and of itself and to believe that, one day, it might even add up to something of worth to others. The early Marx, who touted the dignity of labor as much as he deplored its exploitation, declared that man is "free only" when he "recognizes himself in a world he has himself created."[2]

Marx's phrasing was tailored to the producer society in which he lived, where most people still made or grew things. In today's high-wage countries that is no longer the case, and in our therapy culture there are many kinds of self-recognition that he might have deemed unworthy of interest. Although Marx had something more ambitious in mind than simply the creation of good jobs, the gist of his observation might easily be adapted to the toil of our times. In order to earn a livelihood, we are compelled to work hard at things that are beyond ourselves. If the effort and the product of that effort make us more human, if we feel like the owners psychologically, if not materially, of the product, and if enough of our coworkers feel the same way, then we are on to something quite rare, at least in a for-profit economy— so rare, in fact, that we can ill afford to dismiss any encouraging evidence that comes down the pike.

Inspired by curiosity, this book is a report about the New Economy workplaces that begged for attention in the last years of the twentieth century. Uncommonly flattering claims were made on their behalf. Against all the odds, and underneath all the hype, they appeared to be making a step in the right direction: They offered jobs to write home about. Yet the economic soil that hosted them is the unstable geology of our times and it was prone to move under their feet. Their nascent industry and the skills it bred would not be left to mature in peace. These workplaces quickly mutated under the shape-shifting pressure of modern capitalism, proving to be a fast-moving study for the prospective investigator.

Named to reflect the nonconformist spirit of their work mentality, *No-Collar* documents the quixotic life of these workplaces, concentrating on new media companies in New York's Silicon Alley. Most commentators on this sector have focused on the new technologies or on the whizzbang New Economy with which they were associated. By contrast, my book is about how the employees themselves judged their workplaces. I had been a Silicon Alley–watcher for several years, so I had my own theories (some of them in print) about whether the industry's version of work was a true kernel of hope or just another con game. But I had grown weary of armchair opinion on this topic and resolved to find out for myself. After all, how often in the annals of modern work do we hear employees speak so enthusiastically about their jobs? The window of opportunity for someone to document and analyze this kind of workplace might well be short-lived, and so I undertook my study with the aim of learning from employees while they were on the job.

Accordingly, it is on the basis of those employees' own experiences that this book extracts lessons about the future of work in the trades we identify with the knowledge industries, though I believe they might also be applicable to other occupations. In my account of the no-collar people, who aspired to answer only to newly minted ideas and next-generation technologies, readers will also hear echoes of bygone workplaces. Work patterns and conflicts rarely disappear; they are always being recycled into new forms. Besides, how can the evangelists of the future pitch their wares if they cannot draw upon the thwarted dreams of the past?

Time to Change

However dubious its worth to the mass of the population, each new gospel of work opens an inspirational door for some fraction of society to push beyond its current lot in life. The much vaunted Protestant work ethic meant very little to those driven by hunger and want into the factories and mills of the Yankee industrial revolution. Nor did it make much headway in the antebellum South where the solid paternalism of plantation slavery held sway. But for a good portion of the nineteenth century, the secular formula of this ethic—improving one's station through hard work—brought a real sense of opportunity and purpose to independent artisans, freeholders, and small business proprietors who could see a clear path to betterment through their own punctual toil, thrift, and perseverance. Their success was promoted as a model for society as a whole, and their example inspired a flood of popular tales and tracts (Poor Richard, Horatio Alger, Samuel Smiles, Peter Parley, the McGuffey readers) about the virtues of hard work. A distinct kind of heroic praise issued from intellectuals like Emerson, who eulogized that "a man coins himself into his labor; turns his day, his strength, his thoughts, his affection into some product which remains a visible sign of his power."[3] Like Marx, Emerson was influenced by Romantic ideas about the many-sided, Renaissance dimension of artisanal work, and he believed that the free development of individuality could be realized only through the labor of self-mastery—an idea of especial importance to the growing republic.

Though this work ethic was a Northern European import, the local opportunities and rewards it wrought attracted wave after wave of emigrating artisans. Nowhere was the belief in self-improvement more exalted than in an America still tied to its republican faith in the virtue of small property holders. Nowhere has nostalgia for the heyday of the independent owner-operators run deeper or with more spirited sentiment. Sympathy for the small guy, or regret for his demise, is the bedrock of 90 percent of American popular culture. For every occupation and every profession, there is an edifying story to be quarried about lone mavericks looking to upend some large, diabolic organization through their native wit and zeal.

It is easy to see why. However romanticized, the self-reliant culture of the workshop artisans was gradually dismantled by the hireling ways and punch-clock accounting of the factory system.[4] With the advent of monopoly plutocrats and vertical corporations at the end of the nineteenth century, the individual pathway to advancement was increasingly paved over. Business independents were now edged out of the competition; family farmers were squeezed by agricultural cartels; and free artisans, whose craft skills had been preserved through early industrialization by union control over work rules and stints, were supplanted by the advanced factory techniques of scientific management.[5] The key to assigning personal worth soon lay in the hands of managers and technicians, bound by the efficiency rule of the stopwatch and the cold tempo of high-volume industrial process. For the blue-collar worker, the gradual mechanization of the workplace diminished the ordeal of physical pain on the job, but at the cost of reducing the worker to a servo-mechanism. Office automation eliminated many menial tasks but also introduced white-collar employees to a range of new physical ailments and nervous disorders. In a machine civilization, run by the clock and driven by the stern pace of the assembly line or the data flow, the bittersweet reward for decades of company service was a retirement watch—a ritual to acknowledge that employees' time was finally their own, no longer controlled by manager or machine.

In 1972, a wildcat strike at General Motor's Lordstown assembly plant in Ohio drew a great deal of public attention for the nature of its protest against the inhumanity of the work pace. At an assembly line speed of 101.6 cars per hour—one vehicle produced every 36 seconds—the Lordstown line was the fastest in the world. Its labor force and its local UAW leaders were exceptionally young ("an average age of 24 or 25," and "mustachioed, hip-talking, long-haired, pigtailed and bell-bottomed" in the words of a *Time* editorial). During the strike, they exhibited attitudes ("irreverent of all decision makers," according to *Time*) previously associated with the middle-class students and other refuseniks who had made their mark on the mores of the 1960s. For the most part, theirs was not a grievance over hours and wages. It was a protest against the *quality* of work, and it flew in the face of their parent union's contract with GM, which promised high productivity and labor peace in return for high wages, typical of the postwar compact with corporate America.[6]

The Lordstown strike was provoked by line speedup and by resentment at the activities of GM time-study inspectors, but workers also expressed dissatisfaction with the form in which the company had offered "job enrichment." GM had responded to grievances about the monotony of assembly line work by assigning workers a variety of tasks rather than slowing the line and redesigning the work process in more stimulating ways. Like subsequent landmark strikes—the 1981 walkout by PATCO air traffic controllers and the 2000 Verizon dispute over the stressful demands of Internet time on infrastructure workers—Lordstown was about the human toll of work. Indeed, it was widely perceived as evidence that the ethos of Woodstock—with its protest against the authoritarian suppression of pleasure and its demand for creative expression in everyday things—was being embraced by working-class people. For broader statistical evidence of discontent, it was enough to point to the soaring rates of absenteeism, turnover, walkouts, and sabotage that were being recorded all across the manufacturing sector and beyond.

A year after the Lordstown strike, calls to humanize the workplace took an official form in *Work in America,* a report published by the Department of Health, Education, and Welfare. The report concluded that "a significant number of Americans are dissatisfied with the quality of their working lives. Dull, repetitive, seemingly meaningless tasks, offering little challenge or autonomy, are causing discontent among workers at all occupational levels." The "alienation and disenchantment of blue-collar workers" was matched by "the disgruntlement of white-collar workers" and the "growing discontent of managers," and the public purse was paying the physical and mental health costs of all of this chronic alienation on the job. *Work in America* also lamented the "anachronistic authoritarianism of the workplace," which resulted in a lack of participation in decision-making on the part of employees. In recommending the "redesign of work" in ways that went far beyond job enrichment, the report deferred to the belief that "having an interesting job is now as important as having a job that pays well."[7]

Federal recognition of the problem was bolstered by Studs Terkel's influential 1972 book, *Working.* The widespread oral testimony collected by Terkel affirmed that meaningless work does "violence to the spirit" as much as to the body. A Lordstown unionist, for example, expressed disdain for "the almighty dollar" and spoke more eagerly about his "rights," "the human factor," and "the social aspects" of the job. These sentiments were by no means confined to working-class malaise. For "the walking wounded among the great many of us," Terkel asserted, "the blue collar blues is no more bitterly sung than the white collar moan."[8] The HEW report and Terkel's book appeared at the end of the long postwar boom, a period that turned out to be the twilight of the settled age of mass industrial production in the West. The landscape of work would be buffeted by storms of change over the next two decades, beginning with the massive impact of deindustrialization brought about by corporate outsourcing of manufacturing jobs. Turbo-driven by a shift in investment capital from manufacturing to finance, a new kind of service economy came into being, accompanied by a breathtaking increase in income inequality that would downsize the cherished American middle class to the very smallest among developed nations.

In the interim, corporate America tried to address the problem of the redesign of work through a long succession of management innovations, from "quality of work life" in the 1970s to "business process engineering" in the 1990s. The velocity of change in corporate life quickened into a blur. By the 1990s, the stable and relatively secure environment of the postwar workplace was almost a museum relic. The paladins of the business world were CEOs like Jack Welch and Al "Chainsaw" Dunlap, whose take-no-prisoners style of downsizing exhilarated investors and nauseated employees in equal measure. Fluidity, innovation, and reinvention were the flavors of the day, and Wall Street reacted to little else. In this increasingly financialized economy, executives ordered organizational changes simply to trigger a bounce in the company stock price. As a result, layoffs and cutbacks were legion, even in a strong economy. Even as company profits soared in the boom years of the 1990s, millions of employees were displaced, some of them blithely declaring their independence, as free agents, from the serfdom of the large corporations.[9]

Return of the Artisan?

Given the speed and ubiquity of these upheavals and the grievous toll they took on employees, what did a good job look like at the end of the millennium? Had any progress been made since the *Work in America* report in devising a humane workplace? Where would we look for evidence of personally fulfilling, even challenging, work that brought satisfaction rather than bitterness into the lives of employees? Were there jobs in Candyland? If the answer was yes, the least likely place to find them was inside a large American corporation.

By the 1990s, it was widely believed that the pursuit of the good life was no longer compatible with full-time employment in corporate America. For those raised during the Depression, the large corporate organizations were seen as havens of security for much of the postwar period. Cold War competition with socialism prompted managers to sweeten the pot of welfare capitalism. White-collar loyalty to the company was rewarded by a sheltering raft of benefits that seemed only to expand as union pressure brought similar gains for blue-collar workers. Beginning in the 1970s, this formula of mutual trust was rudely pushed aside and laid to rest in the course of a long season of mass layoffs, first in manufacturing and then in the white-collar ranks. By the early 1980s, the ax was falling hardest on middle managers, who accounted for between a third and a half of all the "demassing" or "delayering," to cite two of the layoff euphemisms of the day.[10] These layoffs were introduced as short-term responses to competitive pressure from Cold War junior partners, Japan and Germany, but they quickly became an obligatory sacrifice to the gods of cash flow and profit maximization. Eventually they were normalized as a prerequisite of Wall Street's approved profile for the investment-worthy company. As a result, layoffs today are no longer the opposite of work in America. They are part of the definition of what work is, or what work is likely to be, in an economy increasingly marked by nonstandard or interrupted employment.

As large corporations lost the trust and respect of employees, they also provoked the scorn of a new breed of management gurus for their bureaucratic stagnancy. The work rules, hierarchies, and rituals of corporate organization were condemned for stifling initiative and creativity and for stunting the appetite of employees for opportunity and meaningful self-application. In *The Change Masters*, her influential 1983 clarion call for a "corporate Renaissance," management theorist Rosabeth Moss Kanter lamented that "great art has not come out of the corporate sector; only dull monotony and Babbitry." "Between Horatio Alger and the recent past," she observed, "we have had only Willy Loman and the man in the gray flannel suit—and stories about the smothering of creativity."[11]

Moreover, Kanter was among the earliest to recognize and praise the "more colorful and expressive" character of the high-tech companies in Silicon Valley and Route 128, "populated by the generation that gave us beads and plumage." These companies were more informal and democratic in their organization and employee culture. They were faster on their feet and more nimble in responding to new market demands, new technologies, and new business problems. They appeared to promote a humane workplace not as a grudging concession to demoralized employees but as a valued asset to production. Kanter and her ilk lobbied hard against the Prussian militarism of the industrial corporation and in favor of companies that would meet these dual demands for reform—championing a humane workplace as well as increasing economic competitiveness—without overly compromising either.

These were the roots of the much publicized face-off between the New Economy and Old Economy in the 1990s. As rising productivity coincided with the Internet stock boom in the last few years of the decade, it became common to identify all digital or online companies as New Economy and all brick-and-mortar firms as Old Economy.[12] Although this demarcation was not always useful or accurate as a way of distinguishing between types of organizations, it is generally true that most of the Internet startups of the period did incorporate the reforms described above. Throughout this book, I use the term New Economy as a historical period marker and to acknowledge its conventional association with Internet companies.

The most prominent feature of the reform legacy was a work culture that embraced openness, cooperation, and self-management. Such habits of work had been discouraged in the pyramid organization of the postwar corporation, and they were verboten in the early high-tech echelons of IBM, RCA, AT&T, GE, and Westinghouse, which emulated military-style secrecy and discipline to the same degree that they pocketed research funding from the Department of Defense. Silicon Valley was less intimate with direct federal funding for research, though the growth of its companies was still fueled by lavish defense contracts. In the Valley's technology startups, an anti-authoritarian work mentality took root, and over time it grew its own rituals of open communication and self-direction, adopting new

modes and myths of independence along the way. In this book, that
mentality is called no-collar, and its practitioners earned the label, in
part, because of their self-conscious rejection of labels, not to mention
status-conscious work uniforms and attitudes. Nonconformity was its
earnest emblem.[13]

Before the rise of the Internet industries, this work mentality had
been primarily confined to high-tech office parks in the outer suburbs. From the mid-1990s, it took on the bohemian trappings associated with the urban downtown areas where new media startups had
begun to locate, triggering rapid industrial growth in center-city
neighborhoods. In this urban setting, the no-collar work style of the
bohemian artist, long established as the signature pariah of the nine-
to-five world, proved as influential as the nontraditional habits of the
computer programmers and engineers. Many of those who formed
the pioneer backbone of the Internet sector had training in the arts
and brought their own maverick brand of individualism. They also
brought their experience in sacrificial labor and therefore a willingness to work in low-grade office environments, solving creative problems for long and often unsocial hours in return for deferred rewards. This aptitude was easy to exploit in companies that operated
on seventy-hour workweeks and offered compensation partly
through stock options. Geeksploitation among programmers in the
suburban information technology (IT) and software sectors soon
found its urban new media match in a phenomenon that I call the industrialization of bohemia.

In the best of these companies, however, employees wondered if
they had found the employment equivalent of the Big Rock Candy
Mountain. Compensation was ample, and it was supported by a broad
range of benefits, including funds for personal development and college tuition. Stock options were a heady attraction not just financially
but because they offered a sense of ownership in the workplace as a
whole. The permissive workplace was designed both physically and
philosophically to chase off the blues. Pioneering a brand-new
medium involved work that was challenging, stimulating, almost irresistible. In the words of one of the employees who figures in these
pages, "it was work you just couldn't help doing." Self-management
was the rule of organization, and individual employees enjoyed near-

maximum control over their own time, work methods, and application of initiative. Released from the indignity of steady supervision, they found that they had adult responsibilities in a youthful environment free of lifestyle discrimination.

In addition to these congenial working conditions, the role of the machine in this workplace was no longer one of impersonal taskmaster but was restored to what many saw as its preindustrial function: a craft tool. The skills required to develop the new digital medium were in short supply, and there was a steep market demand for those in the trade. Some commentators saw the conditions as ripe for an artisanal revival on a scale not seen since the golden age of craft skills.[14] Those with the know-how would belong to a new labor aristocracy, blessed with a strong hand in bargaining over the supply and price of their services. Along with the emergence of these digital artisans, the reappearance of the startup entrepreneur restored the business world's faith in independent, native gusto, just as the organization yes-man appeared to be on the out.

Since the crisis of high-volume manufacturing in the early 1970s, prophets of postindustrialism, such as Daniel Bell, had been forecasting that an information society, based on the enlightened rule of knowledge experts, was supplanting an industrial economy that had been directed ineptly and irresponsibly by capitalists and their stewards. IT was the key to the new benign order, and professional knowledge workers would prove more rational and humane in their planning and allocation of resources than the old ruling class had been.[15] Bell's was an updated version of an old dream of technocracy (fifty years earlier, Thorstein Veblen had proposed "the revolt of the engineers" against "the Vested Interests"), which foretold the triumph of scientific efficiency over the wasteful reign of tycoons.[16] It was a dream in which technology, rather than class conflict, would usher in a new realm of freedom for workers.

Bell's blithe vision of a more compassionate economic order was nipped in the bud by the harsh corporate restructuring of the 1970s and 1980s. Ultimately, the old capitalism was transformed not by engineers but by the so-called shareholder revolution, which brought an end to corporate managers' indifference to stockholders.[17] With the new pressure to deliver value to investors at all costs, long-term

stability and rational planning were subordinated to profit maximization, market leadership, and stock inflation. Under these directives,
the freedom of employees became a low priority. For the most part,
the introduction of IT into the workplaces of the new capitalism resulted in the intensified surveillance of employees. In 2001, the
American Management Association reported that 77.7 percent of
companies acknowledged routine electronic monitoring of their employees' activities, a figure that had doubled since 1997.[18] Software to
regulate the speed of workstation users and to time the length of toilet breaks had become a standard feature of information work. Video-
taping and reviewing of personal email and Web-surfing were becoming more prevalent. It turned out that supervision of workers' time
and actions was even more systematic in the computerized workplace
than it had been under the factory foreman.

If the human promise of IT was being realized anywhere, surely it
was in the artisanal workshops of the Internet industries where routine operations had been shunted aside or temporarily deferred in
favor of technical ingenuity and networking skills. Managers with no
experience in this new media sector had little alternative but to forego
control and cede power to the thinking hand of the employee at the
console.[19] Here, perhaps, was the kind of intellectually awake workplace that Kanter had called for, boasting switched-on employees for
whom work had a redeeming quality not seen since the heyday of the
nineteenth-century strivers. In such a workplace, the zeal of employees was more like a quest for personal and existential stimulation,
closer in spirit to extreme sport or adventure travel than to the sobriety of the self-dependent man who saw himself as a pious and productive member of society.

The best of these companies grew out of the distinctive community
of early Internet users, hackers, technohobbyists, and Web enthusiasts, each bound by a fierce loyalty to shareware, freedom of information, and the ethos of cooperation. Their resident credo—a mix of an-
archist and libertarian convictions—formed the cultural bedrock of
the embryonic industry and offered some makeshift protection
against the incursion of the profit motive. Anti-capitalist sentiment
and posturing were prevalent within the workforce, along with bitter
misgivings about the commercialization of the Internet. Even when

the industry was captured by venture capital and held hostage to IPO gold lust, those within the workforce held on to these convictions with surprising tenacity. Although it devastated their employment prospects, the Nasdaq crash in April 2000 was welcomed by many veterans who had regretted the forced takeover of their fledgling medium by MBAs. The Internet, they agreed, would go on changing the world, with or without the buccaneers on Wall Street.

All things considered, the work conditions of the Internet industries were a far cry from the cubicle inferno of white-collar spleen that Scott Adams pilloried in his Dilbert cartoons. "As good as it gets in corporate America" was a phrase I heard frequently from employees in the early years of Silicon Alley in New York and Multimedia Gulch in San Francisco. Of course, many of them had never worked in corporate America. Either they were too young to have had much adult work experience, or they had shunned any close contact with corporations for political or lifestyle reasons. Even so, their workplaces sounded like a credible response to decades of demands from labor advocates for a humane work environment. Office jobs of any stripe rarely earn laudatory reviews from youthful recruits who tend to start out low on the pecking order.

The Foosball Table as gimmick, Organic, New York (Photo by the author)

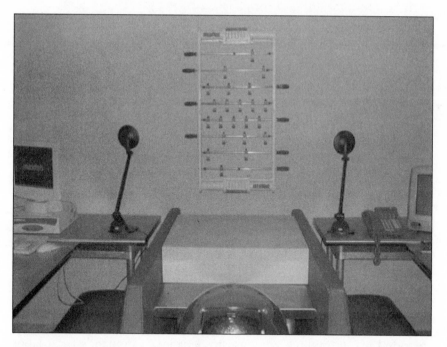

The Foosball Table as Art, Razorfish, New York (Photo by the author)

Initially, public response ricocheted between envy and skepticism. Media scrutiny of these new workplaces was abundant, even though it mostly fixated on dotcom gimmicks like foosball tables and basketball hoops. In next to no time, the Internet gold rush story sucked in all the available currents of public attention. "Follow the money" genres of reporting trumped all others. Reports about the new patterns of work, experiments in company reorganization, and the mutation in employee-manager relations were reduced to a sideshow in the media circus that focused on IPO fever, soaring stock valuations, and insta-millionaires.

Workplace analysis fared no better in the climate of opinion following the Nasdaq crash and the subsequent rash of company failures. Layoffs and crushing market losses dominated every news report from the New Economy, lining its coffin with statistics of ruination just as conclusively as the advancing stock prices had once studded its precarious media crown. Among other things, this near obsession with winning and losing numbers showed how deeply the spread of financialization had impacted media coverage itself. It was becoming habitual to judge all human endeavors through their potential reflection in market value. What valuable lessons were being lost as a result? How many innovations were being thrown out along with the proverbial bathwater of yesterday's stock valuations? These were common queries among employees in the surviving companies, confronted, as they were, with a mood of irrational pessimism about things digital that seemed to have all but supplanted the recent bubble of irrational exuberance.

The Reform Legacy

In the immediate throes of the New Economy recession, published accounts of the crash and burn of company fortunes were read as morality tales about the undoing of greed.[20] This book starts from an altogether different premise. It presumes that the most important influence of the New Economy will be on employees' expectations of work conditions, not on the nature of investment or business opportunities. Even during the boom, most Internet business models were targets of scorn. By contrast, I found it was the social and cultural design of the workplace that stole the affection of employees because it promised to deliver some of that human self-recognition that Marx had written about. In interviewing hundreds of employees for this book, I found that what they prized most was not the prospect of fast money or the memory of stock options that had withered on the vine. Much more common was nostalgia for an irresistible work environment, one that they feared they may never enjoy again in their professional lives. Many vowed to pursue similar work conditions, or seek ways of creating them anew, even if their career paths led to corporate employment outside the orbit of the new media industries. Given the spirited passions that were attached to this oath, it seems likely that these expectations will have some impact on the landscape of work for years to come.

A typical observation about this came from Joni Becker, native New Yorker and Web development veteran of several Silicon Alley companies, who was sitting out the first year of the recession in London, subsidizing her digital art career by consulting for insurance companies. "Any manager worth his salt knew they had to empower us," she explained, "and everyone could see how difficult it would be to reclaim that power and start spouting out orders again. They saw it happen for a while, and they were relieved when the market reined us in. There was a lot of talk about the Old Economy fear of getting Amazoned, but I think the real fear in these other industries was about losing control to employees like us. Too many of us got a taste of the good stuff to stay down on the farm." Eight time zones away, Max Filipacci, who learned programming on the job at a Bay Area agency, had a strikingly similar story. I interviewed him just after he turned down a well-paying job at a large financial services company for less money at a much smaller technology vendor (he was doing it "for the vibe"). "Workers behaving as if they are truly free and truly human," he observed, "are a big threat to corporations, and you don't need an MBA to figure that out." Looking back on the Nasdaq crash, he summed up his experience: "What we learned was that society is not yet ready for us. Not ready technologically, for sure, but also company-wise. The digital age will come soon enough; that's inevitable. Being human and free is what we have to work on; that's the hardest part."

At Razorfish, the New York digital consultancy where I did most of my research, employees had ample opportunity to sample work conditions inside their clients' organizations. Like many of his colleagues, Jake Loury, a client partner who had been trained in dance performance, had not exactly prepared himself for a career where he would be in daily contact with Fortune 500 companies. As the recession spread across every sector of the economy, he was holding on tight to his job: "I'm still not sure that I belong here," he admitted, "but I'm glad I've had the chance to see how corporations are run. When I get a little blue, I think of what it's like elsewhere. What I've seen in other companies is a bunch of rats trapped in a room, poking to get pellets. Not to mention the drug testing, penalties for talking out of turn, and all the other disciplinary stuff." Craig Kanarick, one of the company's founders, confirmed that regular exposure to clients' workplaces was an important source of morale for disgruntled employees: "When they come back from seeing other companies, they're like, 'I'm so sorry. I didn't mean to say any of these bad things. I had to eat lunch in a cafeteria with 400 people, and everyone was in cubicles.' And then they never complain again."

One of the most strenuously promoted career paths in the New Economy was that of the independent contractor or free agent. Their control over time and work options was especially celebrated by liberation management gurus like Tom Peters, who famously referred to "the brand called You" as a profile that individuals are responsible for designing and marketing.[21] For many corporate managers, however, free agency was a convenient justification for the withdrawal of job security. As a manager at AOL explained to me (shortly before his company's own acquisition of Time Warner), "The Peters idea is all well and good, but pretty soon it merges with your typical neoclassical right-wing ideology to the extent that you hear would-be CEOs, and Harvard Business School professors and real-life CEOs saying things like 'To give my employees job security would be to disempower them and to relieve them of the responsibility that they need to feel for their own success.' The next step after that is when these managers begin to view employee benefits the same way—as an act of disempowerment."

Several independents, who were successfully negotiating self-employment, do figure in the pages of this book. For the most part, however, I concentrate on employment in reformed companies, simply because I found they were the most popular jobs. These firms offered oodles of autonomy along with warm collegiality, much of the personal independence of the self-employed, plus all the benefits and monthly paychecks that come with a regular job, and so their employees often spoke of having the best of both worlds. Many were stunned to find out that a workplace could accommodate freedom and humanity, to use Filipacci's words. These qualities were not readily apparent in society at large, nor were companies, especially publicly traded ones, known for promoting them in their capacity as corporate citizens. By contrast, what I found quite widespread among employees was the belief that some kind of improved, if not ideal, society could be pursued *within* a company. In the 1990s, this goal of creating a reconstructed, politically correct company became a fervent substitute for aspirations to social change outside of the workplace. While their younger siblings were using the Internet to launch an anti-globalization movement that protested corporate capitalism all the way from Seattle to Genoa, first-generation websters were inclined to view their own companies as lustrous examples of how capitalism could be reformed from the inside.

All in all, the reformed companies of the New Economy fit snugly into the American grain of optimism about the more perfect society. The opportunity they provided for employees to reinvent themselves borrowed from the national heritage of utopian communities, while their appetite for spontaneity and self-direction owed something to the spirit of the bohemian commune. Most such efforts to follow values that cannot be practiced in the mainstream are short-lived, yet the influence of their example can instigate reform far and wide.

Business history is replete with examples of top-down reforming impulses. In the epoch of the company town, enlightened capitalists tried their own hand at planned communities; "human relations" management was developed in the 1920s to boost productivity by humanizing the workplace; and in the postwar period, corporate paternalism extended its benefit blanket at a pace comparable to gains in state welfare. Each of these examples of reform provided employers and managers a stronger hand in controlling the physical movements, psychological behavior, and loyalty of employees, while staving off the appeal of trade union solidarity or socialist leanings. There is no doubt that employers stood to benefit in similar ways from the reformed organizations of the 1990s, but they started out from quite a different bargaining position. They were operating within a milieu where common ownership, equality of communication, and distributed authority were all taken for granted by employees.

Like any other evangelical community that sets itself high standards of conduct, there were hidden costs of membership. The testimony collected in this book shows how and when employees bumped up against the limits of a humane workplace. Features that appeared to be healthy advances in corporate democracy could turn into trapdoors that opened on to a bottomless seventy-hour-plus workweek. Employee self-management could result in the abdication of accountability on the part of real managers and an unfair shouldering of risk and responsibilities on the part of individuals. Flattened organizations could mean that the opportunities for promotion dried up, along with layers of protection to shield employees from market exposure. A strong company culture was an emotional salve in good times but could turn into a trauma zone in times of crisis and layoffs. Partial ownership, or stakeholding, in the form of stock options could give employees an illusory sense of power sharing, rudely shattered when they encountered the unilateralism of executive decision-making in layoffs and office closures.

Perhaps the most insidious occupational hazard of no-collar work is that it can enlist employees' freest thoughts and impulses in the service of salaried time. In knowledge companies that trade in creative ideas, services, and solutions, everything that employees do, think, or say in their waking moments is potential grist for the industrial mill. When elements of play in the office or at home/offsite are factored into creative output, then the work tempo is being recalibrated to incorporate activities, feelings, and ideas that are normally pursued during employees' free time. For employees who consolidate office and home, who work and play in the same clothes, and whose social life draws heavily on their immediate colleagues, there are no longer any boundaries between work and leisure.[22] Their occupation becomes a support system for everything else. No one who held a New Economy job was immune to this biohazard, unlike in a traditional corporate organization, where it primarily affected only the senior managers and executives.

Utopian communities usually seek to withdraw from the mainstream in order to solve inequities bred under the prevailing economic rules. The companies in this book were in no position to do so, despite the short-lived, and wholly specious, proposition that the New Economy operated by an entirely new set of rules. For most employees, that entailed a confused encounter with the psychology of financialization. It was bad enough seeing your hard-earned skills lose their value in the labor market, as digital know-how became less exclusive or got outsourced to Eastern Europe and South Asia at discount rates. That was a familiar pattern in industrial history. But financialization brought new kinds of uncertainties. Work was no longer something you performed for a fair wage; it was an investment, an opportunity, an asset that you or someone else could leverage as a means to boost a stock holding. Nor was achievement or security tied to work performance; it was more likely determined by the story told by the daily stock indexes. It was small wonder that the family principles espoused by many a company culture were regularly at odds with the story that Wall Street investors preferred to hear. In such moments, the fond pleading of employees and their advocates—"we are a company, not a stock"—was as ineffectual as the wall of a sandcastle before an incoming high tide.

When the accounting scandals at Enron, WorldCom, Global Crossing, and others threatened to engulf all of corporate America in the spring and summer of 2002, every effort was made to make it appear as if the corruption was limited to companies and employees visibly identified with the New Economy. Yet what Alan Greenspan called "infectious greed" was not a contained affliction, and it had taken a much wider toll. The widespread plundering on the part of executives, bankers, analysts, and speculators reflected a clear trend in the general economy. Productive work, as judged by the long-term needs of society or the economy as a whole, is increasingly passed over for business strategies aimed at short-term market yields and ready access to buyouts. Brands and stock prices call the shots, while production skills and jobs, no matter how high-tech or high-value, are viewed as dispensable.

Barring massive reforms of investor capitalism, this trend will only intensify. The no-collar employees who appear in these pages were not only in a pioneer office environment, testing the limits of the humane workplace. As avatars of uncertainty, bruised by the rough passage of market forces, they were also on the front line of economic profiling that was changing the character of work itself. These two conditions—the clement work milieu and the indulgent climate of binge capitalism—could not be easily separated. It may be tempting for some readers to imagine how the former might have developed apart from the latter, but that is not how it happened. In an exclusively market civilization, the *humane* workplace (with its feel-good stimulation and its tests of mettle) has taken precedence over the *just* workplace (with protection for all, democratic control over the enterprise, and assurances of security beyond the job). An alternative economic arrangement would eliminate the need to choose and would try to deliver both.

The No-Collar People

The white collar people slipped quietly into modern society.

—C. WRIGHT MILLS

IN THE TWILIGHT YEARS OF THE AMERICAN CENTURY, THE CHANCES of finding an adequate job appeared to be rising, for almost everyone. Even the wages of workers at the economic bottom, rudely excluded from the rewards of the long boom, were finally beginning to climb. In a skintight labor market, jobless levels dipped (in October 2000) to a thirty-year low of 3.9 percent. This was well below the 6 percent that the oracular Milton Friedman had deemed to be the "natural rate of unemployment," and inflation, contra Friedman, was nowhere in sight. Educated youth seldom had so many ripe opportunities. If you were fresh out of college and looking for a job that might quicken your mind or try your ingenuity, a career—not at all like your father's—with the future stamped on its brow, work that would not cramp your lifestyle and that might pay all your bills and more, then you probably would have made a beeline for an Internet company in an urban downtown. And if you wanted city living in a truly metropolitan vein, you would be employed somewhere in New York's Silicon Alley.

Between 1995 and the time the millennium party wound down, the city's new media sector had created almost 140,000 jobs (with 250,000 in the larger metropolitan area) and encompassed more than 8,000 companies.[1] Unusually, there was something for everyone—MFAs, BAs, BSs and MBAs alike. The fledgling industry needed artsy "creatives," hard-core technologists, and business strategists in equal numbers, and there were even jobs in professional fields—like "information architect"—that simply did not exist three or four years earlier. All manner of fanciful job titles made it seem as though you could invent and name your own field of expertise. The entry bar was lowering by the week. If you hit the job market during a recruitment crunch, you could ask for and expect to receive a salary as high as six figures, plus stock options, despite very limited job experience.

Work conditions in Silicon Alley were far from even and were often outrightly exploitative, but there were some companies that made it part of their business profile to try to offer everything both to their employees and their clients. Several of their names are already lost to history: Sapient, Scient, Viant, Razorfish, Organic, Agency, USWeb, iXL, MarchFirst, Luminant, Rare Medium, Zefer, Proxicom, Xceed. They were the designers and builders of the digital economy, and in industry circles, they were known by a variety of names: interactive agencies, i-service providers, e-consultants, i-builders, or Web integrators. They grew so fast, and in such a volatile business environment, that their identity, organizational form, and product lines were prone to mutate, often from one year to the next, as they responded to market opportunities that opened and closed with startling rapidity. Their owners and managers were always on the lookout for new descriptions and solutions—vague, all-encompassing terms like "digital change management"—that appeared to extend the range of their service offerings to infinity.

There was good reason to swell these service portfolios. In the heat of corporate America's stampede to enter the field of e-business, its senior managers frantically sought outside consultants that could show them the way to survival, if not profitability, in the new medium. They had been persuaded, by a dizzy combination of hype, fear, competitive rivalry, and Wall Street mania, that almost every branch of corporate operations—sales, marketing, production, internal organization, branding, client communications, business strategy—had to be adapted posthaste to function anew in the interactive Web world. Even firms that had leaned heavily on IT in the past required their legacy computer systems to undergo an online makeover. Traditional consulting agencies (like the Big Five—Deloitte and Touche, Ernst and Young, PriceWaterhouseCoopers, Arthur Andersen, and KPMG) lacked this kind of expertise. The fledgling Web agencies stepped forward to fill the vacuum, each expanding their workforces dramatically to meet the demand for full-service houses.

Many had wet their feet as small design shops, building Web sites that functioned as company calling cards. Programmers supplied a technology-intensive back end for the image-rich front end, where graphic designers, information architects, and copywriters made the sites attractive and navigable. But the potential for the Web to transform a broad range of business operations drew them deeper into their clients' organizations—and budgets. Soon they were developing an overall presence on the Web for diverse companies and devising a strategic approach to all of the business needs and goals of their clients. Every aspect of business practice was now in their domain—from the grunt work of Web-enabling bulky databases to the high concept work of digital brand-making. Thus, an initial contract might involve building an intranet or converting a client's entire business structure into digital form, whereas follow-through consulting would offer strategy about how to take advantage of new technologies and marketplaces. Strategy was sexy (because it was intangible) and lucrative (because it was for the long term).

This new consulting model demanded smooth coordination between business strategists, technologists, and creatives in design, architecture, and writing. The Web agencies claimed they could digest the challenge of integrating all three skill areas, because integration was the key to success. To meet the challenge, those with a design background scrambled to swallow technology companies, and those with roots in technology rolled up companies that had an edge in creative experience. All of them discreetly recruited business strategists from the Big Five and the MBA schools, so that clients would be able to enjoy a one-stop service, comprising all the primary skill groups. Without the aid of an industrial blueprint, these companies were trying to pioneer an industrial process that would be key to developing online business for years to come. Every knowledge company that dabbled in interactive media would stand to learn from their successes and failures.

If these Web consulting agencies were trying to be all things to all clients, their human resource policies and official company values promised even more to employees. Gung-ho recruiters were so solicitous of employee satisfaction it often seemed their intent was to squeeze every drop of white-collar alienation out of the workplace. The policies were also designed to showcase their employees to clients and investors. Even their most conservative corporate customers had been persuaded that they needed free-range thinking, on a spectrum from out-of-the-box to off-the-wall. Previously, HR policies had been introduced for reasons of internal morale. In the 1990s, they played a visible role in business strategy. The culture clash between buttoned-down traditional firms and liberated dotcoms was intrinsic to the chemistry, and mythology, of New Economy business.

The Fish Tank

Few firms embodied these principles more fervently than Razorfish, a bleeding-edge Web design shop that had accelerated, in five heady years, from startup in 1995 in an East Village apartment to a global consulting operation, headquartered in the heart of SoHo, and with offices in Boston, San Francisco, San Jose, Los Angeles, London, Amsterdam, Helsinki, Milan, Stockholm, Oslo, Hamburg, Frankfurt, and Tokyo.[2] When the Internet economy foundered, Razorfish contracted steeply and rebranded its identity and purpose, returning to profitability as a leaner, more sober organization. The life span and location of the company meant that its personnel participated in every act of the Internet industry drama. Its founders and first-wave employees played a role in the pre-dotcom moment of Web-based activity in Silicon Alley; its global workforce were able to reap the rewards of an economy of scale, when the firm was flush with revenue and media attention; its post-crash employees witnessed the workplace in survival mode, ravaged by layoffs and reorganization after reorganization; and its efficiency-conscious veterans who outlasted the recession wrestled with the legacy of its fabled culture.

At some point in the mid- to late 1990s, employment in the interactive shops and agencies like Razorfish reached a critical plateau. Work in the Alley was no longer considered a temporary option for financing

Number 4 on
the Silicon Alley
Top 40, 2001
(From the *Silicon
Alley Reporter*)

a downtown urban lifestyle or an alternative career as an artist, writer, or musician. The word was out that it might just prove to be a long-term career prospect. Razorfish had already established itself as the place to be, especially if you had a fresh artistic bent. Its early commercial work had won a raft of awards in graphic and interactive design and in television advertising. At a time when companies and organizations wanted brochureware to advertise themselves on the Web, Razorfish had delivered virtuoso graphics that consistently raised the bar and harvested the respect of other Web developers. When dotcom startups needed a development house to build their company from scratch, Razorfish was a top choice. Before long, the firm's reputation was drawing big corporate clients to its e-consulting services.

More important to prospective recruits, the company's nervy founders, Jeff Dachis and Craig Kanarick, had taken pains to promote employee friendliness that would be the ne plus ultra of company cultures. At every stage of the company's history, employees estimated that their salaries were below that of their peers in rival firms. The discount was for the workplace culture, and more than anything, this culture was reputed to be the quality that gave the company its competitive edge, both in attracting clients and in recruiting the best and the brightest.

Management gurus had been championing the virtues of company culture for several decades, arguably since Douglas McGregor's influential 1960 book, *The Human Side of Enterprise*.[3] McGregor famously distinguished authoritarian Theory X management from a participatory Theory Y style that advocated a more sensitive and caring, therapeutic relationship toward employees. By the early 1980s, companies were being encouraged to develop "strong cultures," with the aim of forging emotional bonds among employees and with the company that would feel just as meaningful as those encountered outside the workplace, among families or friends. Theoretically, the result, from the side of management, would be a boost in productivity and company loyalty. As for employees, they were supposed to acquire newfound respect, garner support for personal initiatives, and enjoy the kind of on-site dignity that had been auspiciously lacking in the age of the organization cog.

By the 1990s, when liberation management was launched through the wild-eyed proselytizing of Tom Peters, culture had become the weapon of choice in a holy war against corporate bureaucracy.[4] Peters and his disciples insisted that a culture of grassroots innovation would free every last creative impulse from employees whose minds were still held down by the bolts and rivets of bureaucratic protocol. When the turned-on Internet workplace made its debut in the media spotlight, it became an object of fascination, fear, and ridicule in equal measures. For the liberation gurus and New Economy boosters, it became an instant poster child for supercreativity and bootstrap innovation. Business traditionalists, who "made money the old-fashioned way," winced at the prospect of losing the cream of the recruiting crop to Internet upstarts who were promising the world to employees and investors alike. Slowest to respond were workforce veterans who had seen management fads and company reorgs come and go and were loath to see this latest stab at employee lib as anything but a scheme concocted by canny managers looking to institute the seventy-hour workweek.

Yet even the most skeptical voiced some curiosity. For one thing, the workplace reforms were part of the basic furniture plan from the outset. Ever since the 1920s, managers had been making sporadic attempts to humanize the workplace with the goal of winning compliance and commitment from employees. In the best of the New Economy companies, these reforms were taken for granted, as default settings, and so employees started out from bargaining positions that were much less favorable to owners and managers than had been customary. If the advertising was even half-way accurate, and as long as they held a monopoly on the knowledge and the skills needed to develop the new medium, production-level employees appeared to have claims on a share of company power that was very rare in corporate history.

In addition, the Internet workplace was alleged to have absorbed a healthy dose of the precommercial spirit of Net culture. Perhaps that would help to inoculate employees against those crafty managerial schemes devised to make workers feel like co-owners while working them to the bone. Until recently, the Internet had been a commercial-free zone and functioned as a gift economy, where goods and information not only were free of copyright but also had to be openly shared and circulated as a matter of etiquette. Advertisements were unacceptable, and private gain was considered a violation of the ethic of shareware and cooperation. It was a widely held belief that the new medium was capable of democratizing communication on a global basis. These ideals were commonplace among company founders and the pioneer New Economy workforce, and they served as a buffer against business as usual, at least for a while. Indeed, the resident anarchism of the Internet fueled the energies and habits of a workplace that was still being improvised.

Which of these versions—the con game or the Good Ship Lollipop—was more accurate? From the outside, it was difficult to separate appearance from reality, largely because of the billowing hype that enveloped the industry. In April 2000, I was struck by a posting on Vault.com, a site for job information on finance, law, and consulting where company message boards are allocated for their employees and would-be employees. The posting, which was on the Razorfish message board, was a peppy rejoinder to some jaundiced comment the previous day:

Dearest Fish—Take Heart

A reminder that you live in the most successful country on the planet, in the most powerful city in the world, in one of the hotest [*sic*] industries in recorded history, for the best company in that industry! You Rock! You're [*sic*] opportunities are boundless. The experience you gain here may provide you the ability to transorm [*sic*] your environment! You're more alive than you can possibly imagine!

The poster's stupefying hubris was perfectly timed. It was April 12, two days before the Nasdaq crash on Black Friday, and Razorfish was on top of its world: handsomely profitable, with real revenue flowing in the door, recruiting hand over fist, and so busy that would-be clients were being turned away. Postings to the Vault board, which even then—before the industry meltdown—attracted a steady and often bilious stream of boss bashing, were anonymous. The fish (as they were officially known, though it was not a very popular term among employees) often wondered if management posted there to boost morale, or put down damaging rumors, or simply to offset all the trash talking. Because of the anonymity, there was no way of telling whether messages like this one had been penned by top brass (complete with misspellings) or whether they came from employees who had drunk the company Kool-Aid.

In this case, it was probably the latter, and yet the poster's self-perception seemed to be indistinguishable from boilerplate company PR. Given the cloak of anonymity, what kind of employee would identify so thoroughly with their company's mission statements? In Silicon Alley, it was common to hear jealous banter about cult-like tendencies among the fish. According to this lore, ex-employees of the church of Razorfish needed a round of de-programming before they could rejoin the outside world. Either these rumors were grudging recognition of the company's ace reputation for employee treatment or a tribute to the effectiveness of its corporate agitprop philosophy.

The Early Urban Prototype

A few months later, I found myself on a conference panel in Amsterdam with Corinna Snyder, a middle manager at Razorfish. In her presentation, she spoke eloquently and frankly about the importance of culture inside technology companies. In the firms that she was familiar with, the process of crafting a culture involved many of the same techniques that are employed in branding. Employees were regarded as if they were clients, and internal branding involved putting the company's philosophical stamp on all services within the organization. According to Snyder, this was a principle that Razorfish practiced (among other things, it helped with employee retention), and the firm advised its clients to do the same, using the new interactive technologies at their disposal. The concept sounded far-fetched to me—or else a little too contrived for employees to embrace—and so Snyder invited me to Razorfish to see how, or whether, it worked.

Razorfish Building, Mercer Street, New York (Photo by the author)

She had been recruited in April as general manager for Triggerfish, one of four New York teams working on client projects. Her team was in the Mercer Street office building that occupied prime Soho real estate, on a street corner that also hosted bijou retailers like Yoshi Yamamoto, Ted Baker, and Facial Index, a gourmet eyeglass store. On its ground floor, Razorfish reception boasted a shrine-like exhibit of personal computers, dating back to the early 1980s. The vintage PC collection, owned by cofounder Craig Kanarick, gave a gloss of mature seasoning to the company, somewhat distinct from the powder-blue '65 Corvette Stingray convertible that he drove, much to the delight of celebrity-porn journalists who were still dining off the Silicon Alley party scene. A jumbo illuminated wall clock, with hands rotating at the speed of a slow fan, forewarned visitors they were entering a zone that ran on Internet time. The back space was walled with exposed brick and featured diner booths that bled into a well-stocked kitchen and a multimedia conference space, half-closed off by automatic garage doors. I had seen this last feature in other Internet company offices and had decided, fancifully, that it evoked the ur-garage of Hewlett and Packard fame, ground zero of the microelectronics revolution in the late 1930s. The only dotcom gimmick on show was a soda machine that dispensed its products when you called in a number from a cell phone. A sodaphone! Typically cerebral for a firm whose company mantra—"Everything that can be digital, will be"—had perfectly captured the messianic certainty of the Internet revolution.

Snyder was in a booth concluding a job interview with a middle-aged man, clean-cut and clearly at home in his business suit and yellow tie. Razorfish, she explained afterward, was now "recruiting for diversity"—adding older business experts to the waves of wunderkinder who had swelled the company ranks during its go-go years. "Right now," she added, deliberately, "we need people who have experience in encountering disappointment, setbacks, and failures." For the generally youthful fish, she explained, "diversity usually means race and gender; it rarely means age, background, or class. Everyone here has a similar educational background, so class origin is not so easy to figure out." One thing, she said, was certain: "There are no WASPs, no prep school people from Andover or Exeter, none of that." That was strictly Wall Street, and it was very important, as I would soon learn, to distinguish everything at Razorfish from the way things were done on Wall Street.

In her mid-thirties, and therefore somewhat long in the tooth for Razorfish, she had been trained as an anthropologist and had written her doctoral dissertation on the post-communist reconstruction of Lithuania. Several years in the trenches of Internet startups had wiped clean the cautious aura of academe. She had acquired the attentive, switched-on mannerisms of the knowledge professional, always thinking on her feet, her cognitive dial tuned by habit to the problem-solving channel. Her office, one of the few walled spaces on the fourth-floor loft, was shared with the company's "technology evangelist." Erik von Daniken's *Chariot of the Gods* lay open on her desk. In the bookcase, Thurman Arnold's *The Folklore of Capitalism* sat alongside several volumes in Lithuanian. There were a few rudimentary management texts—*The Art of Facilitation, Team Work*—that her mother (a veteran manager) had sent to give her ideas, but they had not been cracked.

"Are all the stories about the Razorfish workers really true?" I asked her breezily. Taking my words literally, she explained that the fish "don't understand themselves as laborers. Some of them understand a portion of their work as being like labor, but as imaginative, creative, problem-solving labor. Yet it is not considered creative work if it's labored. The term implies a hierarchy that they don't like to be aware of." "But at the end of the day," she conceded cheerfully, "we do, kind of, punch time cards. We need to report how many hours we spent on a project, since that time is billable to clients." In addition, she pointed out, the percentage of each working day that employee time was utilized offered a "metric for comparing professional service firms against each other in stock evaluation."

According to the company's most recent quarterly statement, which showed record revenue and earnings, 62 percent of its billable employees' time was being utilized, and each of these employees had generated an average of $227,000 of revenue during the quarter. Razorfish was known for its high prices, billing as much as $400 per hour, and so individual employees could estimate to the dollar how much money they made for the company and how much the value of their labor supported nonbillable fish, including the veteran, privileged cadre of floating employees, who worked on "scientific research," "technology development," or "knowledge management." This was not exactly open-book management, but the value of their hourly labor to the company seemed more transparent to employees than it would have been for line workers in any manufacturing firm. I would soon learn that one of the more corrosive internal issues at the company had to do with employees' persistent failure to enter their hours each day. There was some chronic resistance to doing so, and not simply because it was a tedious exercise.[5] Totting up your hours, I was told more than once, reminded some fish of the tyranny of the factory clock that their blue-collar parents or grandparents had labored by.

The fish we had passed on our way into her office were white, alert, gay-ish, and—since potential clients often visited the offices—purposely interesting to look at. Sedately attired in a navy-blue cardigan buttoned at the top and sporting a chiffon scarf, Snyder explained, "I dress like this because I represent the company. They represent the talent. I have to establish legitimacy with a client so that the dreadlocks can go work there. Clients want the dreadlocks, but they don't want to negotiate the terms of engagement with them." Occasionally, clients wanted the full treatment, however, and so she had to wear a fashion-oriented costume, which, she noted, was out of character for her. A quick study of her Triggerfish team members, at their workstations out on the open floor, offered a snapshot of hip downtown attitude. There were no dreadlocks or green hair in sight, but a high quotient of stylishly effective togs and accessories—random barrettes, Betty Page haircuts, oversized digital watches, clunky eyeglasses, lizard skin boots—that were a few notches up the fashion ladder from the business casual of Polo shirts and Docker khakis favored in Wall Street brokerages. When I took a stroll around the office, employees looked me straight in the eye, but there was no affect behind the look. This was New York City, after all, well before the trauma of 9/11.

In many white-collar jobs, the personality and self-presentation of employees has became a routine selling asset. In service sector work, mostly done by women, the methodical performing of what Arlie Hochschild labeled "emotional labor" is part and parcel of the job, and it can have a deadening effect on an employee's real emotional life after-hours.[6] On the landscape of modern work, the demand for emotional labor has risen in proportion to the decline in physical toil. More of the self is engaged, and there is an element of theatricality in the way we are expected to perform our jobs. For creatives in knowledge industries, this was especially true, and Silicon Alley had more than its share of people who came from the performing arts. Seth Goldstein who cofounded SiteSpecific, an early rival of Razorfish, recalled: "There was a sense of casting. You cast your technical person, you cast your creative person, then you show up for the client, and everyone has to look their part. So much of it was about packaging and confidence building."[7]

Whether performing for clients, themselves, or their coworkers, the Triggerfish were capital specimens of a new industrial type. If we were watching a bad science fiction movie about the New Information World Order, an inscrutable, tight-lipped administrator would be exhibiting them to visiting dignitaries as EUP (Early Urban Prototype) models of the no-collar worker. On the reading couch over by the library, some nascent rebel, deficiently programmed with an unauthorized learning curve, would be poring over a history book and figuring out why she had been built this way. We have all seen this movie and can choose, in our mind's eye, between several possible endings.

The Rise of No-Collar

What would the book have told our heroine about her prehistory? She might have learned that the first cohorts of computer programmers were actually women with math and science backgrounds, working for the government on the wartime operations of ENIAC (Electronic Numerical Integrator and Computer). However professionally skilled these women were, their occupational tasks were often clerical in nature and were regarded as routine, at least in comparison to the virtuoso feats of the IT industry's cowboy programmers or the elective hacker communities, both of whom would come to be lionized as culture heroes of the late twentieth century. This differentiation by status and gender foreshadowed the breakdown and classification of computer work into a broad spectrum over the next fifty years—from the pink-collar ghetto of mostly female and nonwhite data processors to the high-price cadres of mostly male and white engineering professionals.[8]

Computer specialists were first labeled knowledge workers by Peter Drucker more than forty years ago, and the slice of the economy claimed by the knowledge, or information, sector, has steadily climbed since then.[9] Although a huge slice of today's economy (from a third to a half of the national pie, according to differing estimates) is claimed by knowledge work, the concept is a baggy one, and it is by no means clear, from theory to theory, exactly which occupational sectors fall under this label. In any case, it makes little sense to generalize about work conditions across a classification that is plausibly shared by high-salaried research scientists and data-entry workers alike. Both are knowledge workers in the same way that agronomists and migrant apple-pickers can be said to be nature workers. Most jobs require some application of knowledge or mental labor, and these days, a majority require some contact with computers to one degree or another.

In this book, the no-collar mentality applies to knowledge workers whose high-tech skills or aptitude for problem-solving wins them a measure of autonomy in a data-rich workplace purged of rigid supervision and lifestyle discrimination. The intangible rewards—recognition, stimulation, responsibility—offered by their jobs are almost as important as the financial compensation. This work mentality is an attribute of those who appear to have information machines at their disposal and is generally not shared by those who are at the disposal of machines. In *The Rise of the Network Society*, Manuel Castells has offered a comprehensive description of the knowledge industry's division of labor and all of its sub-branches.[10] As a rule of thumb, consider my own, much cruder distinction between those who want computers to go faster and those who do not. Technology entrepreneurs pay homage to Moore's Law, which "ordains" the doubling of microchip speed every eighteen months. Yet for most employees who perform routine work with computers, Moore's Law simply translates into speedup on the job. It is not in their interests to go any faster, and indeed much of their workplace creativity is devoted to figuring out ways of slowing down a computer-driven tempo that may already be inhumane. As Marx put it, under these circumstances, "it is no longer the worker who employs the means of production, but the means of production which employ the worker."[11]

For no-collar employees, on the other hand, who fall above the knowledge labor divide, it is generally in their interests to have quicker machines, larger storage densities, and higher-speed access to Internet resources. For them, Moore's Law is usually perceived as a benign principle, authorizing faster tools that allow them to further master and customize their work environment. Ultimately, however, they are in a race to optimize their own time against the time of technology. Unless they stay on top of their game, they will be at odds with the speed of the machine (or the speed at which their competitors use the machine) and will fall behind or even below the labor divide. If their skills become outdated or automated by some sweeping technological upgrade, they run the risk of inventing themselves out of a job, perhaps even of joining the ranks of the technologically unemployed.[12]

Fifty years ago, the first programmers and IT specialists were recruited into large corporate bureaucracies like IBM, GE, and AT&T, where the social hierarchies of the old-line industrial firm held sway. Centralization of authority was further reinforced by the introduction of mainframe computer systems, like IBM's integrated circuit 360 System, with its innovation of software compatibility. In addition, these organizations were benefiting from the bounty of Cold War military spending and had largely internalized the military principles of secrecy, discipline, and loyalty. Over time, management theorists like Drucker recognized that Prussian forms of managerial control would not be able to accommodate the flexible work patterns of the highly mobile, technical craft workers who were so important to these companies and whose skills were in such market demand. The self-government they needed to develop their engineering and programming crafts was at odds with bureaucratic procedure, and so special provisions had to be made for them somewhere off the organizational charts of corporate America.

In a corporate environment where work rules were ubiquitous and where the stratification and classification of every job task were strictly observed, the values, schedules, and dress of the programmers were altogether eccentric: "Their strange work timetable and casual dress attracted criticism. The programmers also disrupted company rules about clocking on and off. This, together with the rewards their market position afforded them at such a comparatively young age, created problems within the company status system."[13] Some management consultants suggested forms of aptitude testing that would weed out the most nonconformist among their ranks.[14] But the more effective, long-term effort at controlling the renegades lay in breaking down the programmers' craft into separate occupational levels. Soon the conceptual work of systems analysts was separated from the product design of programmers, and the routine core production of coding was relegated to a lower skill level. This division of labor was reinforced and streamlined in the 1960s by the introduction of "structured programming," which systematically fragmented work tasks, and later, by the evolution of operating systems and software designed to further standardize the production process.[15] By the end of the century, what had once been the Renaissance multitasking of the early programmers—in control of all aspects of a development project from beginning to end—was fragmented and farmed out to occupational castes all over the world.

The industrial lineage of the no-collar mentality may have had its Cold War origins in these monolithic East Coast corporations, but it would become indelibly associated with the growth of Silicon Valley. In the South Bay, informality in dress, work schedule, and management style was construed as welcome freedom from the puritanical ways of the East Coast corporation. The resident mythology was anti-Establishment and pioneerist, embraced by a warm community of job-hopping engineers and programmers, whose loyalty to companies was flimsy, at least by the standards of Yankee discipline. Open cooperation, risk taking, and easy mobility were considered native to the libertarian culture of the West, and they featured strongly in the regional work culture of the Valley.[16] The bicoastal one-upmanship was embodied in the architectural innovation of the personal computer, fervently championed as a tool of liberation, in contrast to the technocratic authoritarianism of the East Coast computer systems. Who could forget Ridley Scott's famous 1984 Superbowl ad for Apple's Macintosh ("You'll see why 1984 won't be like *1984*"), which implied that the monopolistic rule of IBM was a totalitarian mass of users and employees, moving in Orwellian lockstep? Yet the period flavor of the region's holy war against Central Processing is best captured in Ted Nelson's homegrown cult handbook, *Computer Lib/Dream Machine,* modeled after the *Whole Earth Catalog* and first published in 1974, just before the Altair, the world's first DIY personal computer, was announced. Nelson recalled that the main goal of his book "was to tell people of the evil of IBM, especially in the way they had suppressed the development of interactive systems and computer freedom—creating computer centers, concentration camps for information, where people were regimented and oppressed."[17]

Silicon Valley's earliest models of people-centered policies, including profit sharing, date back to the 1940s at Hewlett-Packard. The HP Way distinguished itself through management reforms and decentralized organization that pushed decision-making to its lowest level. So, too, many Valley startups followed the example of Hewlett-Packard's corporate campus, preserving intact the spirit of a college environment, where tech employees had acquired their monkish social habits and observance of geek dietary laws, along with their self-directed capacity for working without direct supervision, including the gonzo knack of pulling all-nighters to meet deadlines. The HP Way and its imitators fostered corporate versions of the never-never land of the eternal graduate student. The easing of formality—first-name communication, open-door management, egalitarian parking, dogs in the workplace, and no private offices—was aimed at softening traditional forms of conflict with management. Yet the informality was also perceived as obscuring the real lines of power within the organization. In addition, the credo of open exchange of information helped to stave off maturity in the micro-electronics industry—in the stifling form, for example, of proprietary information controls. But it also meant that knowledge and skills were easily transferable, making it all the more difficult for employees to hold on to their bargaining power in the labor market.

In the high-tech suburban enclaves of the Bay Area and the Pacific Northwest, the no-collar mentality flourished in a mainstream, middle-class setting, liberally spiked with California Mellow. It absorbed the health-conscious ethos of the personal growth movements in the early 1970s along with the righteous fervor of the anti-tax revolt of the late 1970s and rode the leading edge of the long economic boom, from 1982 onward, with an air of unswervability. Even though the Valley's brand of regional optimism proved difficult to duplicate, its industrial habitat was copied all over the country and in many regions overseas, including Silicon Glen (Scotland), Silicon Saxony (Germany), Silicon Wadi (Israel), Silicon Valais (Switzerland), Silicon Polder (Netherlands), Silicon Plateau (India), and the Silicon Alps (Austria).[18]

For all its devotion to the art of technical fixes, the silicon fraternity was notorious for its avoidance of problems of society that did not submit to linear solutions. The South Bay became a breeding ground for what Paula Borsook describes as the tech industry's "city-loathing/urban-problem-avoiding bias."[19] Even so, urban-style distress came soon enough to Silicon Valley in the form of pollution, traffic density, unaffordable housing, and income polarization. The ecological footprint of microchip production, which involves more toxic gases and chemicals than any other industry, bequeathed more groundwater contamination and EPA Superfund sites than anywhere else in the United States and posed widespread safety hazards to workers in fabrication plants.[20] Nor could the preferred profile of "gold-collar workers" fully obscure the vast underbelly of the Valley's low-wage workforce.[21] In the clean room, on the assembly line, or on the janitorial beat, these workers were contracted out through almost 200 temp agencies and were segregated in low-grade bantustans on the housing landscape or forced to endure 100-mile commutes from as far away as the Sierra foothills. Higher up the pay scale, immigrant professionals from Asia on H-1B temporary visas were touted as beneficiaries of the American Dream. But they worked for six years on indenture-style company contracts and at reduced pay levels (15 to 20 percent less). The H-1B program, promoted by Valley employers as a response to an alleged labor shortage, was used to drive down the market value of technology skills and push out the industry's higher-priced IT veterans.[22] It was the high-tech version of California's postwar Bracero program, which had brought in a quota of Mexican farmworkers to keep a lid on agricultural wages.[23]

When the ecology of the startups moved to cities like San Francisco, New York, Boston, Chicago, Toronto, Atlanta, and Austin in the 1990s, it was less easy for employees to ignore the collateral damage of the industry's version of turbo-capitalism. The urban new media workforce was a little less white, considerably less masculine, and generally more socially aware than their professional brethren in Silicon Valley. The resident political sensibility was decidedly to the left of the Ayn Randian libertarianism that had taken root in the techno-geek communities of the South Bay. In addition, a work mentality that had evolved in suburban quarantine now took on board the personality traits of urban no-collar traditions, many of them adopted directly from the bohemian art world. These were traits spun from a century's worth of fierce anti-middle-class attitude, and they leaned heavily on the heritage of artists, intellectuals, and nonconformists who had set themselves apart from the workaday world of commercial labor. Added to this was the anti-authoritarian legacy of the 1960s counter-culture. It had nurtured at least two generations of the nonstandard workforce, dispersed throughout the urban underground, and by the time of the recession of the early 1990s, it was feeding into the anti-work slacker profile associated with Generation X. The result was a vast pool of no-collar aspirants, waiting for the right kind of indus-try—one with an indie pedigree—to induct them into the corporate workforce.

When the fledgling Web shops opened for business in the mid-1990s, they attracted coed freestyle staff, weary with waiting tables and steaming lattes, who had cut their teeth on Internet listservs and were open to employment that would not bring any more harm into the world. An added bonus was the promise, touted by homegrown Internet evangelists, that the new medium was going to turn the world upside down. On the face of it, here was the prospect of regu-lar employment, outside of the nonprofit world, where the language of the urban boho was spoken, and the soulless pecking order of mid-dle management had been suspended.

Getting Religion

Meanwhile, in the world of business consulting, a gathering cohort had been preaching a palace revolution in which fast-moving entre-preneurial pockets of energy and capital would topple the rule of the large corporate organizations.[24] According to the gurus du jour from McKinsey or the Harvard Business School, and the editors of maga-zines like *Fast Company*, the self-styled "handbook of the business revolution," all the establishment orthodoxies would soon be over-turned: rigid hierarchies, strictly segmented departments, top-down decision-making, cubicle farms, and forty-year career tracks. Risk-averse "change agents," "idea merchants," and "thought jockeys" would lead the revolution from below. Grassroots entrepreneurs and "crazy managers," like so many sainted guerrilla warriors, would do the work of the Holy Ghost, that is, ignite the Dow index in its bull run toward 10,000 points. If the entrepreneur's righteous labor corresponded to any version of the Protestant work ethic, it was one in which the insoluble grace of God had been neatly supplanted by the providence-bearing stock market.[25]

In the early 1990s, however, when the reengineering fad was still running its ruinous course, and lean production held sway, all of the bluster about the change revolution ran far in excess of its achievements. The pundits had to wait for a properly evangelical cohort of foot soldiers, preferably a youthful one, with something of its own to believe in. Along came the rhapsodic new creed of the Internet revolution, fully imbued with a sense of destiny that instantly separated the elect from the nonbelievers. For the innovators of the new medium, there were no primers or rule books, no disciplinary training, no credentials, and initially at least, no serious funding to corrupt the pure of faith with the promise of fast money. What flourished instead was an ardent conviction that the Web would transform every molecule of the known world, and so the known world was divided up between those who "got it" and those who didn't. The zeal was driven by generational chutzpah; their parents obviously didn't get it.

For the backers of permanent revolution in the world of finance, the dotcommers were a gift from the Great Day Trader in the sky. They needed no tutoring in the arts of nonconformity, and they were predisposed to believe in the certainty of their role in some swift rout of the old order. They also wielded technical skills that, for the time being, no brick-and-mortar corporation could match and would scramble to commission. It was easy to see how, overnight, the Internet startup became the word-made-flesh of the fast company, playing by new rules. Luckily, too, for Wall Street investors, the Internet was a new medium, and so profits would not have to show up for a few years.

Most important, perhaps, this new medium came along at a time when corporate managers were questioning the meager benefits delivered by two decades of lavish investment in IT infrastructure. While computer technology had grown to become the single largest capital expense for firms, there was no evidence that it generated business value in proportion to its cost.[26] Above all, there was the troubling matter of the "productivity paradox," famously summed up in Nobel economist Robert Solow's throwaway line: "You can see the computer age everywhere except in the productivity statistics." No respected economist had been able to prove that computers had an appreciable impact on the figures that mattered.[27] Nor, it appeared, had the IT revolution realized its boosters' promises of reducing work, commuting time, or costs. At exactly the moment that managers were beginning to demand better returns on their IT investment, the Internet evangelists leapt on stage to announce a new way of wringing value from these costly purchases. The result was a new round of infrastructure investment, driven by the promise, and fear, of Internet commerce and services.

Kissed by millennium fever, the new industry was bolstered daily by signals from Wall Street and the GDP figures that seemed to corroborate the righteousness of the Internet creed. Corporate profits showed rapid growth from 1994 through 1996, coinciding with the Internet's debut in the business world. More significant yet, it was reported that between 1995 and 2000 output per hour in the business sector of the economy rose at an annual rate of 2.8 percent, double the pre-1995 rate and equivalent to the growth rate during the golden years of 1950 to 1973. Analysts attributed this phenomenal growth in productivity to the delayed effect of IT investment and to the first fruits of Internet business activity. Their speculations were touted as fact by media boosters and received official backing from research by Federal Reserve economists.[28] With the claims of the Net apostles apparently corroborated, corporate America was given the green light to prepare for mass conversion.

Before venture capital began to wash through the sector in 1997, the Netsters had pursued their passion for new media software in an environment more akin to a revival meeting, where the gospel of Netscape or Java was expounded to novitiates. After 1997, the passions for social change that had been pinned on technology morphed into a general crusade for corporate change. Building the reformed company would now be the equivalent of the New Jerusalem. The political aspirations that had been kindled by pioneer talk about the Internet were channeled into company building. To younger recruits, this was a more manageable outlook on change. If society seemed hopelessly corrupted on the outside, the more perfect union might be pursued inside politically correct companies. A veteran Web designer in a Boston startup put it well: "The world out there is like the Matrix, totally dark-side, and it's difficult to see what kind of impact you can have, whereas, in here, we thought we could see the changes every day."

The religious metaphors I have used in this thumbnail account are not solely for stylistic effect, nor do they simply reflect the widespread references to evangelism and divinity among technology mavens and market worshipers in the 1990s. Every technology boom to hit these shores has been accompanied by a swelling chorus of pious adulation and an army of pundits and shills promising redemption, salvation, and transcendence. For all its earthly footing in nuts, bolts, chips, and pixels, technology has spawned more otherworldly dreams of self-completion than the revivalist waves of religious enthusiasm that have burned their paths across the American landscape. Technology has not had an easy time being secular and ordinary.

In a country where, as historian David Noble notes, "an unrivaled popular enchantment with technological advance is matched by an equally earnest popular expectation of the return of Jesus Christ," it is no surprise that machines have long been associated with the restoration of Eden and humanity's lost divinity.[29] In *The Religion of Technology,* Noble tracks the appearance of each surge of millenarianism: from the importation of industrialization (fed by the ardor of the Second Great Awakening and the technological zeal of Freemasonry) to the Last Days climate of the Atomic Age, pervaded by Armageddon thinking, to the mystical imaginings of the space program (spearheaded by a heavily Christianized NASA) and today's Holy Grail environment in which genetic engineers pursue the perfection of man under the aegis of Co-Creation. The more recent advent of AI technology and virtual reality has introduced yet another round of fantasies about deliverance from the earthly prison of our imperfect bodies.

The Internet always had its share of born-again converts, and they were joined, in the course of the stock boom, by the wild-eyed carnival barkers, peddling goods and applications—vaporware—that existed only in the mind's eye or in their potential mind-share of a yet to be realized market. For the most fervent of the ideologues, the high-tech scripture had a New Age flavor. Bay Area gurus, like Kevin Kelley and other regular contributors to *Wired* magazine, preached long and hard about the spirituality of information machines and rhapsodized the "networked intelligence" arising from their use.[30] George Gilder joined the party after he saw God in a microchip, and for church libertarians, obsessed with the anti-Christ of big government, there was John Perry Barlow's infamous "Declaration of the Independence of Cyberspace," penned in response to the indecency provisions of the 1996 Telecommunications Act.

The *Wired* digerati glamorized the Bay Area technoculture in ways unimaginable to the prosaic engineers and programmers who built disk drives and wrote software. In so doing, they were performing a promotional function that had been filled by centuries of role-players whose messianic preaching prepared the way for the carpetbaggers and percentage men to follow. As for the overselling touts in the marketplace and on Wall Street, they exalted the novelty, and gilded the prospects, of each generation of digital application, as have the vendors of every previous wave of technology-inspired speculation: telegraph, railroads, electrification, radio, and automobiles. Each wave, in turn, had hosted a land grab and an investment bubble, followed by an abrupt collapse, yielding fire-sale prices for pick-up scavengers to build more enduring firms.

More important, for the purposes of this book at least, was the potential impact of the new technologies on the shape of work. Both kinds of evangelist, the digital guru and the e-hustler, could draw on a legacy of rapture about the labor-saving promise of technology. In this slightly more secular version of technological utopianism, deliverance from toil and drudgery in the workplace figured quite prominently. From the onset of industrialization, every social thinker, including the most recent silicon futurists, has grappled with the tantalizing notion that technological advances could reduce work to a tolerable minimum and free up our leisure time. A society liberated from overwork came that much closer with the advent of the Internet. After all, it hosted the capacity, as a communications tool, to compress time and distance on a scale unprecedented since the introduction of the telegraph. Yet you would be hard put to find anyone whose experience of the new technology in their workplace had resulted in a net reduction of hours on the job. If anything, the concept of a finite workday had been obliterated by 24/7 access to networks of information.[31] Even worse, time poverty was becoming a mark of stature. Whereas persons of leisure had once enjoyed the highest social status, now it was prestigious to be too busy.

In all the euphoria generated on behalf of the Internet, widespread claims were certainly made about how work was being *transformed*. However, there were precious few forecasts about the imminent *reduction* of work hours, let alone the *abolition* of work itself, unless you count the prospect of very early retirement from the bounty of stock options.[32] Nor did evidence of the spurt in productivity lead to calls for capping the increasingly long workweeks of the New Economy employee. If anything, it introduced even more pressure on the job by setting impossibly high expectations for productivity to continue to double, year after year. As long as the New Economy was on an exponential growth curve, the prospects of relief from overwork and speedup were dim.

Although no one was calling for work to fade away, certain kinds of jobs were slated for elimination. For example, routine Web use promised a reduction in the time that we spend in hunting and gathering goods and services: information, news, entertainment, food, shelter, and the whole cornucopia of consumer items. If everything could be researched, or ordered, or even consumed online, then most of the middlemen—brokers, retailers, salespeople, travel agents, editors, publishers—who ran the current system of distribution would be consigned to a jobless Rust Belt as a result of "disintermediation." Not that this would result in mass unemployment. For the time being, at least until the Silicon Alleys of the world spawned their own pink-slip parties, the explosion of jobs in the New Economy sectors was supposed to be able to compensate for layoffs elsewhere.

The Trouble with Capitalism

Given all the heady talk about millennial changes, it was no surprise that conversion experiences were common among those who took

New Economy jobs. Among industry watchers, everyone knew artists and writers who behaved, after a fleeting bout of new media employment, as if they had been bodysnatched. Even though they were steeped in bohemian lore and language, their speech patterns rapidly yielded to the Internet industry's stilted version of Business English: "We will have to leverage our core competencies in hopes of monetizing our assets, so that our scalability and pre-revenue will translate into a value proposition for our investors and deliverables for our clients." In a juvenile industry anxious to establish its credentials, the technical jargon of the trade—awash in "cross-platform infrastructures," "content aggregators" and "innovation systems integrators"— was deliberately enriched so that it took on a mystique that awed clients. But the exact meaning of the words mattered less than the fact that a convert's language was being spoken—proof that the speaker was a signed-up member.

As for the high-flying entrepreneurs, some were plainly baffled about how the sea change had occurred in their lives, not to mention their own political views. The day before my first visit to Razorfish, I had interviewed Scott Heiferman, who was on the verge of becoming a serial entrepreneur—a rare type in Silicon Alley. In Silicon Valley, where the culture tolerated, indeed smiled upon, the occasional failure (it was an acid test of the truly risk-averse), the most lionized entrepreneurs had started more than one company. Heiferman, preternaturally young and prematurely rich for his station, had built and sold i-Traffic, an online ad agency, and was now struggling to pony up funding for Rocketboard, his sophomore startup that manufactured keyboards with built-in shortcuts for Web surfing.

I'm a real hypocrite basically, because my little story of i-Traffic is that, when I was at school, I was a major anti-consumerist. I did this radio program that was all about skewering the consumer society, and I really viciously hated advertising. My whole thinking was that I wanted to start the first online advertising agency because I didn't want it to go to the bad guys. I wanted to do it right and not let it go stupid and dumb like Madison Avenue. As the company grew and grew, it appeared that we needed the help of people who knew how to run big ad agencies, so I hired three guys from the likes of J. Walter Thompson. Then we were acquired by Agency.com, which is 40 percent owned by Omnicom, which is Madison Avenue in the flesh. So we did kick Madison Ave.'s ass; we stole the accounts, we didn't let them get the business, and the place you're sitting in right now has a market cap of almost a billion dollars . . . and it's being run by the same people who were running the shit that I wanted to crush. So call me a hypocrite or whatever. I don't have any great understanding of how I started in one place and now this place is a part of the Establishment.

Pacing through the Agency.com offices on Broad Street, on the very southern tip of Silicon Alley, Heiferman explained that his business was about being "evangelists for good stuff": "We're not working on the polio vaccine here, but we're helping decent companies, getting them more customers, like CDNow, Disney, Staples, British Airways, Nokia. We will never work for a cigarette company or anything like that."

Cigarette companies occupy the same place on the corporate landscape as chemical weapons in the business of warfare; unlike other forms of trade that may be highly destructive to people's lives and environments, they are considered to be rogue players, outside of the rules of the game. The distinction was a lingering reminder of Heiferman's ultra-liberal past, common enough in Silicon Alley. But how was it affecting the rules of business? What other kinds of clients were on the boycott list?

Over at Razorfish, I asked Corinna Snyder how the fish were responding to their newfound intimacy with the corporate world. She always consulted her team on their willingness to work with clients and admitted that she was often surprised by when and why they drew the line: "Sometimes the things that don't bother them really surprise me. Like the ROTC, for example. Now maybe that's just generational." On one recent occasion, employees had expressed concern about a company that staffed workers who cleaned up after nuclear accidents: "They do stuff with nuclear power," and some fish had decided, "we don't want anything to do with them." Yet Razorfish had recently completed an IBM project for the U.S. Navy without any objections. "No one has problems working for the state," she noted. "But the environment is big—a bigger concern than actual structures of power." Every so often, her team drew up a wish list of ideal clients, and she found they were "strongly drawn to doing work for companies that produce consumer goods," of the kind that "impact on their own lives." The opportunity to do client work for Nike, for example, would rank very high, whereas a bank that makes mortgage loans to Middle Americans would not register at all. It hardly mattered that Nike is as famous for its cruel empire of sweatshops in Asia as for its prowess in branding and marketing. The coolness factor seemed to be the deal maker in any debate about business ethics.

Toys R Work, Funny Garbage office, New York (Photo by the author)

Snyder confessed to being "stunned" by the sheer amount of sacrificial time—seven days a week for four months—that her team had put into building a site for Giorgio Armani. "They're so proud of what they did," she marveled, even though the project lost money for the company, and the divas on the Armani end lorded over her Triggerfish in all sorts of disrespectful ways. As long as there were choices, the groovy brands would prevail over all other clients, even socially conscious nonprofit projects, like the prize-winning anti-hate site (www.tolerance.org) that the company was building for the Southern Poverty Law Center.

Some part of this bias surely had to do with Razorfish's design background. Working with consumer, technology, and media brands that already boasted a high level of design innovation was obviously appealing to the creatives. The professional challenge to build these brands online was irresistible, not to mention lucrative. Clients who competed not on the prices of their goods in the commodity market-place but on the strength of the stories that they told through brand image, coolness, and attitude were throwing money at value-adders like Razorfish, who could win them the all-important youthful market share online.[33] In an economy where corporate feats in brand build-ing and image management were rewarded royally by the stock mar-ket, money was no object when it came to commissioning a digital makeover from the e-whiz kids.

But there was more to the brand romance than finding a good match for the fish, creatively and financially. There were some projects that allowed employees to self-actualize more than others, and they were usually for clients who had made their mark on the map of lifestyle consumerism. Corporate brands that had been intimate land-marks in the pop marketplace were now familiar, comforting pres-ences in the office workplace, and they held the same promise of being able to deliver "serious fun." Aleck Bourbon, one of Triggerfish's infor-mation architects, especially noted for his flamboyant persona and his well-stocked wardrobe, explained: "My generation learned how to model our own personalities by trying on consumer products and roles from movies and TV shows. We grew up being able to pick and choose among subcultural styles and indulge in the ironic consumption of things that were so obvious and overpackaged." He acknowledged that the recruitment of individuals like himself into corporate America was being eased by the prospect of working in "companies that are playing at being companies and run by managers who appear to be anti-man-agerial." Employees could believe they were no more complicit with capitalism in this ironic work environment than they were when savor-ing the cheesiness of The Carpenters and Abba.

Capitalism was a dirty word for most of the industry employees I would meet and interview. What did that word mean to them? For the most part, capitalism was something practiced by other, larger compa-nies, especially those that exhibited rule-ridden bureaucracies, bot-tom-line thinking, bland employee cultures, and conservative business strategies. By contrast, companies that were small, fast moving, innov-ative, entrepreneurial, brand active, and socially aware escaped all such scorn. Bourbon's neighbor put it this way: "I'm not an anti-capitalist. I just think capitalism is flawed. It caters to the largest common denominator, and it's designed, ultimately, to create larger and larger companies, which end up burying the small guys. I'd like to see the alternative flourish. I like that I know my CEO's home phone number."

Razorfish's own corporate values offered absolution to employees, if they needed it, from the perceived sins of capitalism or at least placed them at some distance from the belly of the beast. Joel Landau, a technologist on Bourbon's team, who had a background in non-profit social justice organizations and was an unapologetic Naderite, expressed a typically remote view. "There are some things that happen that are driven by capitalism that do people some good and make the world a better place. I can't think of any off the top of my head," he confessed, "but I think it happens sometimes, and it happens coincidentally rather than by design." "All the same," he added, "it doesn't take a genius to see the imbalance in the system that we service—between the tremendous amount of money and effort dedicated to getting instant messages onto cell phones and the fact that we have an army of people starving on the streets."

For those who were earnest change-seekers and who needed to feel the immediate impact of their daily effort, the breathless pace of the digital revolution offered some satisfaction. Even if they could not see a direct way to transform the conditions that allowed people to starve on the streets, employees could believe their work was changing the world of business for the better. The Armani project was all well and good as an arty showcase. But Razorfish had made its biggest splash so far with its digital makeover of Charles Schwab into a potent online tool for day traders—those would-be Jacobins who had been persuaded that they were siphoning off the mandarin power concentrated in the big brokerage houses of Wall Street. At Razorfish, the Schwab effect had been a powerful stimulant. If a single Web site could strike fear at Goldman Sachs, then surely some of the rhetoric about changing the world with the Internet might turn out to have some substance.

Noisy Arrivistes

Fifty years ago, in *White Collar*, his landmark book about the rise of the salaried office employee, C. Wright Mills had this to say about the company men and women who would occupy en masse the nation's office cubicles and suburban ranch homes for the next forty years:

> The white collar people slipped quietly into modern society. Whatever history they had is a history without events; whatever common interests they have do not lead to unity; whatever future they have will not be of their own making. If they aspire at all, it is to a middle course, at a time when no middle course is available, and hence to an illusory course in an imaginary society.[34]

The same could not be said of the no-collar people, the would-be redeemers of the soul of modern work, who had sworn never to wear the equivalent of the gray flannel suit. Their rise was conspicuous from the outset. Over time, it became quite rowdy, self-congratulatory, and high on attitude, and their confidence in their ability to make their own future was firm, almost unshakable. Their aspirations, tethered early to the charmed career of the microchip and then evangelized through their own self-styled Internet medium, were millennial in scale and temper. Unlike the white-collar people, their history was favored by chronicles of heroism, and their common interests had been the target of exhaustive market research.

In Mills's book and in *The Organization Man,* William Whyte's classic of the same period, the independent men and women of the nineteenth-century had faded, America had become a nation of hired employees, and its new middle class were totally managed personnel.[35] Conformist and inhibited, their individualism and virtuosity were being smothered in an overly bureaucratic environment, both in the office and in the morally stifling culture of suburbia. From the moment that the first cadre of disheveled programmers at IBM flaunted the company rules for clocking in and out, the no-collar mentality defined itself in strict opposition to the conditions described by Whyte and Mills. All of the subsequent homage to rule breaking, free speech, open cooperation, creativity, self-dramatization, play, and nonconformity drew its moral force from offering a romantic antithesis to the organization man.[36] So, too, the revival of the small entrepreneur and the depiction of the free agent as an intrepid career option rekindled the spirit of the independent operator for which Whyte and Mills had expressed so much nostalgia.

Noticeably absent, however, were the frugality, self-denial, and plain-speaking honesty associated with that nineteenth-century world of small enterprise for which Mills especially seemed to yearn. After several postwar decades in which middle-class Americans had been encouraged to find the true meaning of themselves in leisure time and consumption, and where the authoritarian workday was a dreary sacrifice that earned them the right to pleasure on evenings and weekends, the workplace was once again being promoted as an environment where personal identity could be deeply felt and shaped. This was just as well, given the "unexpected decline of leisure" that Juliet Schor had documented in her 1991 book, *The Overworked American.* Even then—before the infamous eighty-hour workweeks of the New Economy—the average American was working one month more per year than had been the case two decades earlier.[37]

To be spending so much time on the job, work had to be recast as an existential challenge, at least as stimulating as a college seminar and almost as stirring as the kind of adrenaline sport or edge travel that beckoned thrill seekers from beyond the shrink-wrapped landscape of modern leisure. With the postwar introduction of "the weekend," and with the prospect of the four-day workweek in the offing (a growing possibility before the OPEC crisis), leisure had been accepted as part of workers' legitimate share in the Cold War prosperity. Freed from excessive toil, they could now choose their own cadence. Yet leisure time had long since been broken down into bite-size, salesworthy fractions by the market researcher and lifestyle peddler and orchestrated to a degree that mirrored, in its own way, the clockwork of the industrial factory. After the 1970s, the jobs economy turned increasingly fickle. With dependable, secure employment as uncertain as the weather in New England, leisure could no longer be guaranteed in any reliable quantity. Work, by comparison, had to be advertised, once again, as an outlet for gratification. But if it was to compete with the kind of off-road stimulation offered by the generational ethos of Burning Man, it would have to shoot much higher.

The rehabilitation of work was nothing new in the tech industry, where feats of endurance, machismo, and burnout bestowed a distinctive cachet on socially isolated engineers and programmers. "Working 90 Hours a Week, and Loving Every Minute of It," proclaimed an Apple T-shirt from the 1980s. "We offer flexible time—you can work any 18 hours you want," was a wry slogan at Microsoft. The new media job of the 1990s had to appeal to broader and more socialized segments of the workforce, and so its test of true grit had to be promoted in a way that spoke to the all-round development of individuals: something like the intellectual equivalent of Teddy Roosevelt's strenuous life. As the posting on the Vault board had put it: "The experience you gain here may provide you the ability to transform your environment! You're more alive than you can possibly imagine!" Or, as Razorfish's own recruitment literature promised: "Invent/reinvent your career . . . by living on creativity's cutting edge."

Inevitably, the reemergence of risk and venture was compared to the nineteenth-century entrepreneurial paradigm that overtook the independent strivers who came up through their steady observance of the Protestant and craft work ethics. After the Civil War, a risk-taking business culture began to supplant the cautious restraint of the small producers, farmers, and artisans for whom Ben Franklin's credo of personal industriousness had made sense.[38] For the upwardly mobile, the business of selling, investing, merchandizing, and deal making was becoming the chief means of advancement. Mercantile trading—the art of making sure that things got into the hands of those who valued them most—was the key to market opportunity and fast wealth. Franklin's diligent habits of moderation and self-discipline had less authority in an economic climate swayed by frontier-style gambling on a scale that ran all the way from the fifty-acre land speculator to the grand larceny of the robber barons and early corporate tycoons. In any event, earning a livelihood by making things was fast losing its guarantee of independence under the industrial factory system.

By the time the no-collar people appeared on the center stage of American history, almost a century later, making things was increasingly something that happened overseas, in developing countries. At home, "adding value" was the name of the profit game, and it was all-important in any description of jobs and services. Standard commodities had a basic market worth, but their value could be boosted by intangible qualities like ideas, brands, stories, or designs. In his influential 1991 book, *The Work of Nations,* Robert Reich argued that with the loss of high-volume manufacturing jobs, the key to national competitiveness in the global economy now lay in what value American workers could add to products and services. Bill Clinton's first secretary of labor especially lionized the status of "symbolic analysts," whose skills in problem solving, strategic consulting, and knowledge management would be paramount. Reich calculated that up to 20 percent of U.S. jobs were occupied by symbolic analysts involved in the creative manipulation of symbols, images, and ideas: engineers, consultants, coordinators, designers, managers, brokers, advisers, artists, marketers, academics, stylists, and so on.[39]

As it turned out, this occupational group was not the fastest-growing in the New Economy. The largest growth would come in the low-wage category Reich had described as in-person services: security guards, cashiers, waiters, janitors, hospital attendants, nursing home aides, sales attendants. However, the caliber and status of Reich's symbolic analysts made their jobs a goal toward which all workers were encouraged to aspire and a model to adopt for their children's education. It was this slice of the workforce, influential well beyond its numbers, that harbored the no-collar people and assigned to their skills a providential sense of timing. Their technologies were revered like the sacred fire that Prometheus stole from the gods, though in cold reality, high tech was one of the few sectors of the economy where the United States still held a leading edge. Weaponry was another, but that was also dependent on microelectronics and software. The other contenders were media and entertainment, the arts, and graduate education, each of which had their own no-collar traditions of work—and, it should be added, overwork.

By the end of the decade, Reich was soberly reassessing the punishing toll on time claimed by "the lure of hard work" in the occupations he had helped to venerate. He himself resigned, in a highly visible manner, from his all-consuming job as secretary of labor—"all other parts of my life shriveled into a dried raisin"—and "downshifted out of a fifteen-hour day in Washington to a nine-hour day near Boston."[40] In making this choice, Reich acknowledged that he had been able to achieve what was increasingly unthinkable for most workers in the New Economy. In addition, in returning to the secure life of a tenured academic, he was assuming one of the most anachronistic positions (Stanley Aronowitz has called it "the last good job in America"[41]) on a job landscape that more and more resembled a game of Chutes and Ladders.

The Golden Children of Razorfish

That is no country for old men. The young
In one another's arms, birds in the trees.

—W. B. YEATS, "SAILING TO BYZANTIUM"

BEFORE THE INTERNET GOLD RUSH HIJACKED ALL THE STORIES ABOUT
the industry, New Economy workplaces attracted media attention because they seemed to represent a soulful future for work in the value-
adding sectors that Robert Reich had so praised. All the same, press
scrutiny rarely ventured beyond stories about the gimmicky workplace
trappings—the foosball tables, basketball courts, massage rooms, and
beanbag circles—or the apparent lack of applied work being done in
these free-form environments. Even as the economic tide turned
against the Internet sector in 2000, I had yet to read an adequate description of how employees executed their work on a daily basis. Nor,
it appeared, had industry insiders or company reps done an effective
job of explaining what it was that many companies made or did.

Most of the published material in book form conformed to the
heroic mold of business literature. It centered on the sterling feats
and psychological dilemmas of entrepreneurs or else focused on the
creation, or loss, of fast money. For example, in *Burn Rate*, journalist
Michael Wolff wrote a memorable account of his thwarted career in

Silicon Alley as a new media entrepreneur. Yet there was no record in his book of what it was like for his employees.[1] So, too, Steve Johnson, founder and coeditor of *Feed*, one of the Alley's foremost Web magazines, wrote *Interface Culture*, an enlightening book on the cultural impact of interactive media.[2] Yet no close analysis existed, in that book or elsewhere, of how the medium was actually being used in the New Economy workplace itself. Certainly, there were many message boards, like Vault.com, where employees posted regular commentary about their working conditions, often in a constructive spirit of public debate. Yet the anonymity of the boards also fostered a genre of vitriolic flaming, grudge bearing, and anger inflation that edged out the more civil debaters.

When I approached Razorfish managers about the prospect of my studying the company workplace, they seemed to understand why a hands-on analysis might be useful. No doubt, they imagined it might be of some use to their internal organization reviews (it had become common to hire ethnographers in technology companies), and so my access was approved. Although the impact of the Nasdaq crash had been absorbed, they had no sense of how quickly their high-flying enterprise would swoon. I certainly had no illusions about being the kind of anthropologist that tried to capture a culture before it vanished, though there were many moments, in the year and a half ahead, when it felt just like that.

After a month or two of preliminary interviews with employees, I was allocated a desk in Razorfish's New York offices in early November 2000. By then, the bull market was running out of steam, the firm's stock was in steady decline, and the agency was facing its first real crisis. Whenever an occasion arose, senior management assured employees that they had always regarded Razorfish as a company and not as a stock. Unlike the market's volatility, which was beyond anyone's control, the future of the company's identity and mission was a matter of fierce debate among anxious employees, accustomed to have their say. Almost overnight, a company, and an industry, that had seized hold of the iconography of the future acquired a rosy past. Dogged longing for the good old days was about to become the new new thing. In part, this was because nostalgia could prove useful for employees who wanted to retain some control over the present. In addition, it appeared that there really was something worth remembering. According to the employees I interviewed, Razorfish was, or until very recently had been, "as good as it gets in corporate America." It was on the basis of that glowing reputation that I had chosen the company.

It had been a good couple of weeks for reminiscing in the city at large. New Yorkers had just enjoyed their first "Subway Series" since 1956, and the baseball series had sparked a serious outbreak of nostalgia for the blue-collar city of yore. On sports and editorial pages alike, columnists seized the occasion to ruminate on the striking changes undergone by the metropolis in the ensuing decades. Grievous losses were mourned. The first, and for some, the most unpardonable, was the exit of the Dodgers in 1957, ushering in a new kind of world where employers would pick up and relocate overnight. All through the 1960s and 1970s, the city steadily hemorrhaged manufacturing jobs until the massive cardiac arrest of the 1975 fiscal crisis placed the treasury temporarily in the hands of Wall Street bankers. Ed Koch's new "global city" of the 1980s welcomed the institutions of the international finance markets with open arms, along with a steady stream of low-wage immigrants from the Caribbean and Central America to service their needs. This shift toward high-salaried financial services paved the way for systematic gentrification of the old blue-collar neighborhoods and introduced the yuppie and, most recently, the Disneyfication and suburbanization of key Manhattan districts. In the course of the 1990s, New York jumped from twentieth to first in a ranking of states by the magnitude of the disparity between rich and poor.

At the time of the last Subway Series, when blue-collar Yankee and Dodger fans were the core of its workforce, New York City was still the nation's largest manufacturing town, with 36,000 factories producing 10 percent of all American goods and employing 50 percent of the city's workers.[3] With manufacturing slashed to 7 percent of the city's jobs (almost half the national level), Manhattan was now the alpha domain of Reich's symbolic analysts—managers, consultants, designers, and financiers—attended by armies of immigrant workers who supported the FIRE (finance, insurance, and real estate) industries at its core. No other great city in history has seen its economy and the essence of its social character transformed so fundamentally in such a short period of time.

For all this rapid change, the mercurial rise of Silicon Alley could not have been foreseen, especially in a city that had no history of experience with the technology business and precious little with risk capital. Within five years, this brand-new industry had attracted 8,500 companies and increased its overall revenue to an annual growth rate of 60 percent, chalking up $16.8 billion in revenue in 1999. It had added more jobs (up to 140,000) than the city had seen in many decades (and 250,000 in the tri-state region) and had imported an entrepreneurial business culture (from Northern California) that championed startups with large infusions of venture capital funding.[4] In many ways, the new, bantam-weight startups had less in common with the massive corporate mills of Midtown and the Wall Street district than with the bygone manufacturing firms. Historically speaking, firms in New York had always been small, with an average of twenty or thirty workers apiece, most often devoted to craft and custom production (high-volume production on a mass scale always moved elsewhere) and thriving through close cooperation. Until the 1960s, the city's industrial geography, while extremely diverse in its range of output, had been composed of eponymous high-density districts (including garment, textile, flower, printing, electronics, meatpacking), each hosting hundreds of crowded loft workplaces.[5]

The city's first mass workplaces were actually white-collar corporations—office towers, where standardized and semi-automated work routines were established on floors stacked up like so many drawers in a filing cabinet. Adapted from factories with a linear production stream, the work flow could just as well have been on an assembly line, as paperwork and data moved through each mechanized unit—dictation, typing, stenography, calculating, billing—and then up through the hierarchy of the floors to managers aloft. The means of automation and communication had changed over the decades, as pneumatic tubes and conveyors gave way to information processors. So, too, much of the data processing had been moved to back offices, where it was performed mostly overseas by low-wage operators. But the basic spatial arrangement of the white-collar factory, with its routine itinerary of tasks and vertical lines of command, remained in place. The ubiquitous cubicle, introduced initially as a gesture to employee privacy, had quickly become a symbol of the denial of individuality and, for some, became the signature footprint of alienation.

Silicon Alley's digital artisans, grouped initially in small Webshops, promised to resuscitate some of the city's former reliance on custom craft and skill. So, too, its principal location—a strip that ran from the original Flatiron beachhead down to Soho, stretching, over time, to 41st Street to the north and Wall Street to the south—promised to restore some of the vibrant feel of the old industrial districts, where the rules of a trade had once passed down through the generations and where, in Alfred Marshall's famous description, "the mysteries of the industry are in the air." This location, with choice watering holes for networking and schmoozing and ready proximity to the city's downtown zones of play, was buzzing around the clock with street life and artful flurry, in contrast to the business monocultures of Midtown and Wall Street. But it was also a geography of necessity, in that the industry's startups took root, on shoestring budgets, during the real estate slump of the early 1990s, when commercial rents in the area between Manhattan's two central business districts slid precipitously.

On Wall Street and in Midtown, commercial landlords owned fleets of buildings and included plush executive renovations among their office offerings. In the low-rise corridor that hosted Silicon Alley, the buildings generally belonged to single owners, who had done little to upgrade them in the wake of the manufacturing flight. The bare-plaster aesthetic of the loft interiors was a perfect match for startup companies that cultivated an edgy image. Razorfish, as always, fit the profile with style. It had been founded in Jeff Dachis's dinky East Village apartment (once the home of Geraldo Rivera), moved up to a loft office on Lower Broadway, and now leased several large floors in buildings in NoHo (corporate offices), Tribeca (its TV/broadband unit), and in Soho (the workforce core), where I had been assigned to the Triggerfish team on the fourth floor of the Mercer Street office.

The Builder's Cause

As I entered the office on the first day at my desk, I noticed the Department of Labor regulations about "Permitted Working Hours for Minors" and "Equal Employment Opportunity Laws" that were

The Triggerfish Floor, Razorfish, New York (Photo by Stephen Turbek)

posted on the pantry walls. Much earlier in the decade, I had lived for a while in a nearby loft, where a yellowed copy of labor laws dating to the 1920s was still glued to the inside door of what had been a button factory. Like that building, the hardwood floor of this loft—bearing scars but freshly polished—had seen many garment workers come and go. Greenhorn immigrants were the first to toil there, cutters and sewers working around the clock to make ends meet in the New World. Whereas they had stooped over sewing machines, well-scrubbed fish with college degrees were now hunched over their laptops, a tad cranky from long hours on their latest client project. The vast open space was interspersed with workstations grouped together in rafts, like boats in a busy harbor.

The garmentos built an industry that would dominate New York City for the first half of the century. At one time, it seemed as if the Silicon Alley entrepreneurs might do the same. In fact, the two industries kept on crossing each other's paths in ways that would come to haunt the employees who appear in this book. I would shortly discover that the fish on the Mercer Street floors had had to remove the sewing machines' moorings and sand off the machine oil before the company could take over from its previous tenant. Garment workers still shared the building that Razorfish used around the corner on

Broadway. Silicon Alley had grown up, cheek by jowl, with garment sweatshops that were gradually displaced further east and back into Chinatown, as rents rose and rose. The gulf between nineteenth-century and twenty-first-century modes of production had narrowed to a finger's breadth.

The entire Triggerfish team was about to meet, as it did every Tuesday morning, to trade ideas, report on projects, and strengthen team bonds. Two boxes of Krispy Kreme doughnuts arrived on cue, and those filtering in at 9:30 A.M. swiveled their Aeron chairs to face the floor's center. A poster for the movie *Matrix* hung off-center on the wall, with a po-faced Keanu Reeves presiding over the scene. Things started out slow with upbeat announcements from Corinna Snyder about the company's new mobility service offering. Razorfish had recently adapted a new motto—"Everything that can be mobile, will be"—to reflect the hope that new contracts in the wireless technology domain would pull the company out of its business doldrums. Unlike the Boston office, Razorfish NY did not have a strong technology base and indeed was losing some of its best tech people for want of challenging back-end work. It was known more for molding ideas about how existing technology could be put to new uses. Although many things had been invented in New York (electric elevators, cast iron, refrigeration, steamboats, sound recording for movies), the city has never had a technology industry, nor does it host a culture that is easily dazzled by new gadgets.

A technologist next to me, his desk displaying the current holy tech trinity of cell phone, laptop, and Blackberry (the preferred email toy of high-tech and financial elites), stood up to pitch the new program: "Mobility at Razorfish isn't just a technical solution; it's about the user experience." "Usability" had lately become the industry's favorite buzzword, and so acknowledgment of the principle of user experience was almost obligatory. Pretty soon, however, his presentation yielded to next-generation rhetoric: "Mobility is not only about wireless; that's just one piece of the pie. It also has to do with pervasive or ubiquitous computing, and so it's all about embedded solutions—voice recognition and biometric identity verification—that can be built into our products. We should be in the business of inventing intelligent objects. For example, we are beginning to see technologies that allow all of your components to talk to one another—your watch, your laptop, your WAPs. They're called ad hoc networks, and they're like a bee swarm." All of this cool new stuff, he reported, was being shaped in the Pervasive Lab, a room on the floor below, and at a Mobility Lab, which the company was building in San Jose.[6]

Snyder introduced the Web site URL for training instructions and suggested that employees gen up on the mobility campaign for their client pitches. The response on the floor ranged from low-key to neutral. Gee-whizzery was nothing new around here. Besides, it was a little early in the day for fish to get worked up. Snyder, who had a stable supply of natural pep, tried to kindle her people: "It's like a tomb in here. You're all wearing bulletproof vests. We need to spike your coffee." The next agenda item woke everyone up. Snyder reported that a client satisfaction survey had given low grades to the company. The general problem, she summarized, was that clients felt Razorfish didn't "listen."

This seemed to strike a chord, and voices from the floor opened up, seizing the opportunity to air some of their anxieties. A tall male strategist in blue jeans, standing by the back wall, stepped forward to agree with the report: "I think it's on the money. There is a real level of resistance to listening among us. We need to get rid of our haughty mentality and attitude and acknowledge that this is a huge problem. Our clients are much older and more experienced, and they think we're arrogant." Raising one hand, as if he were taking an oath in court, he ended with a moralistic flourish, "There's a difference between being inspirational and being overconfident."

No one seemed surprised that some of the designers in the room felt differently. One of them, an earnest young woman in a white polo neck sweater, questioned the clients' perceptions: "Experiments and risk taking are what we live for, and these clients generally don't want it. Is it our job to educate them, or does the culture not support risk taking any more? Many of these clients are learning, but they still don't understand what we do. I don't think they really appreciate that we are adding incredible value to their companies." Her neighbor, a technical writer, backed her up: "We have a reputation for brilliance, and that's why they are attracted to us. We have a great culture and a real personality, and clients want us because of that. But our design work is brilliant in an understated way; its elegance comes through its functionality, so clients are sometimes confused by the result."

Snyder diplomatically reminded her group of the survey results: "Actually, according to the survey, our clients don't think we're cowboys or too risky. What this survey shows is that we are underperforming even in traditional ways. This is a service and relationship business. Trust equals intimacy divided by risk. It won't work anymore to say to clients that we know what we're doing. We need to build this trust."

The references to cowboy arrogance cut close to the bone. Razorfish had done a princely trade on its cocksure vow to deliver the digital future to corporations driven by the fear of being left behind by e-business. Over time, their clients were learning how to do some of this work for themselves, and so the company's self-assurance was eroding. Increasingly, the fish were finding themselves saddled with the swagger that accompanied the company's dizzy rise, especially the brash boy élan of its founders Jeff Dachis and Craig Kanarick, who were regularly featured in the press as the pride of the Alley. Kanarick, the techno-artisan, had made his PR mark with periodic hair color changes and groovester workwear and had successfully adapted the gonzo tech evangelism of the Silicon Valley "it boys" by adding hip urban upgrades that went down well with media and conference audiences. In a decade when CEOs were groomed to behave like aging rock stars, Dachis had risen to the impetuous upstart role demanded of the Internet entrepreneur, skewering competitors and market analysts alike in a shameless manner. A much envied, and much satirized, act, "Craig 'n' Jeff" had enjoyed a sparkling run as the Alley's leading playboys for the past five years. As the market soured, the posture lost its allure and would soon become a liability to the company.

But on that November day, at least, it was the women who were doing all the talking. A weary-looking project manager, standing by the pantry door, still wearing her outdoor fake fur, hollered out: "We've been having culture clashes, and we badly need to have this conversation." At Razorfish, it was acceptable to have open disagreements. In fact, "creative friction" was the name given to one of the company's core principles. Chafing or conflict between employees was encouraged as a source of productivity. There was even a relevant

section in the Razorfish Creative Mission handbook: "Energies released between differing perspectives and working methods can be
harnessed to create breakthrough solutions."

The culture clashes in question had been building over the course
of two years, ever since the company expanded from a design shop
into a full-service consulting agency. Some of the discord had been a
result of company acquisitions, where employees of a competitor firm
suddenly found themselves thrust into the Razorfish pen. A much
sharper source of conflict had to do with the shifting direction of the
company's primary business. Many of the team's designers, writers,
and technologists were still most comfortable with building sites and
systems that gave them personal satisfaction because they were perceived to be at the forefront of Web innovation. If they satisfied
clients along the way, that was an added bonus. Working for the
groovy companies or nonprofits, where this kind of gratification
seemed more likely, could always be subsidized by client projects in
finance and insurance or the ones with blue-chip names (IBM, Cisco,
Verizon), who were the most durable source of revenue. In either
case, the fish were producing something tangible, at least by the standards of their virtual medium.

By contrast, many veteran employees were none too happy about
consulting for large corporations on a long-term basis. Pushing the
limits of the medium was a pretty cool way of paying the bills, but
managing some mega-company's e-business prospects was too much
like corporate business as usual at an established consultancy like
McKinsey or KPMG. "In a standard consulting model, you can't do
mind-boggling things," explained one of the designers, standing up
and moving to the center of the room to claim more attention,
"whereas in a standard building model, you don't usually maintain a
long-term relationship with a client." "Maybe super-profitable consulting work can help subsidize the fun design stuff we like to do,"
suggested the writer, venturing a compromise. The strategist at the
back of the room brought the discussion to an abrupt close by rejecting the distinction outright: "Consultants do actually make things, and
besides, clients want to know we'll be here next year."

No one really wanted to be reminded of this last point, but over the
next several months, it became clear that the future of their jobs de-

pended on it. On one side, the soul of the company—its much-vaunted culture and renown for ingenuity in design—was at stake. On the other, the company's neck was on the chopping block. But this discussion about building and consulting hinted at more widely shared anxieties among no-collar workers about the nature of value-adding work. The advocates of building clearly felt they were rooting for the business of making things that existed in the world and that could be used again and again. They were appealing to a pragmatic spirit that ran deep in the American grain, one that had suffered as manufacturing shops closed all across the United States. Building interactive sites, creating software applications, and designing IT infrastructure all smacked of craft manufacture, and they could lay claim to an honest toiler's pedigree. By comparison, the strategy consultant's trade of servicing clients who were looking to capitalize on market opportunities seemed like an oily art, a game for yuppie hucksters looking for the main chance.

However, not all the fabricators, not even all the technologists, saw their own work as firmly grounded in reality. "With design, you do something, you look at it, everyone's got an opinion about it," explained Todd Drake, the company's lead technology evangelist. "Technology happens in a much more abstract space where all you're looking at is models of things. Code is a just a model of something that is functional. If we're honest with ourselves, all we're building are models. You can't really see it or touch it, except by interacting through some visual representation, and so the visuals actually do something; they are doing useful work. So it's kinda Taoist—you can only really describe it, not touch it. The metaphysics of engineering and hacking can seem like a mystical quest—which is why everyone plays Dungeons and Dragons—but if you've been doing it for a long time, you realize that you're really just playing with models." It wasn't difficult to find a creative who disagreed. Sure enough, a Japanese designer, whom I interviewed the same day as Drake, offered her own spin on his neo-Taoism. She preferred Web design to technology design, she said, "because the product doesn't turn into garbage. You can just erase it and it's gone. Garbage sucks." Because of her religion, she said, which holds that all physical things have a life, she found it difficult to throw anything away. "That's why I like working on the Web. I don't feel so uncomfortable making stuff that simply doesn't exist."

Philosophical clashes between technologists and designers had a long industrial history, stemming from differences in style, socialization, and trade vocabulary. For all that, the two disciplinary groups (the Technology network and the Experience network, as they were known at Razorfish) shared customs and habits of craft that put them less at odds with each other than with the Strategy network. Nor were relations so smooth with the client partners and project managers who made up Value, the fourth of the networks, charged with the task of aligning and coordinating the other three on client projects.[7] In any knowledge organization, there is always a sharp push-and-pull tension between employees on the creative side and those on the business side. Creatives will always feel their integrity is imperiled by bottom-line finance people, while the latter will complain that the narcissism of the creatives makes for inefficiency. At Razorfish, however, the strategists were relatively new, and their authoritative presence as the wave of the future was a threat to the existing balance of power among employees. During my first six months at the company, they were often depicted as alien intruders on an Edenic work environment where creativity and business resolve had coexisted peacefully.

What, then, lay behind the claim made by the strategist in the Triggerfish meeting that consultants also make things? Perhaps it was defensive in part, since the newcomer strategists still had to prove themselves to the golden children of Razorfish. On the other hand, strategy consulting, as an occupation, could not have been riding any higher in the business world. It had played a pivotal role in the so-called shareholder revolution, which reestablished financial control over corporations by reining in managerial autonomy and making CEOs accountable for the equity performance of their companies. Strategists had been the architects of the palace revolution that overthrew managerial capitalism, and on their say-so, executives had finally made the decisions that investors wanted. Every tactic employed by CEOs to deliver an extra fraction of market value to shareholders was introduced at the urging of the strategy hotshots, and their knack for "optimizing" companies was valued above all others as a New Economy priority. Because they were unaccountable to employees (except in the latter's capacity as stockholders), they were often regarded as caretakers of elite outside interests.

Given their pivotal role in the distribution and delivery of value, it is hardly surprising that strategists could imagine themselves to be makers and creators. After all, they decreed the size, shape, and identity of companies, in addition to devising methods for turning the base metal of earnings into golden equity. Their business solutions were technical fixes for clients' problems and in this respect could be seen as part of the infrastructure. Yet their own professional status was saddled with an unhappy consciousness. The business revolutionaries of the 1990s may have applauded the strategy consultants as spiffy change agents, but they eulogized entrepreneurs as the real culture heroes who actually built companies and created wealth. The Triggerfish strategist's comment about making things also tapped into larger misgivings about the value of the profession to society as a whole. No matter how high-priced or blessed by Wall Street, the strategists would always be regarded with skepticism by those employees who judged them as non-producers and likely to side with the client in any potential conflict. Even in an industry that made virtual products and services and that was more intimate than most with the stockholder theory of value, it was easy to detect evidence of the legacy of producer pride.

In the producer economy of yore, labor was viewed as the primary source of wealth and, for that matter, the only true measure of value. No less than Adam Smith established this point. John Locke extended the argument to personal property. If you work it or improve it, it belongs to you by right. Locke's principle was the philosophical core of freeholding labor that guided the early years of the producer's republic, where free men and women owned their own labor and made things for themselves and for the good of the community. With the institution of slavery, these beliefs were flatly corrupted. The advent of industrialization and waged labor threatened them in new ways. Factory owners could now extract value from labor, and the product of labor was no longer the personal property of those who had worked it. Nonproducers who profited from this system—merchants, lawyers, bankers, speculators—were in the same blighted corner as the owners. In living off the sweat of others, they violated the integrity of the self-reliant freeholder citizen that Jefferson and others had revered.

Although production has largely moved elsewhere, that sense of indignation has not entirely eroded. It flared up in the scandal over the collapse of Enron, a company that specialized in turning things, like raw energy, into commodities and then into financial instruments to be traded online like stocks. Nothing could have dramatized better the gulf between an economy of tangible things and a spin economy, contrived to siphon off profits by cooking the numbers and telling the best stories. More to the point, the scandal exposed the ways in which profit and stockholder value flowed exclusively to consultants and executives. Rank-and-file company employees who had been brought into the stockholding system through their 401(k) plans were left out in the cold. Their anger fueled widespread misgiving about the merits of financialization and put on public trial the cozy relationship between executives and consultants. The ensuing crisis of confidence in investor capitalism, and in corporate America as a whole, raised a new round of questions about the public utility of consultants and other agents of finance. What do they actually do? And is it of any long-term worth to society?

We Dream, We Do

What companies like Razorfish actually do had recently been a matter of public curiosity, suspicion, and occasionally, ridicule. *Sixty Minutes II* had broadcast the company's single most embarrassing moment earlier in the year, when Dachis and Kanarick were chosen to represent the industry in a segment on Internet companies. Interviewer Bob Simon asked Dachis to explain ("in English") the company's purpose. "We've recontextualized what it is to be a services business," Dachis replied. Simon asked for something more concrete. "We radically transform businesses to invent and reinvent them . . . ," Dachis ventured. This was still too vague for Simon, who allowed a harrowing silence to follow. Kanarick finally rescued Dachis by killing the question with a crisp response ("Business strategy"), but not before the industry's lingering aura of mystique had been converted into a dark cloud of mistrust for millions of viewers. The term "recontextualizing" instantly took pride of place within the office humor of Razorfish employees, and the industry as a whole.

The segment was predictable *Sixty Minutes* fare, but it preyed on several different species of anxiety. In the world of *Sixty Minutes* populism, plain speech is always a sign of virtue, and professional jargon is usually an indicator of duplicity and cant. The villains always speak with a forked tongue, which the debunkers expose. In this instance, the bad guys were the new kids on the media block and therefore a threat to old media's monopoly on public speech and information flow. *Sixty Minutes* represented the acme of broadcast media pride and was not about to miss an opportunity to take the contenders down a peg or two. In addition, the public image of the industry was nourished by larger-than-life profiles of twenty-something millionaires who were judged to have come by their wealth far too easily. Even in a winner-takes-all capitalist economy, the legacy of the producer republic and the Puritan work ethic requires the victors, at the very least, to show that they have worked hard for their spoils. Bob Simon was trying to confirm the widespread suspicion that dotcommers were selling snake oil, at vastly inflated prices.

Internet insiders who watched the segment would have recognized the voice of a company in an uncertain business landscape, where the identity of firms could mutate from quarter to quarter. It was also the voice of a juvenile industry trying to establish its legitimacy by adopting the lexicon of Business English and adding a convoluted spin or two of its own. The need to appear and sound mature in the presence of parents—clients, business analysts, and the general media—had lately become paramount. Josie Baxter, the designer who had been so vocal in the Triggerfish meeting, noted that "as a company grows, its people increasingly use this kind of codified language, which is made up of shortcuts or passwords for things that we actually do. I feel it was a lot more real when we actually had to be articulate and explain ourselves." Many of her colleagues were Web veterans for whom the industry was an expedient opportunity to carry on inventing and tinkering with the new medium. They saw the business lingo as a handy alibi, or cover, to shield them from too much unwanted scrutiny. All the talk about monetizing and leveraging and recontextualizing was simply a way of buying time to do their thing in a work setting that gave them lots of free rein. Razorfish had more than its fair share of employees like this. As Baxter observed, "it's only recently that they have put their heads up and noticed that something else is going on."

But for Baxter, the jargon in the *Sixty Minutes* segment sent a direct message. It belonged to the rhetoric of consulting; it was not the language of those who made things. "If you're a consultant," she pointed out, "you talk about the clients you have worked with. If you make things, you talk about the things that you have made." In her opinion, the company "had turned the corner on this issue." In a business landscape where brands are towering landmarks that attract high-flying investors, the names of clients are passports to gainful recognition. By the 1990s, making things was much less lucrative than making brands, and if you become a publicly traded company, as Razorfish had been since its boffo IPO in April 1999, the pressure to make money for stockholders, according to Baxter, "obliges you to distance yourself from the activity of building."

Even if it was headed in a direction that Baxter didn't like, Razorfish hardly matched the dotcommer stereotype that the *Sixty Minutes* segment had been mining for effect. For one thing, it was not a dotcom, since it did not rely on traffic to its Web site to sell goods or information. Razorfish had built dotcoms, but its primary business increasingly lay elsewhere. Nor had it peddled an iffy business model to venture capitalists and engineered an IPO without having generated very much revenue, let alone a drop of profit. In fact, the firm had produced substantial revenue and had turned a profit in every quarter from its inception. As for the millionaire mystique, salaries had risen handsomely in tandem with the company's success, but in my time at Razorfish, I would not encounter a single employee who had joined up with the chief intention of becoming rich.

As for Silicon Alley as a whole, the statistics about compensation told quite a different story from the public cliché of tattooed slackers raking in the lolly. The most comprehensive industry surveys of new media employment in New York City from the years 1996–1998 consistently showed the average full-time employee earning less than $40,000, about half the equivalent in old media industries like advertising (at $71,000) and TV broadcasting ($86,000). These figures, compiled by PriceWaterhouseCoopers and the New York New Media Association, did not factor in the value of stock options or other forms of deferred income, which were enjoyed by more than 40 percent of the workforce. Yet any informal sample of industry employees would confirm that few benefited overall from these options. Other surveys gave considerably higher salary estimates, but none that came anywhere near to matching the public stereotype of stratospheric wealth.[8]

To fully appreciate the *Sixty Minutes* exchange with Dachis and Kanarick, you would have to ask why this story, and others like it, had been assigned in the first place. Internet stock fever was a requisite news item from 1998 to 2000 and then again in its death spiral phase. Understandably, there was immense public interest in the business activity of companies like Razorfish. But word had also gotten out about the jobs themselves. What if they really were as good as they sounded? Workplaces that guaranteed personal dignity, encouraged individual initiative and ingenuity, and allowed employees to be their own boss? What if this kind of job was sustainable, and what if it spread into the general workforce?

Satisfying the Internal Client

Two years earlier, when Baxter left her job in a Chicago advertising firm to join Razorfish, she encountered "the kind of work you just couldn't help doing." It was a new and unanticipated kind of pleasure, and she found herself sharing it with colleagues she had never expected to enjoy so much. Patricia Lopez, a project manager on the Swordfish team who had moved from a telecom company in New Jersey, described her own experience in a way that was common enough among her peers: "When I first came here I remember thinking, there's absolutely no way on earth that a company like this can exist, that it can be run the way it is, with so many intelligent and dedicated people, and where the perks and the stress are totally balanced so that you don't feel you are selling your soul to the bosses." If anything, the impact was even greater on those who hailed from noncorporate backgrounds. Paul Beniger, a jazz musician who had been "kicking around the nonprofit world" for several years, recalled: "I was in shock for a full six months. The institutions I had been at had socially conscious missions, but the good intentions didn't always extend to their own employees. Razorfish was like a workers' paradise by comparison."

All of the fish had their stories about Camelot, except for recent recruits who joined after the Golden Age, and then they had a Silver Age story to tell. A standard feature in these glowing accounts was praise for fellow employees, whose integrity and passion for their work had made the task of cooperation and consensus building all the more satisfying. Internal mobility across disciplines also ranked highly. Because the organization was relatively flat and fluid, many of the fish found it easy to shift from one area of expertise to another, learning a range of skills in the process. Indeed, the workforce boasted more than one crack professional who had started out as the company's receptionist. Others found the environment especially useful in exorcizing the evil spirits of their prior training. Melinda Katz, an MBA with a High Goth wardrobe, stepped away from business school, where she had "encountered the most morally and ethically challenged human beings you could imagine," into a Razorfish job, where there were "no politics, no bullshit, no careerists, no ladder climbing, no brown nosing, no sniveling, none of the weird social dysfunctions that you encounter everywhere else." In this work utopia, she said, "I was met with a constant wave of permission to test myself, without any of the usual pressure, or threats, about succeeding."

Some veterans like Cecelia Clough, who had become titleless (a privilege of old school employees), interpreted this sense of permission as an opportunity to practice her loyalty to the company: "I've always tried to fill a critical function that brings value to the organization. I look around, see what needs to be done, and then more or less define a job description and a title around that." "Enjoying this autonomy," she explained, while reaping the rewards of full-time employment, meant that she "had all the benefits of a company woman without having to be one."

Younger recruits, less identified with the career of the company than with their own, particularly relished the absence of direct supervision. To be treated as "responsible adults" who could be left to their devices to complete their work, whether in the office or at home, was a blessing for freshly minted college graduates. Many inferred that the *real* world of adult employment (beyond Razorfish) would not tolerate this sort of thing. They likened their experience to a postadolescent realm of adventure, even though their self-directing role within the company organization was freighted with more than the usual share of risk and adult responsibility.

The permission ethic allowed employees to use the office as a potential funhouse, where self-dramatization and performance contributed to work and play alike. The majority of the fish were new to New York City and found that they could get an easy social fix in the workplace or on breaks with their fellow workers at a nearby bar or club between stints on a project. Clough recalled the Gen X experience of herself and fellow slackers who "perfected the art of fun in the early 1990s, when there was no meaningful work out there. When we finally decided to get serious, there was no reason to discount, no reason not to bring that perfected art of fun into the business experience." Naturally, the founders had made it their business to "satisfy the internal client," and so the fish had perks that were common to the industry—in-house masseur, video-gaming room, gym membership discounts, regular social excursions, and some very famous parties.

Recreation Room, Razorfish, Boston (Photo by the author)

Yet employees had much more to say about the grassroots im-
promptu sport than the built-in perks. Many described it as a privilege to share a workplace with colleagues who could conjure up a di-
version or scene by improvising their wit, dramatic talent, or sense of
occasion. The dancer who would crank the radio up and take his
freestyle moves out for a five-minute spin on the loft floor. The writer
who circulated an unsparing critique of the business jargon she overheard in the course of the day's work. Or the chanteuse who randomly
accompanied the 4 P.M. calisthenic break with standards from her
Broadway repertoire. The fun could materialize digitally but was
more likely to happen in real time and space, as if to offset the burden
of online application.

Henry Castells, a programmer who had abandoned the "Silicon
Valley monoculture for a taste of urban diversity," insisted that the fun
had to involve a healthy dose of cynicism: "We practice cynicism to
the point of rejecting whatever we have been spoon-fed, whatever we
have been programmed to believe about how workplaces are supposed to be, including our own management's version. In the Valley,
companies played along with the tech hype, but here I quickly discovered there was a passionate will to take nothing for granted, not
even what Razorfish Corporate said."

Clough attributed this passion to the experience of her generation
in the recession of the late 1980s and early '90s, "when the world at
large did not cooperate with our expectations." She recalled: "We
were highly educated people, and we decided that if the world wasn't
going to validate us and our worth, then we were not going to validate
conventional wisdom and its worth. So the psychology of young adults
like us was to refuse to participate in the status quo." Once they decided to make their mark on business by creating an alternative to the
status quo, "lo and behold, the economy started to cooperate." By
contrast, those who came of age later, in the new go-go climate,
"found themselves in a highly cooperative world that embraced all of
their aesthetics and aspirations," and so they developed "a psychology
of entitlement without accountability." For the most recent Gen Y recruits, the fun was no longer something they had cultivated and re-
fined; it was more likely to be taken for granted, along with the other
benefits offered by HR.

Yet Clough's Gen X perspective could always be trumped by the bragging rights of boomer employees, a few of whom had managed to slip onto the payroll. Tom Fallows, a technologist who cut his teeth in the Bay Area hacker counterculture that gave birth to the legendary Homebrew Computer Club, formed his views on the politics of hedonism while living in Haight-Ashbury in the late 1960s. When it came to risk taking and spontaneous play, the twenty-something fish did not even register on his scale: "It was the outrageousness, or the potential outrageousness of Razorfish, that attracted me to the job. But they are all much more conservative than I expected, both at work and in their playtime. No one's risking themselves; no one's taking big chances."

A seasoned graduate of the hippie romance with human-scale technology (which had given birth, in its own way, to the personal computer), Fallows was more charitable about his colleagues' belief in the utopian potential of the Internet. The company's Golden Age had crested the wave of true believerism in digital change, and he was heartened that many of the fish had held onto the conviction that the medium really could usher in a world where people's needs could be better harnessed to resources. Yet Fallows had been disappointed to see much of the energy unleashed by this conviction being channeled, in the industry at large, into a narrow profit-taking orgy. Employees, he said, were itching to do pro bono work and to see their skills make a social impact beyond the upsides and downsides on the stock watch. So far, at least, Silicon Alley had not bettered the technology industry's notoriously weak record of philanthropy and social involvement.[9]

Change fever had taken its toll in ways that were being felt internally. Some of the blessings of the Golden Age had begun to reveal their hidden costs. Josie Baxter's discovery of "work you just couldn't help doing" meant that she was consistently putting in the kinds of hours for which Net workers had become renowned: deeply caffeinated seventy-hour workweeks, where the rest of the world simply dropped out of sight, and when there were days off, they were spent recuperating.

Janice McIver, a project manager with extensive industry experience, had left the frenetic Bay Area for what she hoped was the calmer climate of New York, because she had been "in way too deep." "There was no downtime, no chance of being civilized," she recalled.

"I simply did not know where the work stopped and I began." By the time she joined Razorfish, the work crunch that led up to the IPO was over, but the projects were coming thick and fast, and the office was still more of a first than a second home. At a School of Fish session in Europe on personal values, "I finally realized I had nothing to put on the table about who I was, except for my work. It was sad and stunning to me." To the credit of management, she reported, she had been put on a special program, along with the company's "biggest workaholics," that emphasized the need to salvage life outside of the workplace.

Kathy Vanderstar, a writer and self-described Luddite who had been raised on an Oklahoma cattle ranch, tried to explain the appeal of long hours: "Definitely, there was a certain coolness to being in a kind of sweatshop, a coolness to staying late into the night. It was intoxicating at first. Look at me! I'm in New York and I'm working really late! Then, of course, you realize that it sucks. But, even then—and this was the strange part—it was still a rapturous feeling." Her boyfriend, Barry, was a programmer who worked at Oven, a nearby Internet firm. He described a related kind of narcosis: "I used to get a real kick out of taking my laptop and all my work home. I was wired for so long and had problems sleeping because I could always go over to the computer. When I'm in front of a laptop, something happens to my brainwaves, and I'm basically wired for long periods of time. It's like a drug." In the Silicon Valley culture of engineers and programmers, there was a boy bravura to working on the edge of burnout, and Vanderstar acknowledged that part of the appeal of keeping vampire hours lay in a woman's prerogative to compete.

In the industry as a whole, the distribution of laptops to all employees was decisive in securing their long hours, regardless of their work location. Scott Kurnit, one of the Alley's most successful entrepreneurs, bragged about his experience at running MCI/Newscorp's iGuide: "This was a company that worked all the time. This was a company that handed out laptops to everybody. This was a company that checked email on weekends" and "cooked up ways to compete" on Sundays. The same hard-boiled swagger applied to About.com, his next enterprise. "We can run twice as fast as other companies, as long as we have the people here who get a kick out of doing that. So we do our best to get people here who do. Run faster, run harder, be smarter, be better, get compensated, get rewarded for it. . . . It's not that we mean to kill our people. We don't. We're not a sweatshop—but we mean to actually free you up while having you work all the time."[10] In moments like these, when their bosses puffed themselves up, the tongue-in-cheek analogy that many Net workers drew between their workplaces and garment sweatshops must have seemed all too real.

At other times, the recognition and caring enjoyed by the fish inside their own industry bubble could breed unrealistic expectations about the corporate landscape of work. For example, the Razorfish policy of satisfying the internal client could set employees up for dispirited dealings with clients who had no particular reason to lavish them with praise. Vanderstar described the frustration of trying to get the same encouragement from clients that they got from their own colleagues and managers: "I guess we're all people that have had successes in school, and we've always gotten pats on the back, and here at Razorfish there is lots of recognition. Great job, you're doing a great job! And so we expect that from everyone, and that's not life in corporate America." It was a predicament that many office workers might view with envy.

Mel and Fanny

With lush Camelot still visible in the rear view mirror, the road ahead was uncertain, and it might lead through the corporate badlands. "We're one step away from cubicles," joked Vanderstar, though she knew full well from her visits to the offices of clients that Razorfish was still an Eden by comparison. By November, the pipeline of orders was drying up, and most fish were spending their days preparing and delivering pitches to prospective clients. In Silicon Alley, the number of dotcom sudden deaths had been mounting daily—over 20,000 layoffs between the April fall-off on the Nasdaq and third-quarter statements. Razorfish did not escape unscathed. With third-quarter earnings sharply down and its early customer base shriveling away, one-tenth of the global workforce were let go in the last week of October. In the New York office, the layoffs took almost two weeks to execute. "The Band-Aid was very slowly peeled away," lamented one veteran, who had been enlisted on a Morale Team to help repair the damage. Just as bad, the layoffs were announced by way of a euphemism—a "performance improvement plan"—that made employees cringe and inspired all sorts of gallows humor. For fish who had grown accustomed to an environment that could only reward and never penalize, the emotional toll was particularly acute. After all, the family romance of the company was one of orphans raised by a pair of enterprising but watchful older brothers. Siblings are not easy to fire, and managers who were confronted with the task had no experience to fall back on.

Many of the fish I initially interviewed had so entirely taken self-management to heart that they were only just beginning to notice that the company had a senior management group. Old school veterans were still living off the esprit de corps of their startup years with Kanarick and Dachis, while newer recruits had scant contact with the corporate officers who were housed in a different building fifteen blocks to the north in NoHo and who appeared to exercise no visible control over work schedules and goals. All of a sudden, or so it seemed, the upper administrators began to behave more like corporate managers, and their decision-making became all too visible to production-level fish.

Taking a page out of the Harvard Business School textbook, the first of several "reorgs" was introduced to pump some accountability into the organization's flat structure and to build confidence among investors. In a series of email communiqués that were judged to be very top-down for Razorfish, management announced that project teams should now be pursuing ten-year, multimillion dollar contracts with mega-corporations. These Fortune 500 clients would replace the more diverse client list that had made the company's name.

Dachis and Kanarick had earned points for nurturing employees during the firm's mercurial growth, and the company's record of low turnover spoke for itself. How would this empathetic environment fare in the downturn, when more layoffs seemed inevitable? Silicon Alley was already awash with stories of ruthless downsizing and callous conduct on the part of managers who had shut shops overnight and fled, leaving wages unpaid and severance packages undelivered.

Other employers, with an eye still on the prize, had floated hopeful press releases about their new business plans before firing off rounds of pink slips. For an industry that was supposed to have inherited Silicon Valley's tradition of esteem for business people who had failed once or twice, there was no evidence that these new insolvencies were being regarded benignly. A punitive air prevailed among the brick-and-mortar citizenry, for whom the scapegoating of dotcommers was becoming a popular sport. The wrath was commonly shared by investors of all stripes, cruelly deprived of their Nasdaq fix. But the most curious response of all could be found among industry insiders. *Schadenfreude* does not quite capture the mix of rancor and glee that possessed industry voyeurs of the carnage, who made Philip Kaplan's fuckedcompany.com the Web site of choice for spectator sport or fresh news from the killing fields.[11]

Web consultancies were insulated to some degree from the brunt of the dotcom collapse. Razorfish, in particular, had always been promoted as ahead of the pack or, in one indelible Dachis boast, as "six or seven generations ahead of any of our competitors."[12] But no amount of bravado would save his company from being sucked into the layoff vortex. Some veterans who had been in the industry since the days of the CD-ROM boomlet in New York in the early 1990s saw a silver lining in the first round of cuts. They had lived through previous shakeouts and had seen business come back even stronger. In addition, there were some who welcomed the opportunity to do some housecleaning. "Razorfish is a self-cleaning oven," I had been told by more than one employee. "Folks who don't belong culturally tend to phase out." The layoffs were a way of shedding the incompatibles who had been hired during the recruitment explosion, when a rising body count assured a higher stock valuation.

But it was impossible to ignore the mounting stress levels. "It's so primitive," lamented Camille Habacker, a sparkling fashion plate who was Director of Content for North America. "People here are having migraines, breaking out in hives, rashes, panic attacks, serious physical manifestations of mental trauma." Named by her parents in honor of Garbo's greatest role ("I have a high standard to live up to"), she herself seemed unflustered. But she expressed alarm about the erosion of the company culture where she played a very particular role:

"I'm supposed to be one of these motivational people who keeps everybody together, but I have to admit I am way too emotionally invested in Razorfish. If we can't rescue the soul of this company, then we are truly fucked." As a middle manager, she had a vantage point on employee distress: "My people are freaked out by this thought. If it goes down the toilet, where am I going to work next? In what hellish corner of corporate America?"

Habacker, a veteran of three years, was a lustrous example of the company's employee philosophy, "Invent/Reinvent your career." An English major from a small coal-mining town in western Pennsylvania, she slipped through the net that would have snared her in her Russian Orthodox family of teachers and took a master's degree in technical communication at Rensselaer. When she swept into a corporate consulting firm in New York, she discovered she had a true knack for business ("which is scary," she confessed, "because I hate thinking about money"). Better still, she recognized that she could combine this talent with her flair for theatrical performance.

Hired as Razorfish's very first information architect, she became the company's own "it girl" when she successfully pitched the Schwab contract (with "the help of fishnet stockings," she joked) for the site that made Razorfish's name. Although she had helped to create the content groups at each of the company's offices and was fully loyal to the creatives on her team, Habacker's fascination with the art of business set her apart. As a result, she did not share the preference of her designers and writers for lifestyle clients. Media and entertainment companies may have been more at home with Razorfish's "groovy factor," but, she pointed out, their own groovy employees were difficult to work with. Habacker favored the "wow factor" in winning over "more straightlaced but much smarter" financial services clients. "I think what's made me successful is that I don't buy into the jargon. I walk into a meeting with clients, dressed like this [she had a notably baroque taste in vintage clothes], and I curse a lot. In the time for introductions, when everyone talks about what they do outside of work, I say, 'Oh, I own a burlesque club, and in my off-time, I'm a stripper.' There's about three seconds of discomfort in the room, and then everybody really listens to what I have to say."

After I had attended a few of her project meetings, it was easy to see how clients, and colleagues, would be swayed by any one of her presentation skills—comic timing, storytelling talent, visceral communication, candid confidence. Underlying the staginess, however, was the same earnest, self-dramatizing quality I had first seen in Snyder and then in so many others. It was the manner of the ever-alert knowledge worker, caught in the act of thinking for herself, never in possession of the rote response (like the organization cog) or the categorical answer (like the academic), but sorting, visibly, through a series of semi-formed ideas, like so many digital applications, in search of a solution to a problem that had not necessarily been posed. It had probably started out as a computer programmer's awkward mode of improvising a social self. In this urbane setting, it had hardened its contours and acquired some polish and was becoming the approved method of performing your no-collar skills in public. It also showed that you worked, or could work, for a fast company.

Habacker typified the panache of the old Razorfish, while her business savvy marked her out as key to the client-facing future of the company. Before long, she would move yet again to take up a pivotal role in the new Business Development group. For all her prowess in the digital field, privately she was a nonbeliever who didn't use a computer or personal digital assistant once she stepped out of the office. After two years of fourteen-hour days on the job, proving herself and learning the trade, she had tried to establish some boundaries between work and play. Like many of the fish, who were afterhours artists, actors, musicians, or DJs, she had a sideline that had turned into a business—The Slipper Room, a modernist burlesque club on the Lower East Side that she owned with her artist husband, James. Both Dachis and Kanarick were investors and had their own cocktails on the menu (the "Dachismo," three airline bottles of vodka, with tonic, and the "Craigar," a radically modified Bloody Mary). But the live ethos of Camille and James's mom-and-pop operation—in the flesh and unmediated—was the very antithesis of Razorfish's virtual bailiwick.

In addition, the club's rules of burlesque performance were strictly traditional—no stand-up, lip-synching, raunch, or campy minimalism. Instead, the acts featured as much spectacle, choreography, and drama as the classically tiny stage would allow. "Classic burlesque is not just strippers," James expounded over martinis. "It has to have a political element. It's basically political farce that looks at your times and comments on them." On Saturday nights, as part of "Mr. Choade's Upstairs/Downstairs," the couple performed delicious routines as Mel and Fanny Frye, showbiz hosts who had seen better days. Mel was a schmaltzy Vegas promoter, with a frightful ear for standards, and Fanny was his pill-popping wife and cabaret partner. Camille also appeared in other acts, playing a variety of ditzy but slinky roles that evoked Cameron Diaz in pasties and G-string. A typical cast of characters for the evening would include a sword-swallower, a dandy crooner with bright blue eyes and robotic affect, named Albino Andy ("discovered in a small club in Squirrelwood, New Jersey") a torch singer named Dirty Martini with an arch standpoint on life, and naturally, a succession of brassy female dancers with weather-balloon bosoms.

Onstage at the Slipper Room, the Director of Content for North America (Photo by Ronnie Sunshine)

Offstage, the couple insisted that they have "old-fashioned values." They both come from families where their parents "were madly in love," and so they were nurtured, not spoiled or neglected. "We believe in good manners, we live within our means, we don't leverage ourselves," explained James, "because debt is wrong." "We believe in a nation of polite individuals, who make an effort to dress a little and who give a shit." Camille nodded in agreement as James completed his speech. "Right now, we have a society of rude, pushy people who think the end is near, and they should grab what they can get. We believe that you have to earn your place in society."

Their concern about integrity carried over into frustration about things back at Razorfish. "Everyone agrees that working at Razorfish is as good as it gets in corporate America," she acknowledged. "The trouble is that Razorfish has duped everyone into thinking they're not part of corporate America. These people honestly don't believe they are part of the mainstream. What are they thinking?" she gestured theatrically. "They're working for Schwab, Ford, IBM. They're working for the Man." "That's right," interrupted James. "That's what your book should be about. How the counterculture was duped into thinking they are not working for corporate America. It's like a wolf in sheep's clothing." "What I'm praying for," concluded Camille, "is that we can run with the wolves, but be the quirky wolf."

The Finest Hour?

By mid-December, the wolves were getting hungry. Management issued a fourth-quarter warning that revenues would be down 35 percent from the previous quarter and that earnings, expected to come in at 2 cents a share, would suffer a 17-cent to 22-cent loss. Some investors lost no time in announcing a class-action lawsuit (the first of several, all dismissed in due course), alleging that Dachis and other executives had violated the Securities Exchange Act by giving false and misleading statements about the company's finances over the course of the previous six months. With this news, Razorfish stock plunged another 35 percent and would end 2000 in the same sorry camp as most other technology stocks—down 98 percent. So far, in this bleak December alone, Web companies had issued almost

10,000 pink slips, and more than forty companies closed their doors by the end of the month. A regular "pink-slip party" in a Chelsea bar had become the social event du jour for the newly jobless. The recently axed showed up to pin memorabilia, including worthless stock option certificates, on a "Wall of Blame," featuring their defunct business cards. Company swag was displayed in a Museum of Un-Natural History, and prizes were awarded to contestants for Best Layoff story ("No more ultra-casual dress code means I can sit at home in my suit and tie").

All of Razorfish's chief competitors—Agency, marchFirst, Scient, Sapient, Organic, iXL—faced a similar shortfall in earnings, and all had announced substantial layoffs in response. The company's stockholders were clamoring for blood, and Dachis had been slammed in the investors' phone conference on the day the warning was issued. Few doubted that the ax would fall again. Yet Dachis stood his ground, opting for loyalty to the fish over accountability to the stockholders. Just before the earnings warning went out, all of his employees received an email announcing the decision not to lay anyone off. Dachis asked them to be "brave and strong." It was a cri de coeur, guaranteed to revive the swooning morale of the fish and to inflame the company's Wall Street critics. Lehman Brothers instantly cut Razorfish's price target, titling its company update, "The Fish Is in Choppy Waters." Other Wall Street analysts followed suit, openly expressing scorn for the no-layoffs decision. Steven Birer, an analyst with Robertson Stephens, direly warned: "I have concerns about the company staying in business if they continue to follow this path. It sounded like [CEO Jeff Dachis] believed it was all market related, not company specific, and I think that's denial." Wall Street had spoken and was accustomed to getting its way.

Dachis called a general meeting for all of the New York fish. The gathering was scheduled for the third-floor loft of the Mercer Street building. Chosen for its symbolism, this was where the company had begun its rise three years earlier. The Christmas lights looping down from the sprinkler systems and the half-lit menorahs scattered around the room lent extra warmth to a space that held fond memories for veterans of the startup days when there had been only twenty employees, sharing the same pizza orders. Employees filtered in slowly from the other downtown offices. Subdued, even for the early hour, but not somber, they filled the air with a low buzz. Preceded by Sophie, his jaunty, omnipresent weimaraner, Dachis briskly entered the loft, wearing a dapper business suit and skinny black tie. Kanarick, in a dark blue mod outfit, his hair waving up as it reached his shoulders, followed suit. They waited patiently as the firm's general manager warmed up the crowd. The fish were about to hear their leaders explain why they were not being laid off.

With all the heavy artillery fire from Wall Street, Dachis was by no means assured of a cheering home crowd. In the trenches, the consensus was that management had become too distant and much too top-down in their decision-making in recent months. Dachis was aware of this. "It's amazing how many of you have never met me," he began his speech. "We know that, at times, we suck at communicating. Here's my cell phone number. Open, honest dialogue is what we based this company on." Originally trained in drama and dance, for which he had earned the moniker of "Dancin' Jeff" among his detractors, Dachis had learned how to draw on his stage skills to round out his stump CEO sermon about the company vision. Now he was going to deliver the updated version. "Everything that can be digital, will be," he began. "If that turns out to be wrong," he teased, pausing for effect, "then we have a problem."

Launching into a lesson about the fundamentals of digital business, he reminded us of the principle of disintermediation. In the "old producer/distributor model of business," all of the middlemen—"the union guys who do the trucking and delivering of product"—get a small cut. "In our model, all those middlemen get laid off. Everything that is physical can be compressed and lubricated, and will be. Whether it's tomorrow or in five years, it will happen." By now, his audience could see there would be no turning around. The scripture would not be revised. "Our vision is consistent and clear," Dachis continued, moving into third gear, "and has not altered one iota. There's a circus out there which we never wanted to be part of, and now the circus is over. We were never about the Internet or the dotcoms. The stock will go up and down. We're a company, not a stock, and we're playing to win the revolution, not the stock market. This company is a company of true believers."

As Dachis piled on the defiance, Kanarick stepped in to back him up: "The easiest thing to do is lop off 600 jobs. But a baseball club that loses three seasons doesn't drop out. The Mets have a bad month, they don't fire the team." "So how will we survive over the next few quarters?" asked an employee in the front row. Dachis reminded us that the company had $85 million cash on hand (at the current burn rate, that would last for two quarters) and $50 million more owed by clients. For twenty straight quarters Razorfish had been profitable, while most companies in the Internet business had lost money. "We're not going to feed the beast of revenue simply for the public markets. . . . I'm willing to wait out two quarters [of losses] until we get our shit together. We have less than twelve months to do it. We are going in this direction; come with us."

It was a bold performance and, perhaps, Dachis's finest moment. The conviction that employees always come first and that stockholders are not in the saddle must have warmed the hearts of veteran fish and steeled the nerves of the fresh conscripts. In six months, we would know if it had done the trick.

Fixing How You Feel

Get ready to meet such exciting new pals as the rather muddle-headed Gramma Nutt, the warm-hearted Queen Frostine, and even (shudder) the black-hearted Lord Licorice. Before you begin to play, you might want to read The Legend of the Lost Candy Castle on the game platform.

—Candyland, A Game for 2 to 4 Players

LEISURE, WE COMMONLY ASSUME, IS THE EXACT OPPOSITE OF WORK. It is optional as opposed to obligatory, and it is something we pursue in time that is not owned by our employer. Some workers have been able to retain a clear-cut sense of their "own time," as quite distinct from company time. Waged service employees and punch-clock industrial workers, especially if they belong to unions, can still organize their lives in a way that echoes the slogan of the labor movement for shorter hours in the mid-1800s: "eight hours for work, eight hours for sleep, and eight hours for what we will."[1] Professionals and the self-employed have never observed these boundaries very strictly. For white-collar employees of all grades—from the upper clerical through the managerial ranks—the prospect of doing so has eroded greatly in recent years. The ubiquity of cell phone and laptop use and the advent of flex time threaten to dissolve entirely the boundaries between work and leisure. We often think of the result as unhealthy, because we regard work in general as a baleful pollutant when it spills over into our homes and after-work environment. The harried profile of the yuppie workaholic, whose entire life is a series of networking opportunities, is regarded as the worst illustration of a civilization that cannot keep sacred and profane things in their proper place.

It is less common to think of leisure and free time spilling over into the workplace, yet this was a feature of many New Economy companies. Predictably, it provoked a good deal of unease among national managers whose charge it is to worry about work discipline. For employees in the general workforce who enjoy some discretionary control over their working time, neo-leisure has become a familiar presence in the office. Managers have had to accept that Web surfing, video games, news and pornography consumption, email and bulletin board correspondence, online solitaire, broadband entertainment, and a cornucopia of other diversions are now a routine part of every office workweek. In many workplaces, these activities have to be factored into accounting for employees' time on the job.[2] However, in new media companies, neo-leisure was not simply tolerated as an unavoidable cost of doing business in the information age; it was actively encouraged as a way of adding value to an employee's output. Play was viewed as an activity that could catalyze ideas and serve as a battery source for recharging flagging energies at the workstation. The permissive workplace could take a playful turn at any moment, and however spontaneous the result, it was still part of the business plan.

In this kind of environment, serious fun was key. It had been a stock component of the postmodern emotional tool kit in the 1970s and 1980s. In leisure activity, it had even taken on a workman-like air, as in the *Saturday Night Live* catchphrase, "Are we having fun yet?" It was no surprise, then, that the 1990s workplace would adopt fun as an industrial tool for jump-starting the engine of innovation. To play along, you had to contribute some usable wit that would improve the hour. Those who could not or did not know how to play were likely to be phased out over time. Fun was no longer something to be deferred until the weekend, nor was it quarantined for special occasions, like weekly beer bashes or seasonal parties. With joie de vivre all but mandatory in the offices of New Economy firms, events like the company party had a distinct role to play in the financial and emotional calendar of Silicon Alley.

Party Loyalty

Less than a week after Dachis's plucky stand against Wall Street, it was party time at Razorfish. The choice of this year's venue for the holiday party was loaded with wry symbolism. The fish moved all the way down to the financial district and occupied a sumptuous six-story mansion that served as a clubby retreat for one of the most elite of Wall Street institutions, the Downtown Association. Lining the walls were faded prints of Old New York harbor along with portraits of the captains of industry, finance, and politics who had composed the club's storied membership. Volumes such as *Burke's Peerage and Baronetage* and *Gentlemen's Clubs of London* filled the library shelves. Nothing could have been further removed from the company's cooler-than-thou ethos. Thanks to a bar on almost every floor, the lavishly stocked fête fizzed along, in spite of the patrician surroundings. Dancers curved the air behind a scrim in the main room on the third floor, creating silhouettes just like the opening credits in a James Bond movie. The dancers had been hired along with the DJ crew, but well-lubricated fish soon took over their role. "That wouldn't happen at most other companies," bragged one reveler by the bar. "They wouldn't know how to dance so well."

Most office parties are carnivalesque to some degree. They are supposed to reveal a side of the company or institution that is ordinarily masked by the routine exercise of hierarchy. Rules of office etiquette are temporarily suspended, the bigwigs unwind their coils, and the cubicle dwellers take immoderate liberties. Almost the opposite applies at companies like Razorfish. The office party has a significance more akin to a high ceremony of state, where keystone values are ritually expressed. All of the decisions that go into the event are closely scanned and interpreted by employees and onlookers as if they were intended to send a formal message about the company's current standing in the business world. To outsiders, fed by media clichés about decadence, Razorfish might have been just another giddy dotcom, where Ecstacy was dispensed at the reception desk and parties were simply an extension of the workday. Naysayers who minimized the excess also missed the point. The hedonism of company culture was carefully crafted; it could be as articulate in expressing a company's profile and aspirations as the corporate portfolio.

May Day Party, 2001, Razorfish, New York (Photo by the author)

There were some new media companies, such as the cybercasting Pseudo.com, that saw a promotional opening in trying to fit the profile reserved for over-the-top notoriety. CEO Josh Harris's free-for-all bacchanals (culminating in a million-dollar end-of-the-millennium bash, called Quiet, that lasted for an entire month) were planned as Warholian happenings. Harris's heavily themed blowouts (gladiator combatants, on occasion, drew real blood) functioned as lurid advertisements for the industry's capacity to make excess into something artful. For Alley denizens, the Razorfish parties usually had something more nuanced to say about the industry for which the company was a leading emissary. Some Razorfish offices in Europe hosted monthly dance parties, like the legendary SIGI events in Hamburg and Stockholm. They were effective recruitment tools for the company, but they also served as stylishly engineered showcases for the industry as a whole.

The first May Day party at Mercer Street in 1997, for example, was a carefully scripted rite of passage for the Internet industry's move into the upscale SoHo precinct. The choice of culinary fare (Krispy

Kreme donuts and White Castle burgers) and entertainment (strip-happy belly dancers and Brazilian lounge music) helped to establish the company's pre-IPO reputation for ultrahip knowbrow. A year before the Wall Street party that I attended, the company airlifted 1,200 global employees for a long weekend of revelry and internal branding at that most tongue-in-cheek of destinations—the Mandalay Bay resort in Las Vegas. Naturally, tales of debauchery abounded. Yet the real purpose of the event was to show that Razorfish—having made several recent acquisitions, including the technology-heavy Boston shop I-Cube—could be inventive in merging entirely disparate company cultures. Some employees described the effort as resembling a middle-school dance, with each group—pocket protector–wearing I-Cubes and glittery wig-toting Razorfish—standing on opposite ends of the gym. Others remember it as the high-water mark of the halcyon days. The event, titled Fish Fry 1.0, was memorialized in a glossy ninety-eight-page booklet of images that could have passed muster as a high-fashion designer catalog or as a luminous documentary record of a rock star tour. There can be very few period artifacts from the industry's heyday that capture so artfully a company's shrewd use of ebullient, photogenic employees to promote its native dash and gusto to prospective clients.

Employees had their own take, of course, on these high-profile events, and the Wall Street party was no exception. By the time I arrived, hotfoot from a plebeian Pink Slip holiday bash, where partygoers were asked to "come dressed in the swag of your demised company," the deep leather armchairs on the top floor of the club had attracted some dedicated cigar smokers. They were fervently engaged in passing judgment on the company's prospects. Among them was Maria D'Angelo, a content developer and steeltown baby who was one of the very few employees I'd met from a working-class background. "Most folks here probably feel quite at home," she remarked. "How so?" I asked. Expertly flicking her scarlet boa back over her shoulder, she explained, "It's just like a Princeton eating club." Her partner, who worked for a Midtown advertising firm, interrupted this acerbic line of thought. "This place was chosen in order to tone things down," he assured me, "to make sure no one gets too crazy." "Ever since the IPO," he elaborated, "management have had to play down the wild reputation of the early May Day parties." Josie Baxter pitched in, "Now that we're becoming slaves to our big corporate clients, this is an appropriate place to be." She had stopped by to confide, to everyone in earshot, that she was about to jump ship to join a smaller company. "To keep the faith," she explained.

On the way to the coatroom, I ran into Shel Kimen, also wearing a boa, who was one of the company's self-styled culture ambassadors and after-hours DJs (she had just completed her set on the second-floor turntables). She had played many roles inside Razorfish, circulating between management and the rank and file, and so she functioned as "the people's version" of what she called "the corporate memory." When morale was low, part of her job was to improvise ways of restoring enthusiasm. Judging by her bubbly mood, her night was far from over, but she took the time to soberly offer her assessment. "It's an ironic choice for a Razorfish party," she said carefully. "Very, very ironic," she added, just as carefully. As usual, the company was doing a little role-playing, but for Kimen, the message this time around was a little foreboding. This might be one of the last occasions when Razorfish could pretend, for one night of fancy dress, that it was a real Wall Street company. In the months ahead, it would probably have to *behave* like one.

Pain Consultants

The plan for the holiday party had been executed by the recently formed Morale Team, six core members and several ancillaries who had been assigned to lift wilted spirits after the October layoffs. Potted plants on employee tables, group outings to the Big Apple Circus, a cookie-baking contest, and a clothes donation drive for the homeless were other initiatives on the team's plate. One of the self-styled "morale ninjas" described the group's purpose. "If you're unhappy with your work, or you're having trouble with your manager, you go to HR to fix it. If you're having trouble with your job, then you come to us. We try to fix how you feel."

"Fixing how you feel" was a company spin on the legacy of industrial psychology. In a work environment with a high quota of personal autonomy, emotional management ranked high as a relevant skill, especially among employees who expected serious attention and encouragement on the job. Employees with time on their hands were obliged to engage in therapy raps with their colleagues. As I circulated around the offices, I regularly passed clusters of two or more fish who were discreetly but passionately recounting the impact on their feelings of some new aspect of company reorganization. A climate of profound vulnerability emerged in the several months before the second round of layoffs in February 2001. This was the downside of the permissive workplace, and it was just as melodramatic as the upside. As job security deteriorated, fish mourned the steady loss of layers of protection; they spoke repeatedly of being left undefended, shorn of rights, and bereft of options.

There was no entry in the free agent pocket encyclopedia for this long drawn-out passage of trauma. It was a species of anxiety unique to the full-time employee in an age after the repeal of corporate paternalism. Like an amputated limb, the old protective bond of security could still be felt as if the social body of the workforce were wholly intact. But loyalty and trust were no longer viable, and the reliance on self-management meant that individuals were exposed to risks and uncertainties that would ordinarily apply only above their pay levels. In times of crisis, the heightened strain of these responsibilities took a much greater emotional toll on full-time employees than it did on freelancers. One crucial multiplier of the anxiety was the amount of time employees spent learning new skills just to maintain their employability. Since there was virtually no formal training on the job, the kind of professional development that was needed simply to keep up with their fast-moving field was entirely self-directed. Employees learned new skills from other colleagues while problem-solving on projects, but most of the training had to be pursued on their own time (as much as 13.5 hours of unpaid time per week, according to one survey of New York's new media workers).[3]

But some of the pain also clearly came from damage done to the nervous tissue of the company culture. When fish, at all ranks, spoke about "losing our culture," it was palpably felt, as if you could see it draining off at the edges. Razorfish culture was experienced as much more than a cliché, even though it belonged to a long history of creaky management concepts cooked up to stave off the disaffection of employees. Managerial handbooks are chockablock with advice about how to prepare for resistance to culture change and how to smooth it over. Naturally, opposition to change increases with the perceived strength of the culture. At Razorfish, ingredients of love had poured into the mix, so there was bound to be heartbreak in the offing.

Corporate techniques of employee motivation had come a long way in the course of the century. By the 1920s, the promise of advancing oneself through self-employment was no longer feasible as a general inducement for employees of large corporations, and strikes and work stoppages had made it too costly in the long run to rely on coercion and fear as the basis of labor discipline. Union opposition to the strict regimens imposed by Fredrick Taylor's efficiency experts had halted their spread through industry, leaving unproven their actual impact on output. In any case, the Taylorists, with their stopwatches and clipboards, had treated workers as self-interested individuals with limited needs, and managers soon found that they could get better results if they recognized the psychology of informal group norms among their employees.

Elton Mayo and Fritz Roethlisberger's famous study of AT&T's Western Electric workers in the late 1920s is generally regarded as the origin of modern managerial ideas about how to boost productivity and soften conflict in the workplace by responding to the social and emotional needs of workers. The "Hawthorne effect," named for the telephone assembly plant in Cicero, Illinois, where the experiments were conducted, implied that workers were more productive when they believed that managers were actually paying attention to their work conditions.[4] They worked even harder and with more loyalty when they felt themselves to be voluntary participants in, rather than servants of, workplace goals.

Mayo's theory of human relations advocated employee consultation as an alternative to Taylor's efficiency cult of scientific management.[5] Employees who were treated like responsible, independent adults would be more compliant (and efficient in the long run) than those who were regarded as machine parts. Moreover, Mayo's ideas were also widely embraced by corporate managers because they were a palatable alternative to socialist explanations of labor conflict.[6] According to his doctrine, discontented workers were not really dissatisfied with a system of capitalist ownership that exploited their labor; their chief complaint was that they were not treated more humanely, as complex individuals with more sophisticated needs and priorities than those governing the basic necessities of life. The system of monopoly ownership, so much under threat of government intervention, if not proletarian overthrow, in the 1930s, could survive, Mayo promised, only if employees were provided with a sense of participation in the company's affairs. In the decades since the Depression, catering to the perceived social and emotional needs of employees became a basic principle of management practice and the mainstay of acres of volumes of business literature, each preaching the importance of self-fulfilled employees to corporate profits. It has also prompted no end of employee cynicism. William Whyte summed up the general attitude in 1951, when he observed, of the organization manager, that "no one wants to see the old authoritarian return, but at least it could be said of him that what he wanted primarily from you was your sweat. The new man wants your soul."[7]

The postwar boom years were a time of near full employment, when the labor market came closer to being a seller's market and when extra incentives had to be offered to attract and retain valued employees. As a result, part of the burden of the workday shifted away from the employee. "Management now had to earn the right to a fair day's work from employees," argued Jack Barbash, and did so by offering more attractive compensation packages.[8] Managers found themselves adding to the laundry list of perks and benefits to maintain the cheerful cooperation of employees. CEOs, government policymakers, and union leaders had all agreed on a common commitment to match productivity gains with wage increases. Yet salary increments and benefit upgrades ultimately proved to be an insufficient form of compensation for the banal execution of soulless work tasks. In the wake of the "revolt against work" in the 1970s, all-round gratification on the job would be championed as the therapeutic cure for the work blues. In response to the movements for personal growth and inner change that had mushroomed out of the counterculture, efforts to create corporate soul and enhance morale were focused on the self-development of workers. Managers underwent sensitivity training in how to promote "employee empowerment."

After the 1973 *Work in America* report capped a decade of rising discontent about alienation on the job, widespread workplace reforms were introduced. The Quality of Work Life movement had its brief moment in the sun.[9] For the most part, however, reform in the 1970s and 1980s was driven by responses to industrial competition, especially from "Japanese management," whose emphasis on teamwork and collective self-discipline was perceived to be the golden solution to the Western disease of deficient motivation.[10] A swift succession of management innovations followed: "quality circles," "problem-solving teams," "customer-centered goals," "worker empowerment," "employer involvement," "job enrichment," "autonomous work groups," and "company culture." Each were guided by theories of reorganization such as total quality management, just-in-time, lean production, business process reengineering. Some local variants of the fads took on cultish dimensions, as EST-trained managers introduced consciousness raising and hypnotic techniques to release human potential and enhance the positive thinking of the group.[11]

After the publication of Tom Peters and R. Waterman's *In Pursuit of Excellence* in 1983, a colorful succession of management consultants held sway over business thought, each promoting their own concept of reorganization as the key to motivating employees in a change-sensitive environment. Some testified to the irreplaceable value of creative employees; others preached that employees were wasteful fat to be trimmed from the ever leaner core of a company's competency. Their claims, evidence, and remedies diverged quite widely. In the case of Peters, even his own theories contradicted one another from book to book and ultimately lapsed into incoherence. In response to this inconsistency, the high-flying consultants insisted that the New Economy was driven by chaos and therefore inconsistent at its root because it was constantly in the process of reinvention. One result of this shiftiness, as John Micklethwait and Adrian Wooldridge pointed out in *The Witch Doctors*, was that "the life cycle of a management fad shrunk from ten years to one year."[12] How did employees respond? Joanne Ciulla observes that while some fads create a "sense of euphoria among participants" (rather like the Hawthorne effect) by raising the "expectation that employees are going to be enriched and

empowered," the bounce is usually short-lived, until the next program, reorganization, or group goal comes down the pike.[13]

Not all the reforms were skin-deep, however. Although employee
participation was often paid only lip service or was used by management to tighten its control,[14] there was real follow-through in some in-
stances. For example, in GM's much-praised Saturn plant in Spring
Hill, Tennessee, unions and management cooperated fully in every aspect of decision-making and production.[15]

In response to the influx of women into the white-collar workforce,
all sorts of new programs were introduced to ease the pressure on
dual-income families: child care centers, flex time, job sharing, paid
maternity leave. Interestingly, Arlie Hochschild's study of a Fortune
500 company that had embraced many of the new management concepts found that employees rarely took advantage of the new family-
friendly policies to spend more time at home. On the contrary, they
spent even more time in the workplace because they experienced less
stress there, got more emotional support from coworkers, and came
to believe that the new set of corporate values—stressing empowerment and valuing the individual—offered more respect and dignity
than they got in the family home. "In this new model of family and
work life," Hochschild speculated, "a tired parent flees a world of un-
resolved quarrels and unwashed laundry for the reliable orderliness,
harmony, and managed cheer of work. The emotional magnets beneath home and workplace are in the process of being reversed."[16]
The workplace became a haven; the home was more like a factory
where chores were conducted with drudge-like efficiency. The company, she concluded, had successfully usurped values associated with
families, churches, and community life and was forging a new kind of
moral capitalism. Moral, at least, as long as it needed its employees.
Not long after Hochschild's study was published, many of the employees she studied were laid off as the company underwent some
reengineering of its own.[17]

The Permission to Give Permission

Most of the employee goodwill that managers had built through
decades of human relations programs was swept away by the waves of

downsizing that rolled through the white-collar workforce from the early 1980s onward. With the exception of the early 1990s, the economy had been in pretty good shape, and corporate profits were healthy, so the mass layoffs were viewed as a particularly callous form of betrayal.[18] Global competitiveness continued to be the favored rationale behind the cuts, but they were clearly aimed, in the short term, at boosting stock prices, and they lent themselves, in the long run, to a transfer of power away from managers to shareholders and their board representatives. As a result, any prospect of trust in the accountability, let alone sensitivity, of corporate America to employees was shattered for at least a generation, leaving the door wide open for the romance of the startup, the lure of free agency, and the entrepreneurial promise of the alternative, New Economy company. It did not help that management fads like "company culture," which preached the importance of people, were being introduced at a time of maximum downsizing.

Many of the industry employees whom I interviewed had stories about parents who had put in forty years at the same large company, only to fall under the ax of reengineering. Not one expressed even a passing interest in the benefits of a long-term career with a single employer. Field visits to clients' offices that resembled scenes from Fritz Lang's *Metropolis* confirmed their worst assumptions: cubicle infernos, slothful bureaucracies, anonymous work relationships, and artificial culture. This last item was often viewed as the most doleful, since companies like Razorfish had the real thing—an authentic culture. If it was true, how did this culture differ from all the other human relations efforts that had been devised to restore the team spirit of employees?

In the tight labor market of the late 1990s, Fortune 500 firms had begun to offer a new deluxe range of employee perks, from concierge services, like dry-cleaning pickup, to fully paid sabbaticals. By comparison, most of the supplementary benefits enjoyed by the fish were quite ordinary: tuition reimbursement, a referral fee for recruitment tips, personal wellness funds, car service for those working late, on-site massage, and a leadership training program called Catapult, which whisked off select employees for a three-week stint in the Costa Rican rain forest to learn new ropes. The skillfully crafted parties and the regular social outings ("drink tanks") were not so easy to duplicate at Procter & Gamble or Merrill Lynch, but they were common fare in the Internet industry. Nor were the scooters (for a year or so, a select way to move around the office) regarded as distinctive to Razorfish itself. In any case, all of these tangible perks would evaporate as the company's struggle for survival sharpened, and cost-cutting took its toll. None were mourned with exceptional remorse, at least not in comparison with the erosion of self-engineered fun.

Each in their own way, the fish agreed that the recipe for good culture at Razorfish had less to do with perks, goodies, and sweet toppings offered from above than with the flavors that welled up from below. Yet the identity of the vital ingredients proved a little more elusive. On the eve of her departure, Josie Baxter tried to recall what she had most appreciated about the company culture. It was what she called "the permission to give permission, to yourself and to others." The phrase was her attempt ("hopelessly abstract," she admitted) to describe the "growth of a mentality that had not been planned or calculated," and which "had gotten out of control, but in a good way." Her colleagues had used what she called their "award of autonomy" to create their own unanticipated rituals of work and learning. The result had been a spirited accomplishment to her, not something she could put in her bank account or 401(k).

A writer colleague on one of her team projects, also on her way out, put the matter more bluntly: "There was the official party line on culture, which was enforced fun, and then there was what we created for ourselves." This distinction seemed to be crucial for most employees, though it was so intangible that few could point to defining examples. Tim Basco, an information architect who would survive many rounds of layoffs, tried to explain: "On the one side, there's the company's definition of culture, and I can describe it: We're all supposed to be edgy, passionate people. That's the marketing package with which Razorfish brands itself out there in the world. But when culture comes from the corporate office, that's what I call The Culture. It's different from the thing that happens among us vibrant, interesting people when we interact with each other. Our own vibe of 'anything can happen' is more of a reflex thing, and it's what nourishes us."

For a middle manager like Corinna Snyder, who could not partake of what she affectionately called the "people's culture ghetto," the obligation to promote The Culture was too obviously engineered: "I felt like I was driving the old Culture Train up from Kamchatka to do some agitprop." With her academic background, she found that "it resonated so much with the Soviet anthropology experiment of the 1920s and 1930s" that tried to engineer a new proletarian culture. In a company that showcased its employee culture with such vigor, employees had to feel that they partook of something spontaneous that Razorfish had not sanctioned, but which fed off the official permission in unpredictable ways. In other words, the fish had to believe they possessed their own counterculture, even within a company that was supposed to be a counterculture.[19] To better understand this, we have to take a closer look at the official culture that was promoted by management.

In the firm's heyday, all new recruits were issued a booklet titled, "Razorfish Creative Mission." To demonstrate the transparency of decision-making within the organization, the booklet included a section on "guidelines for executives." On the cover was a no-collar employee whose head was consumed in an incandescent cloud of light and energy. Inside were twenty pages of company philosophy, detailing what kinds of employee behavior were actively encouraged. "Creativity" in all forms was the core value, and it was celebrated on every page, though mostly in an unchewed lingo that aped Business English: "We are working toward an improved efficiency where new kinds of thinking expand the limits of intelligent thought. Unprecedented thinking often comes into being in a nonlinear manner. Opposites, inconsistencies, and ambiguities produce creative sparks." This principle of entertaining "mutual opposites," which philosophers might recognize as neo-Hegelian, was called "creative friction." It "occurs by holding conflicting thoughts in the mind simultaneously," and it can lead to "creative collaborations" between employees, especially when they have "conflicting cultural and disciplinary viewpoints."

The booklet routinely made a point of distinguishing Razorfish practices from those of traditional companies, notably in the case of interdisciplinarity and the promotion of free, anti-conformist speech: "Repressive companies harm creative thought when deviant thinking represents a threat to continued structures. Creativity's power to undermine is also its power to enlighten." Other habits that were championed included time out from work ("periods of disengagement from our principal activities"), playfulness ("creative play yields tangible results"), and tolerance for other employees' rhythms ("when someone on your team expresses that they have no ideas, we should understand that an innovative idea is probably forming and about to emerge"). On the off-chance that new recruits might think all of this was still a little too formal, they were reminded that "Razorfish is a group of skilled and passionate amateurs that are also experienced professionals."

Many of these concepts could have sprung from notes taken for a course in poststructuralism (central to the college education of many fish). They were a typically avant-garde take on management notions that had become the fundamentalist diet for Fast Company and Harvard Business School evangelicals. Interpreted literally, as a prescription for internal policy, it would be hard to imagine a less punitive work environment. This would be a place where personal failure was regarded as an opportunity, dissent as a basis for understanding, and inattention as a source of innovation. As for the work product, it would be a harmonic blend of beauty and functionality, in the lineage of the arts and crafts tradition of William Morris. Not only would the human qualities of employees be indulged, but they would lie at the core of the company's brand character.

If the "Razorfish Creative Mission" was in the line of descent from the Hawthorne effect, and not some new genus altogether, then it had clearly taken the idea of human relations to its elastic limit. Empathetic respect for employees was no longer simply a stimulus to productivity or a concession to stave off labor conflict (though these were hardly irrelevant factors). Here, it was championed as the company's primary asset, the key to its competitive edge in the marketplace. In an economy where any skill or service could be subcontracted, full-time employee culture was one of the very few assets that could not be easily duplicated. It was a "core competency." By that same token, the company was expecting a lot from its recruits in return. The emotional tool kit that employees took to and from work along with their laptops was full to overflowing. Social skills and other forms of emotional competence, which were ordinarily confined to their private lives, were needed in a change-prone workplace.

Lewis Coser wrote about "greedy institutions"—the sectarian order, the utopian community, the family—which made all-consuming demands on the energy, loyalty, and commitment of their voluntary members or employees.[20] In a similar manner, New Economy employees sacrificed excessive portions of their lives to the continued health of their companies, and in this respect these firms were as greedy in their own way as the monolithic corporations of the 1950s. But the types and degrees of emotional involvement differed from the forms of neo-feudal loyalty that Coser described. They included not only professional passions but also attention to a range of needs and anxieties of fellow employees. This emotional involvement had the formal quality of therapy, at least, and at times approximated the complexity of an intimate relationship. These organizations, I would conclude, were experienced as *needy* rather than *greedy*.

Indeed, emotional intelligence, a rarefied psychology concept gussied up by consulting guru Daniel Goleman, got a lot of play in New Economy management circles.[21] An emotional intelligence industry had sprung up, where employees could undergo training in the art of emotional identification and emotional management. There was even an EQ test to assess their abilities. With so much volatility in the workplace, corporate managers saw the financial benefit of having employees who could cope with the additional stress and enable others to do so. Certified EI practitioners, of course, were on hand to estimate the exact amount of added value that companies could count on. As for the financial return of company culture in general, Terrence Deal and Allan Kennedy, self-described intellectual godsons of Tom Peters, had provided a widely cited estimate (on the basis, apparently, of zero research or evidence) that a firm with a strong culture "can gain as much as one or two hours of productive work per employee per day."[22]

Regardless of the expectation of returns, was it even possible to maintain this level of empathy and respect for employees in a corporate setting? Certainly, it was more difficult in a large organization than in the intimate setting of a startup with less than fifty workers. After the Razorfish workforce ballooned, the core values were invoked more often in lip service than in practice. The mission statement booklet was no longer issued to new hires, and the policy of creative friction was less and less in vogue. On the other hand, fish who came onboard during and after the company's expansion were not obliged to make the same self-investment as the earlier culture-bearers, nor did they feel so accountable for the fortunes of the company.

As one of the original golden children, who had devoted herself to what she called "cultural preservation," Cecelia Clough felt that the newer recruits behaved as if "the world owes them." Echoing JFK, she explained that her cohort was more likely to ask, "What can I do for the organization?" whereas "the younger folks are asking themselves, 'What is the organization going to do for me?'" As someone who saw the company as a brilliant collective achievement on the part of her circle, her perception of the newcomers as Johnny-come-latelies was easy to understand. These later recruits, however, were more likely to see their job as a limited contract with set boundaries and were therefore able to distinguish more clearly between their own interests and those of management. Even Clough was willing to acknowledge this might be a healthier mind-set in the long run.

No Evil Child of Postmodernism

Core values and mission statements were all very well, and managers pushed them as best they could, but the task of motivating employees in a New Economy company was best accomplished by peers out on the floor. There were some fish who naturally took on the role and others who were paid to do it.

Shel Kimen, who had offered the final word on the holiday party, was the best equipped by far. A self-described "anti-corporate female from punk culture" who was an instinctive "advocate of the people," she liked to describe her kinship role in the company culture as that of a "troublemaker" and "rule breaker." No one doubted her integrity, and she was the very last person you would mistake for a flunky for senior management. Bleach blond, with a nose ring, combat boots, and prominent tattoos (one of which boasted the Chinese characters for brown rice and green tea—the detoxifying diet that she frequently fasted on), Kimen had a flawless track record as an ambassador for open communication. As a die-hard holist and devotee of positive thinking, her countercultural credentials were less Big Apple than

Bay Area, which is where she caught the Internet bug in the early 1990s. Silicon Graphics, which "had a reputation as a big bad company," saw her potential as a way of accessing the new youthful Web scene, and so she was hired, as she joked, "to help them not look so evil." In *Fast Company* parlance, she would have been their change agent.

Recruited to Razorfish as an information architect, she was soon moved into a middle management position as a way of tapping those ambassadorial skills. In the small-scale days, a managerial role among the fish was not an easy concept to grasp, define, or perform. After the expansion, it was even more of a challenge. Her allotted niche of motivational management had to involve some boosterism, Kimen reasoned, but it could not allow for dictation or cheerleading. "How do you create a structure so that people can see the rewards of creating their own excitement, so that they'll want to do it? Not by forcing change on them or imposing a policy that says 'It's time to have fun now!' But by creating an environment that invites and encourages and gives people permission to participate without explicitly saying so." Because she was such a communitarian soul, Kimen had been helpful in engineering the company's official reorganization—called Forlen-kla (Swedish for "simplify")—which had ushered in the professional networks and phased out the communitarian teams. However, she was ambivalent about its outcome and was much more attached to everyday tactics for lifting morale (like emailing fish in every office around the world to turn on their music at 5 P.M. for an international groove-in).

Other tactics were less direct. One day, Kimen told me that she had a plan for "a group of ringers in each office, who would be given a tool kit of fun, creative ideas and things to do. They might be told, for example, to take a bunch of magazines and, in the middle of the day, cut out pictures and paste them on the walls, and then walk around and invite people to participate and start to play. No one would know they had been told to do it." Kimen did not want, nor could she afford, to be seen as a "tool of the establishment," handing on decisions from above. If anything, she had become what she called a "custom manager," personalizing relationships so that she was different things to different people and actively seeding ideas where they might take root, as if spontaneously. Whether or not her plan had prompted it, a "people's wall" of drawing paper was hung on the fourth floor some weeks later, and it quickly filled up with sketches, doodles, and slogans. It grew into an example of the survivor art that had become common in Internet companies, just a genre and a half upstream from the artwork of convicts on death row. The idea circulated up to the Boston office, where it took on a more catered form; crayons and collage materials were set aside on tables for employees to make RAZ ART.

People's Wall, Art for Survivors, Razorfish, New York (Photo by the author)

Kimen's species of motivational spin belonged to a new generation of management techniques that took their cue from the art of viral marketing. Viral was the term Internet mavens used to describe the speedy electronic propagation of word-of-mouth communication, and viral motivation was essential to employee psychology at places like Razorfish. It involved some ventriloquizing of the mind-set of employees, but it was aimed chiefly at sowing and scattering impulses among employees in order to stimulate self-motivation. Strategic sneezers would pass on a benign virus with an enthusiasm that would infect others until it was fully established in the organization's nervous system. This was also how Internet evangelists talked about the contagious spread of the Net gospel outside of industry strongholds. Every layoff victim, no matter how embittered, would carry the digital revolution antibody as they went forth into the real corporate world. Or so went the talk.

After the first round of layoffs, the fish were more wary of motivational initiatives in general. Whether out of amusement or fear, they were inclined to view all such tactics, even the viral ones, in a conspiratorial light. The need to separate "our culture" from the company's "Culture" sharpened, and it became critical to the psychology of employee survival. Yet the line between the two had never been easy to detect. Kimen herself was a case in point. Most employees I interviewed saw her as a voice of the people and even as a thorn in the side of management. Her own ambivalence was quite fathomless. Did she ever feel she was selling a line and was able to do so because of, and not in spite of, her superbohemian identity? She admitted that when she started working with large clients, there were great pools of doubt and moments when she thought, "I'm going to turn into this horrible corporate monster." But then she was hardly alone, since most fish felt the same way.

Shel Kimen, Management Performance Art (Photo by the author)

Ultimately, Kimen got by on her own zeal for fomenting change in large organizations. She thought of her job as a "subversive form of corporate performance art." This appetite for change for change's sake, she admitted, was second nature to her generation, "who had seen a lot of Obey Your Thirst ads." It was rocket fuel for her ceaseless efforts to "restore the magic" at Razorfish, and it overrode most of her doubts about her mission. Her preferred self-image, like that of so many other Web pioneers, was of "carrying the flame for an ideal" that would "change the world" and "humanize the business world enough to stop treating people badly."

Weaned on a generational culture that had been branded with slogans like No Fear, Kimen did, however, have one abiding dread—that she had been fooled. There were times, she confessed, when she saw the Internet industry as "the evil child of postmodernism" and when she felt duped by her desire to believe in the magnitude of change. Her cohort had been "the good people who wanted to make stuff free, to give it all away, and find another way to live, and yet, because we live in an American world so shy on values, it was a perfect opportunity for capitalism to pull on our heartstrings." What she did for the company, however, was mostly exempt from such misgivings. Razorfish was still, and perhaps always would be, a struggle for the good. The bad stuff happened elsewhere. On a business trip to the Stockholm office, Kimen had a sharp revelation. Her hotel featured a choice of music—techno, ambient, hip-hop—in the elevators. In her room she found DVDs of independent, artsy movies and a guide to underground DJ events in the city. She had stepped into a market niche, and the hotel knew it. "I thought I was some kind of rebel in the business world," she confessed, "but I'm not. I'm the fucking target audience. And that is a weird, very weird, feeling."

The revelation had left its mark because it hit Kimen where she played, not where she worked. It was a shock for her to see how far market calculation was reaching into the underground arts culture where she was most truly homesteaded. Razorfish was one thing—everyone had to earn a living. But the living part should have the option, at least, of being off-limits. Following Kimen in her after-hours career as a DJ did indeed take me to some out-of-the-way places and scenes, far removed from the social vibe at Razorfish, which, for her,

was pervaded by "East Coast Brahmin" habits: "wine and lots of talking." She was becoming a regular at fringe happenings all over the
city, many of them linked to the Burning Man diaspora, a decentralized network of events where performance and circus art, experimental music, paint, sculpture, spoken word, and spontaneous phenom-
ena converged in a bubbly brew.

A visit to one of her gigs, called "Leave No Trace," took me back to
the Wall Street district and its deserted late night streetscapes. Cos-
tumed figures in hooded capes, jester caps, and brocade lurched onto
the cobblestones outside a tenement house on Pearl Street. Inside
were three floors of revelers, many sheathed in full-body latex, others
with a dirt pancake on their skin, swirling from room to room through
the improvised light shows. High-tech gas masks and chemical protection suits beckoned from the bad future, a bearded titan in chain
mail from the harmless past. A towering fellow in a silver suit performed a wordless cartoon drama on a stage, using sound and gesture
to illustrate the action. A riot grrl band rocked the upstairs lounge,
and a DJ shrouded in a cavernous hoodie spun together ethereal
loops on the ground floor. Off to the side, the occupants of a vapor-in-
flated tent swapped stories, cocooned from the carnival of free spirits
outside.

This was not Halloween, and there was no gothic death vibe. It was
all white magic, and the action in every space and corner was fluid,
nonrepetitive, and without threat. Kimen, in an all-white costume,
was spinning nimbly around the dance floor periphery. "This is the
only place in this town," she asserted, "where you can say hello to a
stranger and get a very friendly response." She may well have been
right. When I left at 3 A.M., she was well into her DJ set, threading the
air with a free-form, sweet-and-savory soundtrack, the kind of
music—smart but not cerebral—that she described as "abstrakt eclec-
tia and experimental barks." She was no longer in that world where
parties were an integral part of a company's business model. All the
same, I was struck by a sign at the door, as I exited, which advised,
"No Spectators, Participants Only." It was the Burning Man motto,
and somehow its mood of mandatory edge seemed as appropriate to
the canyons of Wall Street as it had been to the deserts of Utah.

Steel Tables

Eager for tangible evidence that no-collar work attitudes had spread beyond their silicon stronghold, the business media fixated on the flourishing of loose dress codes in corporate offices. This occurred first in the innovation of Casual Fridays and then in the more general establishment of "business casual" as an acceptable norm. At a time when the issue of mandatory uniforms for service personnel holding McJobs was skyrocketing, America's business class had begun to shed its own occupational livery. Among other things, free dress was a new way of distinguishing the servers from those being served. It was also a response to a lavish marketing campaign launched by Levi Strauss in 1992, which bombarded 30,000 corporate HR departments with educational kits that promoted the virtues of casual wear in offices. The campaign was so successful that by the end of the decade, one-third of all U.S. companies had gone casual five days a week, and fashion industry groups like the Tailored Men's Clothing Association had retaliated with their own dress-up campaigns. The Men's Apparel Alliance, an ad hoc group of haberdashers and clothing outlets, amassed funds, PR hotshots, and a spokesman, designer Joseph Abboud, in order to combat the trend.[23]

These style wars were closely analyzed for their symbolism, but they also impacted jobs in the garment industry across the world. The trade in formal business wear tended to support high-wage employment, among Italian manufacturers, for example, whose national industry had been carefully nurtured through state policies and union involvement. By contrast, the casual wear revolution that swept through corporate America was a product of the global sweatshop, in poor countries where cheap labor could be combined with military discipline.

Characteristically, the Razorfish response to Casual Fridays was Dress-Up Fridays, when employees donned corporate drag. It was also an in-house practice to snicker at companies that tried to create an edgy insta-culture by importing a Sony PlayStation or a Ping-Pong or foosball table. This was common enough in the stampede to stake a claim in e-commerce, when brick-and-mortar managers started their own digital divisions and retrofitted offices so that their hip young recruits could copy the handheld camera style of the Internet startup.

Next to business casual, the reorganization of office space was most often portrayed as a sign of radical change. It was hailed as a revolt against the prisonhouse of mental toil lampooned in the Dilbert strips: the cubicle farm of partial-height privacy partitions with suspended fluorescent-lit ceilings overhead, periodically sited potted plants below, four-walled middle management offices along the windowed perimeter, and paneled executive suites on the top floor. The constancy of this rigid office design and its formulaic expression of hierarchy had come to typify the failure of imagination attributed to the large corporation.

The classic postwar expression of the mega-corporation was realized in Skidmore, Owings & Merrill's (SOM) 1957–1961 design for IBM headquarters in Armonk, New York. The semi-automated lines of white-collar production that had been organized vertically in urban office buildings now took on a horizontal form in the sprawling environment of the suburban office park. The SOM design added new layers of military regimentation to a workspace already heavily regulated through the administration of rules and tasks. According to MOMA's chief design curator, Terence Riley, the building "epitomized the emergence of a corporate culture built on the lessons derived from the war effort in terms of scale, organization, and discipline."[24] In time, it contributed to Big Blue's reputation as one of the most inflexible of corporate machines, whose technocrats toiled with soulless efficiency on its centralized mainframe systems.

SOM's subsequent modular plans set the standard for the mass production of office design for several decades, while Herman Miller designer Robert Propst did the same for furniture systems with the introduction of his Action Office. Almost from the outset, designers offered variations to counter the rigidity of these system templates. These included Propst's own 1968 Action Office 2, the first open-plan cubicle system, with entirely movable walls and panels, followed by countless other custom adjustments to the universal plan for warehousing employees. Despite these humanizing modifications, the cubicle pen prevailed in North America, unlike in Europe, where more active, unionized workforces resisted the open-plan systems in favor of preserving privacy. The ubiquitous American cubicle, as Christopher Budd points out, came to "represent a form of individual housing that neither provided privacy nor fostered interaction."[25]

In stark contrast to these system-based environments, the emergence of mobile digital technologies helped give birth to the "wild child," in Riley's phrase, that is today's more flexible workplace. The no-collar job, after all, can be done in a bedroom, in a café, or in an open field. In February 2001, MOMA hosted a large exhibition, *Workspheres,* devoted to the design of new workplaces, ranging from the latest ergonomic furniture for the traditional office to groovy mobile hardware for the nomadic office.[26] *Workspheres* was a big hit on Silicon Alley, and I saw several Razorfish employees at the opening. If the show had an orientation, it was to exult in the newfound capacity of no-collar workers to free themselves from constraints of time and space. In part, a trade show for commercial design companies, the exhibition also commissioned whimsical proposals for the further dispersion of work away from nine-to-five office locations. A QWERTY keyboard jauntily stitched into in a pillowcase (Hella Jongerius's "My Soft Bed") elicited mixed feelings—seduction and repulsion—among visitors all too familiar with the bittersweet plague of multitasking in a 24/7 world of online availability. They would be reminded, by design consultant Larry Keeley's contribution to the catalog, that American workers already average two thousand hours of work every year, by far the highest rate in the world, outstripping even the workaholic Japanese by seventy hours.

According to curator Paola Antonella, the show catered exclusively to "a condition that stems from abundance," and therefore it focused on the most advanced, high-tech sector of the workforce. Consequently, it had nothing to say about the majority of office workplaces, where computer technology is used for the systematic surveillance of employees or to control the speed at which they work. These forms of regulation contrast sharply with the autonomy enjoyed by no-collar knowledge workers. For most low-wage information processing or data entry workers, their digital tools have nothing to do with creativity or play or empowerment, or for that matter, any of the principles enshrined in the Razorfish handbook. Their machines are sources of musculoskeletal damage, psychological disorders, chronic stress and

fatigue, and for the women who predominate in these pink-collar occupations, reproductive problems.[27] Ingenuity on the job mostly takes
the form of slowing down the work regime, beating the system, and
trying to sabotage its automated pace. The cumulative loss of productivity from computer downtime caused by employee sabotage is
surely one of the best kept secrets in corporate America.[28] The
amount of productive time lost to sabotage alone would help to explain the "productivity paradox," which for decades had baffled economists, unable to find empirical proof that IT boosts productivity.

Surveillance and sabotage belong to an old story about the routine
use of new workplace technologies to control the behavior of employees.[29] Part of that story also involves the resistance of workers, like the
original Luddites, to new technologies introduced in order to automate their skills, standardize the application of their knowledge, and
reduce their status to passive operators of machinery. Nor were no-
collarites exempt from this de-skilling. For all the independence offered by their new digital tools, the digital artisans knew that software
upgrades could automate overnight the programming and designing
savvy that had taken them years to learn. Speedup took its toll. Delays
in completing and delivering client projects were often attributed to
the self-absorbed temperament of Web designers. Their attention to
detail could easily be construed as a narcissistic fixation if it proved to
be a drag on the tempo of the work flow.

Stephen Turbek, one of Razorfish's very first recruits, agreed that
programs had become much more standardized and acknowledged
that "it's a big ego hit for the designers," but added nonchalantly that
"they seem to be rolling with it." Although Turbek had learned several
crafts in his time at the firm, he had been trained in industrial design,
and so he had a frankly commercial background. In fact, he described
himself as "a small 'd' kind of designer" to distinguish himself from
the kind of designers who "believe in themselves as artists" and for
whom "the goal of the thing they are making is to express an idea or
to reflect themselves." Commercial designers, he reported, are
trained to let go of the product. But Turbek also noted that "they are
not taught to stand up for themselves so well and are unable to give
push-back on projects, so they end up working really late hours, especially at the end of projects, because they have to do the manual

labor" after last-minute decisions have been made. He was one of the few veteran fish I interviewed who did not pine for the old days. In fact, he said that he welcomed the "corporatization" of the company, if only because it had reduced the workload of most employees. The camaraderie was "intoxicating," he recalled, but "for a year all we did was work, twelve to sixteen hours a day, seven days a week."

Turbek had been at the MOMA opening and had taken an especially keen interest in the show. He had run his own furniture company for a while, and so he had assumed much of the responsibility for designing the Razorfish offices. In contrast to the trophy interiors commissioned by companies like DoubleClick and Screaming Media (in the fashionably raw Starret-Lehigh building on the West Side) or Oxygen Media (in the old Nabisco factory in Chelsea, another high-profile site for new media), Razorfish's New York offices were quite makeshift. Their signature feature were the brushed steel tables that formed the basis of every workstation. Often cited as Razorfish's answer to the famous desks made out of four-by-fours that belonged to Jeff Bezos and every other employee at Amazon.com, the steel tables were the result of Turbek's cost-conscious decision to go for "cheap, fast, and changeable" furniture. With the company in constant flux, flexibility was a priority.[30] Purchased for $150 from a Bowery restaurant supplier, the tables were pushed together, four to a group, to form rafts. The rafts were positioned at angles to one another to break up the appearance of galley rows. The overall physical effect, spread across the large loft floors, was uniform but asymmetrical and had the social feel of a trading floor. Over time, Turbek had monitored employee responses and modifications to the layout. Some had placed curved screens in front of their stations for privacy or nesting, but the blueprint format had stayed intact by general consent and had been duplicated at most of the other offices.

More distinctive than the physical layout was the policy of mixing together employees from different professional groups. Each raft of tables was supposed to include creatives, technologists, and strategists. This arrangement was intended to discourage subculture cliques and to encourage the sharing of trade skills and knowledge among employees who had to work side by side on client projects. Interdisciplinary seating was aimed at the goal of a streamlined industrial

process, harnessing talents and tasks that would have been compart-
mentalized in a more conventional office plan. It also reflected the
New Economy dogma that the brightest ideas came from unlikely
sources, such as casual encounters between employees from different
microcultures. According to this doctrine, distraction from the task at
hand was no longer a brake on productivity but was essential to the
thought process of the knowledge worker. Even the large office furniture manufacturers had recently recognized this principle in their
new designs. *Workspheres,* for example, featured Resolve, the new
Herman Miller system, based on 120-degree angles ("nature's favorite
angle," according to creator Ayse Birsel) and designed for greater
connectivity between employees in a shared space.

Certainly, there were fish who took the opportunity to learn skills
from their neighbors, and some even reinvented their jobs accordingly. Over time, however, the system eroded, as employees drifted
from the interdisciplinary seating plan. The pull of professional sub-
cultures proved to be quite strong. Technologists, especially, gravitated toward one another, electing to work in secluded packs in "war
rooms" when they were on a group deadline. Turbek admitted he had
come to revise his thinking to incorporate the need for "internal co-
hesion or knowledge sharing within the individual jobs." This change
of mind had come from his observation of employees in the workplace, and he distinguished it from the top-down arrogance of auteur
designers who imposed their social engineering by fiat. The most notorious example had been Gaetano Pesce's ultra-mobility design for
Chiat/Day's New York offices. Employees had no dedicated work
space and were required to find a place (not an easy prospect) within
the office to work with their laptops and cell phones. This free-for-all
model of hoteling had been a very public failure. "Quite simply, it was
not designed around the way people want things to be," observed
Turbek. "Employees," he added, "are looking to be guided a little.
They can be redirected about 15 degrees, but not 90 degrees."

Craig Kanarick, who helped engineer the Razorfish layout, described the effort to maintain the space as nonhierarchical:

Jeff and I were right out on the floor; nobody was facing the walls, so
you never saw the backs of people. For the first two years, the finance

group was out on the floor with everyone else, until they had to start locking stuff up in cabinets, and even when Jeff and I got offices we made it so that they were more glass than wall and had no ceilings. The offices made it look like we were executives, but my desk was right up against the glass wall, with another person facing me, and Jeff's desk, in the same office, touched mine.

By the time I interviewed Kanarick, his office was four-walled and ensconced in the corporate building several blocks away from production-level employees. Scrupulously tidy, with a Zappy electric scooter parked in the corner, it also boasted, on a book stand, an atlas-size Helmut Newton book of stylized erotica. On the wall outside was a Kanarick visualization of an Adlai Stevenson quote: "The free mind is no barking dog, to be tethered on a ten-foot chain."

Eagerly anticipating his upcoming vacation time on Mustique, the exclusive Caribbean island where he had a co-op share, Kanarick expounded at length on the difficulties of managing a large company. "Thirty is the magic number," he asserted, "and then things change dramatically." When he talked about his ideal version of Razorfish as a place of work, he made it sound as if it belonged more in the Personals section than the Employment section of classified ads:

> People say they are going out on a date, they go out to a party, out on the town, out to dinner, whereas they go into work, into jail, into the hospital. Going out is a really wonderful thing; going in is really bad. If people said I'm going out to Razorfish, then I'd feel we've created something really special. If I'm going to go somewhere everyday, it damn well better be a good experience, and if everyone else shows up there everyday, I can't just bribe them. I don't have a crew of really expensive prostitutes here that just get paid to show up. They had to really love what they're doing, and love showing up, and love the culture.

Love seemed like a high standard to expect of employees and probably not a very healthy one. Even so, I had interviewed dozens of fish whose passion for the company probably went beyond the zone of comfort, and much of it was refracted through the personal charisma of the founders. Yet there was no explicit geography of power. The authority imparted by Kanarick and Dachis was difficult to locate, and employees often spoke of its flow through the company's offices as indistinct and diffuse. "There is no central source of permission," explained a project manager from Rumblefish. "Authority in this place is like love; it's like the light in another room. You see it but you don't know where it's coming from; it's just there, it's like an ambience. It's self-created, but it's also fashioned from the outside, and each feeds off the other."

If this quality proved irresistible to some employees, there were still practical choices to be made about how to use the open workplace. Although they generally had the freedom to choose where and when to work, the fish were encouraged to be onsite frequently, to recharge the culture battery. Nevertheless, a serious bout of self-application on a project invariably meant working at home. The gregarious office and its corresponding noise level made it difficult to sustain concentration. Donning headphones was the only way of ensuring privacy and peace. The open environment was a high-voltage energy source for more youthful recruits, but maturing fish tended to lose their enthusiasm for it. The plan was intended to foster a resourceful mix of people and ideas. In practice, it often demanded a high degree of homogeneity among employees, because it required a consensus about noise and activity levels, taste, morality, and the public sharing of personal habits.

No matter where employees were working physically, they were all connected through an intranet. In a sly tribute to the ship's central computing system in *Alien*, it was named Mom. Among its features was an interactive calendar for each employee to book meetings with colleagues. Anyone could schedule an appointment if a slot was free. Everyone's daily schedule, even those of senior managers, was rendered transparent. Like all knowledge technologies, it was a system where the virtue of common access also doubled as the threat of total oversight.

A Whistlestop Tour

By some New York kind of consensus, in a city that provided more than enough aural stimulation, hardly anyone played music aloud in the offices. Entering the San Francisco office, on my Razorfish tour in the fall of 2000, I was greeted by a fierce blast of AC/DC. Music here was all but obligatory, and employees, almost 130 of them, vied over what went onto the playlist. The result, I was told, was like a family whose members all had different musical preferences. Bending the air with reverb and high gusto, the acoustic impact of Angus Young's thunder chords was being amplified because the center of the building had been hollowed out, and each floor rose like a gallery around the atrium floor.

San Francisco Office, Razorfish (Photo by Nilus Designs)

A new manager had recently installed a four-walled office for himself, and the symbolism of his closed door was being taken badly by fish who were passionate about the controlled chaos of their work space. Everything, including performance reviews—even the recent layoff process—was conducted in the open. The instructions for Nilus deMartin, the office designer, had been to produce "a design that expressed creativity rather than a 'we are totally successful' look." Given the periodic influx of sightseers from the business world, this choice was strategic. "We're like Marineland," explained Bonnie Pratt, an information architect from Montreal. "We've become a regular stop on

Silicon Valley tours." Although many of the visitors, especially those from Asian companies, were startled by the open environment, she reported that younger employees who had never toiled in a cubicle farm were equally dumbfounded by the curiosity of the tourists. "I'll never be able to work in a place that's not like this," she herself lamented. "I'm spoiled for life."

In San Francisco, the company had acquired an iconoclastic design shop, Plastic, with a heavily tattooed workforce, and so the Razorfish integration had been friction-free. However, in the Boston office, which enjoyed a stunning overlook on the Charles River, there was much less unanimity. I-Cube, the Cambridge technology acquisition, was stacked with hard-core programmers, many of them South Asians on H1-B visas, who had not responded enthusiastically to the raffish Razorfish ethos. The result was starkly evident in the office design. A maze of chest-high partitions had been introduced as a compromise between the open Razorfish plan and the eight-foot gray cubes of the I-Cube technologists. Management had retrofitted the offices without input from the design group, and there was no Razorfish stamp on the space other than the company's palette of colors on the walls. "For whatever asinine reason," explained Liam O'Connel, a content developer, and poet in his free time, "designers really do need a nice work place, and they need to sit in the same place for a period of time. Technologists don't care where they sit, don't care what the place looks like, and couldn't care less if they have to move every day." Recently, he reported, there had been some agreement on the need for changes: the bland carpeting and the hung ceiling would go (no-collar workers usually want to be able to see the wiring and the ducts). But the downturn had changed all that, and by the time of my visit in March 2001, survival art was on the walls, and management was asking employees to opt for "voluntary separation" (but not getting too many takers).

Unlike in New York, there were bowls of fast fuel in the kitchen— Nutrigen cereal bars, Ritz Bitz sandwiches, M&Ms, Hunt Potato Chips—to energize technologists on a long stint. Whereas other offices had shunned pool and Ping-Pong tables as dotcom gimmicks and therefore very uncool items to have in the office, both had been preserved here. The I-Cube brand was still present, on mousepads, screensavers, pens, and mugs, and the management organization had retained much

The Semi-Cubicle Space, Razorfish, Boston (Photo by the author)

of its hierarchical structure. Clearly, the Boston office had been the result of a top-down acquisition, not a level merger of two different cultures, just as the Fish Fry get-together in Las Vegas had foreshadowed. Employees I interviewed agreed that creative work was not adequately understood or recognized, and none of them believed they had seen much of the "famous Razorfish culture" that other offices enjoyed.

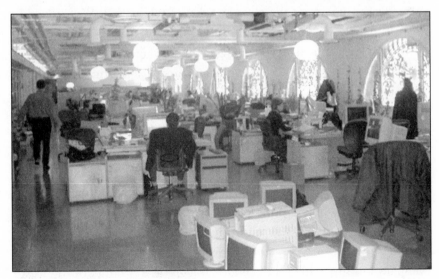

Smithfield Offices, Razorfish, London (Photo by the author)

Undoubtedly, the most singular Razorfish office location was in London, upstairs from the meat market of Smithfield. Eight centuries after its medieval heyday, when it flourished just outside the city walls, great sides of beef and flocks of poultry were still being hawked on the street level of the market. The odors of the trade had largely dissipated by the time the fish showed up for work. Their office, managed by vegetarians, was stocked daily with bowls of organic fruit. Inside, a Paul Oakenfold soundtrack was gently warming up the day with waves of light, bouncy trance. On the previous day, Louis Armstrong had presided. The London office (the result of a relatively smooth acquisition of the design shop CHBi) was bright and roomy and enjoyed full, open plan floors with stained glass windows and well-integrated plant life. At the back, a History Wall, devised by an employee, offered a vivid narrative of some of the events and personages that Smithfield had hosted in the course of its long life:

> Being outside the walls, it enjoyed a degree of freedom and licence that the more buttoned-up city could not quite control. This was a place to come and have fun, the original West End. It was a chaotic place, full of movement and energy. Gin palaces, taverns and opium dens all crowded together in the alleyways, feeding off the trade that flowed out through the city gates and in from the country. Great art was kicked up out of the mess and dirt of the market. Writers and artists mingled with cutpurses and whores in the tangled alleys. They fed off the colour and life, breathing in the air where monasteries stood next to brothels, hospitals next to meat markets, and printing presses next to gin rooms.

The Wall's author paid special tribute to "the people of Smithfield who died here for causes they believed in," while "others created things that still amaze the world." He ended with a footnote to the fish: "We do not shy away—we make our mark." The assertive tone was modest only in comparison with the American bragging style that had won the company's repute. The London fish I interviewed also took the opportunity to exercise some native skepticism about the company culture, which they tended to view as a product of American business schtick. Sarah Wooten, a technologist who had spent a little time in the New York office, observed: "It's a very British thing not to be terribly self-confident or terribly public about things. Your mum would laugh at you if you crowed the way that North Americans do." "Over here," she added, bluntly, "Jeff and Craig were always seen as a pair of wankers." Others declared their pride in a different work ethos, embracing the view that "Europeans work to live, whereas Americans live to work." Wooten was more appreciative of her New York colleagues: "Sometimes, however, they are so professional they're scary as human beings."

In the area around the market, the "rookeries and slums" described on the History Wall had long vanished, and the "great melting pot of trade, of science, of art, of revolution and of charity . . . where life was never sanitized or hidden away" was filling up with sleek cappuccino bars and pricey wine stores. This was Clerkenwell, where rents had risen steeply during the city's boom years. The surge had been even more spectacular in Shoreditch to the east, another dotcom haven, where the avant-garde art gallery scene had cut a gentrifying swathe through a stolid working-class area of the city. In London, it was the art world and not the dotcoms that supplied the media circus with fresh fodder. Impressed by the sassy ascent to international prominence of the Young British Artists, Tony Blair's New Labour government had showered attention on the creative industries, and the digital sector had benefited accordingly.

Under the policies of Chris Smith, Blair's minister of culture, media and sport, artists had been asked to play more functional roles in society: assisting in the improvement of public health, race relations, urban renewal, special education, welfare to work programs, and economic development.[31] Above all, Smith's policies required state-funded arts activities to show a good return on investment (ROI, as the MBA's put it). These stipulations caused quite a ruckus.[32] Many artists felt they were being groomed to be model citizens or offered a role more akin to entrepreneurial social workers than to traditional creative artisans. In the United States, recent policy documents, such as the NEA's *American Canvas* (1997), promoted a similar profile for the fundable artist.

On the face of it, such policies were designed to make artists more accountable to society in the work that they do. But their real significance lay in a reverse proposition: the mentality of artists was becoming too valuable to be left to artists themselves. In a value-adding economy where creativity is glorified, it was no surprise that attention would turn to artists and their work styles. Indeed, their traditional work patterns seemed to fit all the requirements of the no-collar knowledge worker. Sure enough, many had found their way into the offices of the digital economy, where, as we will now see, the industrialization of Bohemia was already well under way.

The Industrialization of Bohemia

I saw the best minds of my occupation destroyed by venture capital, burned-out, paranoid, postal, dragging themselves through the Cappuccino streets of Palo Alto at Dawn looking for an equity-sharing, stock option fix, HTML-headed Web-sters coding for the infinite broadband connection to that undiscovered e-commerce mother lode in the airy reaches of IP namespace. . . .

—Thomas Scoville, "Howl.com"

IN HIS BOOK *BOBOS IN PARADISE*, DAVID BROOKS OFFERS AN extended description of a "new upper class" that fuses bourgeois and bohemian values and whose apotheosis is the blue-jean capitalist, preaching liberation management and ingesting organic food. Most of the story Brooks tells about this truce between traditionally warring parties focuses on patterns of taste, consumption, and habits of self-expression. "Marx," he writes, "told us that classes inevitably conflict, but sometimes they just blur." "The values of the bourgeois, mainstream culture and the values of the 1960s counterculture have merged," he concludes.[1] Yet Brooks's warring parties have little to do with what Marx meant by class conflict. The conflict between the bourgeoisie and bohemia has always been the result of generational friction or sibling rivalry within a dominant class. Bohemians, then and now, have been attracted to the cause of class conflict as much for aesthetic as for political reasons, but their antiestablishment interests are usually much better served by the maintenance of the bourgeois status quo than by the often repressive outcome of class wars. In this regard, Brooks, as a self-defined "bobo," seems no less confused about class identity than Gustave Flaubert or Jack Kerouac had been.

Brooks's cheerful depiction of the bobo is basically an elaborate market profile of an upscale consumer, and it could be used as such by the marketing departments of any Tom, Dick, and Harry in the gourmet retail business. If we look beneath these alterations in the sumptuary style and etiquette of individuals, we will find a much deeper revision of industrial personality. A portrait of the work process ought to provide more telling evidence of this change than Brooks's vignette of the bobo consumer. It will show us what happens when the routine pace and rhythms of industry are reprogrammed to accommodate an artist's work mentality that once flourished in defiance of industrial routine.

To recount this story properly, we must begin with the traditional urban habitat of artists and consider the changes wrought on this environment by their new industrial recruiters. For most of the postwar period, urban downtowns were the last places you might have expected to see signs of industrial growth. By the late 1980s, some pundits were wryly suggesting that commercial property values might be saved if portions of center cities were allowed to revert to pasture. Yet within a decade, many of these city economies were prospering and had seen the appearance of new urban industries for the first time since the 1960s. Ever since the flight of manufacturing, city managers had been full-time supplicants, ever vigilant in wooing companies that showed any interest in locating within their borders. By the 1990s, there were clear winners and losers of this courtship game. The losers were scrambling to make room for casinos, and their downtowns, if they were alive at all, were stamped by the mammoth footprint of sports stadiums, museums, and retail entertainment centers. The winners had capitalized on niche opportunities in the value-adding economy. Their growth industries, grouped in the high-end tier of producer services, were generating jobs in spades. This growth was less evident in the high-rise enclaves of their central business districts than in the old manufacturing downtown neighborhoods, where the facial marks of dilapidation were profiled and accentuated as indices of vitality, youthful regeneration, and glamour.

The new media companies that moved into these zones could not afford prime commercial rents, but their no-collar employees did not want, in any case, to work in plush corporate towers. The bare-plaster, low-rent ambience was as much an aesthetic virtue for the employees as it was an economic necessity for the owners, and it proved an effective and visible way for the companies to advertise themselves as grassroots alternatives to corporate America. Like two generations of artists before them, they would be playing an equivocal role in neighborhood gentrification. The same formula that had driven residential gentrification for three decades would now be applied to the commercial zones of these old neighborhoods, where depressed rents made property ripe for speculative development. From the perspective of city landlords, the digital economy was not a messianic movement bent on delivering a millennial future; it was a high-protein stimulant for zones in transition, and the shabby chic of its boutique companies and human capital was a perfect engine for pumping value into depreciated land assets.

Nowhere was the cost of this transition more deeply felt than in San Francisco, where in the late 1990s, 70,000 new jobs were being created each year. The city had become an annex of Silicon Valley and the hub of a New Economy commuting zone that stretched from Santa Cruz in the south to the Russian River in the north and as far as Stockton in the east. Twenty million dollars of venture capital were washing daily through the city's economy by the fall of 1999. Unlike in New York, the new media sector had become the largest single source of employment, and the high-price growth of this monocrop was crowding everything and everyone else out. Residential rents had already inched above Manhattan's nosebleed prices, and as downtown leases ran out, landlords quintupled commercial rents (to a high of $80 per square foot for Class A space, the highest asking rate in the nation). Longtime residents of bohemian and working-class areas, like the industrial warehouse sector below Market Street (SoMa), the South Park quadrant, and the Mission district to the south, were being squeezed out daily. Artists of all stripes, along with other low-income groups, were faced with extinction in a city renowned for its maverick, countercultural spirit.[2]

The irony of this predicament escaped few, least of all those employees who had been attracted to the Bay Area for its natural and cultural advantages. Like discerning tourists looking for an unspoiled beach, they had arrived on a surge of people and money that threatened to destroy the very reasons for being there. Barry Christgau, an engineer who had moved from the Midwest in the late 1980s to work for Sun Microsystems, acknowledged the contradiction: "I came here for the mountains, ocean, and the liberal lifestyle, and to be with the brightest of the breed. Now people come for the money—the city is full of MBAs and BMWs—and the environment is being ruined. I'm by no means not guilty, and it's a strange feeling to know you are a vehicle for things you don't really agree with. I wish the boom would end." Christgau could see how turbo-capitalism was making the city unaffordable for those with no stake in the gold rush. He lived in the lower Mission district where neighborhood activists had taken to occupying the buildings of companies that were displacing nonprofits and artists' spaces. Incidents of arson were being reported. "You have the right to choose to live and work anywhere," Christgau remarked, and added cryptically, "but you don't have the right to live and work anywhere."

Gulch of Pain

The week I visited the San Francisco Razorfish office, in late November 2000, Proposition L, a city ordinance that would have curtailed the expansion of office space for the Internet industry, was narrowly defeated. The company stood to benefit from the outcome since it was due to move, shortly, from its offices in SoMa to a larger space on the edge of Portrero Hill. Yet most employees were aware of the growing conflict around office expansion and were deeply ambivalent about the move. "I'm doing this job to fund my art work," explained a Web developer who also made what she calls "community sculptures." "But the way things are going, there won't be anywhere left in this city to do my stuff." Like many other progressive, arts-minded Internet employees, she had found herself with one foot on either side of a battle line that crisscrossed a landscape in the throes of another gold rush.

In a city with an unrivaled record as a laboratory of social and cultural innovation, the species of gentrification that blew in with the Internet business models had a complex makeup. For one thing, the Net economy took root in San Francisco rather than Silicon Valley precisely because it was a refuge for alternative thinking and boasted a resident labor pool of creative workers. Community use of the Internet had been pioneered in the rave scene, on listservs like the Well, and in a frankly noncommercial climate of experimentation. The city was home to *Wired,* which cast a glamorous fervor around all things high-tech and was heir to a legacy of homegrown utopia in influential publications, from the *Whole Earth Review* of the 1960s to the *Mondo 2000* of the 1980s. Everyone who was not a Bay Area newcomer could say, "It was a culture before it was an industry," and it was common among scene veterans to make a distinction between Web people—devoted to the ideals of transforming communication, shareware, and free information—and dotcommers—who were widely regarded as gold diggers.

In fact, San Francisco had been built on land speculation, beginning with the grabbing of lots in the two years between the raising of the American flag and the chartering of the city in 1850 and continuing with the gold rush and wave after wave of railroad speculation. Portions of the city had a long history of real estate inflation in boom times. South Park itself was a working-class Filipino quarter before it became the epicenter of Multimedia Gulch (Mayor Willie Brown's name for the Internet district north of Portrero Hill), but its origins lay in a much earlier land boom, in the 1860s, when it was developed as an elegant enclave for the city's pioneer mercantile and professional elites.[3]

When city artists were last faced with displacement—during the boom of the 1980s—they had fought back and won from City Hall a special live/work ordinance that permitted the conversion of formerly industrial space into studios. This 1988 measure bypassed building codes and affordable housing stipulations. In the course of the next decade, however, it became the loophole of choice for developers to circumvent the city's annual cap on new office construction.[4] Through a loose interpretation of this ordinance, new media companies could define their new premises in SoMa (where development had been all but frozen since 1986) as something other than office space.[5] As Rebecca Solnit and Susan Schwartzenberg point out in *Hollow City,* their passionate account of the "Siege of San Francisco," Internet companies and their employees looking to locate in a cool district with industrial lofts and warehouses were the ideal clients for landlords who had learned how to manipulate the live/work ordinance.[6]

In response, anti-gentrification sentiment ran high. Some of the street protests had a carnivalesque air, recalling an earlier ritual declaration of the demise of a counterculture: Death of Hippie, in Haight-Ashbury, in October 1967.

DEATH NOTICE

It's time . . . Please join us in person or in spirit as we mourn the passing of San Francisco Culture. At two o'clock on Saturday, October 21th we will convene at Union Square and proceed up Market Street bearing a coffin to the Steps of City Hall. The procession will include a marching band and police escort ending with speakers, performances, and celebration. Maybe you've watched this unique city's culture, built on diversity and a thriving art community, being strangled by blindly managed growth in recent years. What happened? How can we influence the social impacts of our new economy? (We request that all participants wear somber attire befitting a funeral march.)[7]

Other protest groups, such as the Mission Yuppie Eradication Society, were less polite, encouraging the aggrieved to vandalize SUVs parked on the street or to trash and torch "yuppie bars." Formed as a unity lobby, the Mission Anti-Displacement Coalition focused on the industry's penetration of the predominantly working-class Latino (and formerly Irish) district that had recently seen the invasion of avantgarde sushi restaurants with valet parking.

One favorite target of the coalition was Andrew Beebe, the highly visible owner of Big Step, a client server software company that had taken over a building that was central to the Mission's sense of community. The building, which had been used by nonprofits, had been occupied by protesters, and Beebe was being demonized as a rapacious dotcom archetype with formerly progressive beliefs and credentials. I caught up with the beleaguered, ponytailed Beebe in the executive lounge of the San Francisco airport. In his capacity as one of the first players from the Internet industry to be tapped by the Chamber of Commerce, he was en route to a San Jose meeting of the Chamber and was preparing for a disagreement with other members on the battle over Proposition L. The business community, he said, had "circled the wagons," and he saw himself as a renegade on the issue, pushing for sustainable growth. "I'm gonna sound like one of those Californians who says, 'Now that I'm here, fuck everybody else who wants to move in.' But I believe that balance is good for the community, and I don't see the benefit in having the city overrun by one type of development."

"The early scene here was totally organic," he recalled "No one was in it for the money." But the romance of the Web and the gold lust turned out to be "mutually desirable," he added. "As a romantic soul with big aspirations for what technology can do to change the world, I can realize these aspirations much faster with 20 million in the bank, maybe even 200 million." However cavalier about his ambitions, Beebe was simply giving the jumbo version of what all artists with an Internet job had said to themselves: "I'm only doing this to subsidize my art."

On the subject of his Mission building that had been occupied, Beebe displayed mixed feelings. Gentrification was "a legitimate thing to be up in arms about," yet he regretted the targeting of his company. "A lot of our people at the core are actually progressive, but they have developed a very narrow view of the world because they've been so busy or single-minded." Beebe acknowledged that he trained employees to focus on nothing but business, 24/7, and was only just realizing that "there's more to life than cranking our product and getting to the gold." The day before, he confessed, he had missed an off-site meeting because he "was having so much fun building a child care center around the corner of our building for the local neighborhood group." On the other hand, Beebe felt that his company had been unfairly demonized by activists looking for a scapegoat: "One of our problems," he explained, "is that 40 of the 100 remaining Marxists are living within ten blocks of us. They are people who don't agree with capitalism as a system, and they make our mayor [Willie Brown], who is a pretty progressive guy, look like a fascist by comparison." Much of the blame, he believed, lay with the landlords who ordered the evictions and then collected nosebleed rents from companies like his.

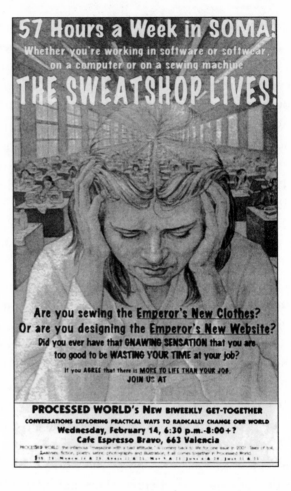

**No-Collar
Sweatshops
in Soma**

In the Mission, for example, landlords (mostly non-Latino) rented on a month-to-month lease and could quadruple their asking prices at will. It had become common for SoMa landlords to demand company stock before they would lease to startups. Unlike the highly visible Internet entrepreneurs, whose business profile required them to seek publicity and to cultivate flamboyant personalities, landlords knew how to remain faceless and had a long history of evading public scrutiny. All the same, there were few participants in this citywide drama who could claim the moral high ground. Even the anti-gentrification activists were derided by Mission locals as "old yuppies," who had arrived twenty years before, with their Apple Macs and mountain bikes, and were now trying to drive out the "new yuppies" with their SUVs, cell phones, and East Coast MBAs.

Like the artists, performers, and writers who were also Net employees, community art groups had scant reason to turn their backs on the Internet sector, since so many of their clientele worked for new media companies. Jonathan Youtt, cofounder of CellSpace, which occupied a sprawling, multilevel, 10,000 square foot warehouse in the Mission, estimated that half of the people who used the facility depended on paychecks from the New Economy. CellSpace had grown out of a puppetry collective into a center for collaborative arts that was 95 percent volunteer run and had broad ties with community initiatives in the Mission and beyond. Offering performance and exhibition space for dance, art, opera, spoken word, film, music, and roller-skating, the warehouse was also a hive of artisanal activity, hosting workshops for metal, sewing, wood, sound, food, digital connectivity, and multimedia production. In a venue like this, it was easy to see the continuity between the preindustrial and the postindustrial arts and crafts. Digital activity was not a distinct realm of gee-whizzery, eclipsing all that had gone before. It was simply one among several crafts for creative expression that had evolved over time, and it was made available here as just another medium for community use.

On the night I visited Youtt, yoga and kung fu classes were in session, along with "tango for protest" and a benefit for groups pushing for the city to create a public power utility. Locals were lining up to use the computer terminals. Youtt, attired like a whimsical magician with streetwise trappings, acknowledged that "artists are often quite unaware of their role in gentrification and don't see themselves as a problem." Those most devoted to their own personal growth (the practitioners of "art for art's sake") are the ones who "end up having the most physical impact on the city." The community arts movement had a different record because of its direct involvement in neighborhood initiatives and its view of art as a vehicle for community initiatives and empowerment.

Youtt was optimistic that the digital medium would prevail over the dark side of its commercial exploitation. "There are enough hackers and other Web originators," he estimated, "to make sure it stays true to their liberating, commercial-free intentions." As for the developers and entrepreneurs who had colluded in the evictions, Youtt turned necromancer in forecasting their ruin: "If you enter into this kind of deal with the devil, it means that your whole business is doomed, as far as I can tell. Karmically doomed." Over the next several months, his prophecy would bear fruit, with or without help from the spirit world. By the end of 2001, failing dotcoms had produced a large surplus of available office space, and rents dropped as much as 50 percent in the SoMa submarket.[8]

Silicon Urbanism

Techno-futurists, from Alvin Toffler to Nicholas Negroponte, had forecast that computers would have a decentralizing impact on work. Power, population, and wealth would no longer need to be concentrated in metropolitan centers. For many purposes, and for many types of employees, it was predicted that the physical sense of place might become obsolete. Yet this scenario of dispersion had not materialized, as a quick glance at the overheated economies of urban downtowns would show. The dramatic job growth and soaring rents in older metropolitan centers like New York and Chicago was nearly matched by smaller cities like Boston, Seattle, Toronto, Denver, Portland, San Jose, Salt Lake City, San Diego, San Francisco, and Atlanta. It was the same story in Los Angeles, where a combination of unemployed IT workers from the decimated aerospace industry and a glut of underused warehouse space on the West Side had fueled the digital buildup. If anything, there had been an overconcentration of new producer service industries in downtown venues, along with a recentralization of human capital and know-how. In principle, much of the New Economy could be run and serviced by virtual means. In practice, the physical footprints of its geographical division of labor were very tightly mapped onto the existing infrastructure of high-speed backbones and data hubs: the old Arpanet centers of Boston, San Francisco, and Washington, or at the termini of intercontinental fiber-optic cables, in Los Angeles, New York, San Francisco, and Washington.[9]

Outside of the media, fashion, and culture industries, most large corporations still had no explicit need for central urban locations, but that had more to do with cost accounting than with the introduction of advanced technology. Science-based knowledge industries, including hardware and software complexes, continued to concentrate on the high-end suburban periphery: Santa Clara County in Northern California; Irvine and La Jolla in Southern California; Raleigh-Durham in North Carolina; Route 128 outside of Boston; suburban Austin, Texas; Redmond, Washington; and the Colorado Front Range. The urban growth in jobs in the digital industry was a result of several factors: a ready supply of underemployed creative workers, an available network of Web-based skills pioneered by urban artists, and a temporary supply of substandard office space at depressed rental prices. In some cities, such as New York and Chicago, financial industries, along with their attendant business and legal services, also saw a boost in growth. If this buildup had anything to do with IT, then it was a result of feedback from the centrifugal impact of technology. Saskia Sassen has argued that the technology-driven dispersion of operations across the global economy made it all the more necessary for transnational firms to have links to centers of coordination for managing their far-flung production units and diversified product lines. These urban service centers were composed of layers of specialized firms—legal, accounting, consulting, business, and IT—which needed locational access to key resources. The central agglomeration of these supplier services and activities coexisted with the tendency to distribute production offshore.[10]

It would be wrong, however, to see this urban growth primarily as the outcome of new technologies playing out their industrial potential. Nor, in the case of the Internet companies, were they merely the fabrication of investors and analysts pumping hot air into the Internet stock bubble. Silicon Alley was just as much the result of precision boosting by an urban growth machine calibrated to cycles of real estate speculation that depend on the periodic obsolescence and rehabilitation of building stock. In New York City, the real estate slump of the early 1990s presented a clear opportunity for new kinds of business, and it also promised a huge return to everyone with a vested or peripheral interest in the subsequent inflation of the city's real estate market.

Aside from the boosterism of the industry's own media (the *Silicon Alley Reporter*, *@NY*, *New York Software News*, and *Alleycat News*) and trade groups (New York New Media Association, New York Software Industry Association, and the New York eCommerce Association), the city's newspapers, magazines, politicians, and lobbyists all played a loud role in cheerleading the rise of Silicon Alley. The idea that New York was a silicon boomtown could not get enough press.[11] City and state government also stepped in to subsidize the industry, offering attractive tax abatement packages and Internet-ready space to promote industry spin-offs in other parts of the metro region (BronxSmart, Silicon Harbor in Brooklyn's Red Hook, CyberCity in Long Island City, SI Hub on Staten Island, HIWay 125 in Harlem, and Info River Valley in the Mid-Hudson Valley) that were deemed in need of economic stimulation and regeneration.[12] At an NYSIA "Software Summit" I attended in November 2000, the keynote speaker, Senator Charles Schumer, delivered a typical tribute to the digital faithful: "When they look at the future of New York, they should look at this room. Ten years ago, this city was near the bottom of any company's list, and we were bleeding jobs. Now we are the world center of ideas, and ideas have become the dominant economic force. In short, you have been a godsend to New York."

Many moneyed interests happened to converge in applauding the rise of the new media sector. Typically, in a boom economy, a point is always reached when the interests come into conflict with each other. As rents explode, so does the cost of doing business. The return on corporate investments is threatened by the increasing rents and land speculation. One fraction of the capitalist class, investing in land, is at odds with another, investing in companies or their stock. In the newspapers of record, editorials begin to agonize about the evolving conflict. The city is too expensive for new business, they warn, and companies hit with rent hikes begin to make noises about relocating.[13] Regardless of its other dimensions, the correction that began with the Nasdaq crash in April 2000 and snowballed into a general recession offered the only market solution to this growing conflict. Rents stabilized and then dropped, and stock valuations swooned as the down cycle of depreciation kicked in, seeding the way for the soils of opportunity to play host to the next boom. Because of its monocrop Internet economy, San Francisco was the hardest hit by the technology slump. Less than two years after the Nasdaq crash, commercial rents had fallen by more than 50 percent, and prices were back at their 1998 asking rates. Yet they still retained a massive appreciation from pre-dotcom levels.[14]

In New York, where the new media sector accounted for only 5 percent of the city's income and employment, the loss of the World Trade Center (erasing a full third of Lower Manhattan office space) proved to be a much greater blow, since the financial services industry accounted for more than 25 percent of the city's economy. Again, however, it was necessary to take a long view. Although its firms' fortunes had been mixed, Silicon Alley was a serendipitous response to a problem posed by the report of the Wagner Commission on the future of the city in 1987. The Wagner report, commissioned by Mayor Koch and issued just three months before the crash on Wall Street, challenged the city to come up with ways of developing the commercially depressed valley between Manhattan's two central business districts.[15] This challenge loomed even larger in the course of the real estate market collapse of the early 1990s. The interactive companies of Silicon Alley—spreading out from the midpoint of the Flatiron District—fit the bill perfectly. Not only did their entrepreneurs covet scruffy space, but they retrofitted the old building stock with high-tech infrastructural improvements that permanently boosted its value. Best of all for the building owners, most startups quickly outgrew the space they rented, moving on to larger premises before their leases ran out. This allowed landlords to rent again, at higher prices, fast-forwarding the market into a high-altitude bonanza.[16]

The Value of Street Life

Boom times come and go, mostly to meet the appetites of investors and speculators for prodigious short-term returns. In the case of Silicon Alley, however, New York had not just played host to a boom industry. The stuff of urbanism was a prime ingredient of the industry's growth because Silicon Alley companies turned city rhythms and urban attitude into profitable product in much the same way that realtors had turned ex-industrial grit into added property value. In *The New Geography*, a book on the spatial impact of the digital revolution, Joel Kotkin argues that location still matters in the New Economy because skilled high-tech employees have become "sophisticated consumers of place." Companies that need innovative no-collar employees are obliged to locate where these workers want to be—in vibrant urban centers that offer high-quality stimulation and services.[17] Yet the value of these urban qualities far exceeded their role in services consumed by workers off the job. Urbanism was also playing a significant role in production itself. The best place to view this was in the offices of companies like Razorfish, which tried to capture some of the hum, scurry, and sociability of urban street life, not to mention its surface transport—Rollerblades and scooters.

In an October 2000 *New Yorker* article, Malcolm Gladwell noted that the qualities of street vitality that Jane Jacobs had celebrated in *The Death and Life of Great American Cities* were increasingly prized within office workplaces. Open-style offices were now busy public spaces where "ideas arise as much out of casual conversations as they do out of formal meetings." In order to get the most innovation out of employees, the office space had to be very social, with employees from all professional groups interacting regularly. In other words, the office had to host the diversity of uses that Jacobs had once argued for in urban planning: "the workplace equivalent of houses and apartments and shops and industry."[18] Some companies had run a long way with the mixed-use neighborhood idea. Gladwell cites the Los Angeles office of Chiat/Day, designed after the ad agency's disastrous New York experiment with "nonterritoriality." Boasting a Main Street, a Central Park with café tables and greenery, and basketball courts off to the side, the L.A. warehouse office was a conscious effort to emulate a bustling streetscape. Similar efforts were mounted by more traditional companies that had created their own internal e-divisions. In London, the new e-commerce unit at British Airways was housed in glass-walled offices built around a cobblestone walkway known as "the street" and lined with coffee shops, modern sculptures, and waterfalls. There was also an indoor olive grove, for contemplation, where noise was forbidden, to ensure mixed-use of the office space. In other corporate offices, street cobblestones became a familiar part of the carpet pattern.[19]

Most Internet companies shied away from such cheesy efforts to impose the street on the office, settling instead for a spontaneous, disorderly feel, as if ideas were more likely to walk in from the street itself. While the principle behind the idea of the urbane office seemed to make sense, employees had their own preferred patterns of society, often favoring the camaraderie of their professional microcultures to the diffusion model of knowledge-sharing championed at places like Razorfish. (This point was somewhat replicated in the geography of domiciles; the technologists tended to live in suburbs and commuted, whereas the creatives lived in Brooklyn, and the MBAs in Manhattan.) So, too, fish working together on a long-term project tended to end up seated together, so that big clients had their own "company towns" inside the office, where knowledge and ideas were shared mostly among the team members rather than among the fish at large. Project employees from those client firms were often happier to work there than in their own corporate offices, and their presence helped to ensure that Razorfish ideas also flowed in the client's direction. As a result, any model of how information and ideas circulated within the office would have to show the drag, or gravitational pull, of territorial neighborhoods as well as the eddies formed around proprietary pockets.

But the analogy that Gladwell drew with the urbanism of Jacobs had a larger social dimension he had not quite anticipated. In her book, Jacobs had adopted the standpoint of the cosmopolitan intellectual, fiercely opposed to "dullness" in all of its forms. As a result, *Death and Life* was a natural, if sentimental, advocate of diversity and disorder in street life, qualities that its author, like most cosmopolitan intellectuals, saw as artful and exciting.[20] Like the classic bohemians, then, Jacobs viewed as a virtue what had once been a necessity for working-class residents. In neighborhoods like her own Greenwich Village or Boston's North End, family life had been conducted on the stoop or the street because the tenement homes and apartments were often overcrowded. For these families, public street life was obligatory, and suburban privacy, when it was offered, proved to be quite inviting by comparison. From the 1970s onward, professionals in the new urban service industries, who could otherwise afford the privacy, embraced in full the principle of urban vitality in neighborhoods that their parents might have abandoned a generation earlier. Their ability to pay a premium for the urban principle made mixed neighborhoods like Jacobs's Greenwich Village largely unaffordable for the lower-income population that had been the original source of diversity and with whom declassé bohemians had always peaceably coexisted.

By the 1990s, New Yorkers had long grown used to seeing artists' communities serve as a beachhead of choice for residential gentrification. In areas like Greenwich Village, SoHo, the East Village, Tribeca, Chelsea, Dumbo, Williamsburg, and Fort Greene, the pioneering of bohemian enclaves had become an indispensable element of the industrial real estate cycle.[21] In the 1990s, a similar cycle of gentrification began to work its way through commercial real estate, with Silicon Alley as one of its leading edges. Just as the new urbanites had made the cost of a Village address prohibitive for low-rent residents, so, too, the Alleycats' taste for raw urbanity in the workplace would boost commercial rents and price out the broader mix of businesses that serviced lower-income customers. Artists had played a leading role in residential gentrification. Now their presence in the workforce was having a similar impact through the industrialization of bohemia.

The Value of the Artistic Life

In the 1960s, the art-making activities at Andy Warhol's Factory caused a stir by showing how artists could create art by imitating the mechanical principles of industrial production. According to Warhol's credo, art was not only about the unique expression of creative individuals or the one-of-a-kind artifacts they crafted; it also had something to say about rhythms of mass manufacturing and the culture of commerce. Thirty years later, by the time Warhol's Factory building on Union Square was being occupied by Razorfish rival Scient, Silicon Alley managers were moving in exactly the opposite direction. They were trying to fashion a business that imitated all of the attributes of artists—their habitats, lifestyles, clothing, work patterns, and custom individuality—and they were seeking to incorporate all of these into a work temperament that could be recognized by clients as a reliable industrial process. By then, and partly because of Warhol, the stereotype of the avant-garde artist subsisting on the outer fringes of society was less and less rooted in reality. The art boom of the 1980s had placed artists at the fêted center of Manhattan high society, as their art became targets of investment for corporate collections. Some were star celebrities; most were a quick study in the business of self-employment, as entrepreneurial in their pursuit of funding as any startup owner. Consequently, stepping into the world of New Economy business was not that much of a culture shock for artists.

By the late 1950s, the cheap rents that had sustained urban downtown pockets of bohemia since its mid-nineteenth-century genesis in Paris were beginning to dry up. As manufacturing leeched away from the city, artists who took over the vacated factory lofts enjoyed wide open floors where workspace doubled as living space. This live/work ethos was embraced, to some degree, by upscale buyers who later endowed loft living with real estate allure.[22] Nonartists could now purchase many of the trappings of a creative, bohemian life without having to work at living it.

The Web shops of Silicon Alley introduced a further phase, when they imported this lifestyle component back into the workplace. The lofts were reclaimed for industry, but the work they hosted looked more and more like play, and employees were encouraged to behave like artists and keep artists' hours. The Alley's neo-bohemian culture helped sustain the belief that this kind of work was a viable alternative to corporate America. This belief (it may be more accurate to call it a willing suspension of disbelief) was especially important to contrarians with an arts background, who had been trained to scorn the conditions of a middle-class work environment, as well as the routine rhythms of industrial time.

Like Razorfish, several of the pioneer Alley Web shops grew out of attempts to stake an artistic presence on the Web. Even after the companies established a commercial identity, many maintained their own digital art department, if only to attract attention, in an attention economy. Avalanche had borderequalszero; Agency supported Urban Desires; HotWired had the RGB Gallery; and Total New York hosted the legendary ada'web, a "digital foundry" curated by an employee group (under the direction of Benjamin Weil) that commissioned well-known artists like Jenny Holzer, Julia Scher, and Lawrence Weiner to produce online projects. In an arrangement that was not untypical, the noncreative employees of Total were encouraged to spend "creative time" with the ada'web group as a way of recharging their batteries for client projects. Tinkering with the arty side of the medium had been an amateur passion for most Web veterans. As companies were established, it became a routine element of the job.

Personal digital doodling was perceived to be of benefit to the work process and product, and employee time devoted to this form of play was factored into the workday.

Ada'web did not survive Total's acquisition by AOL in 1997; it was disbanded and its archive was taken over by the Walker Art Museum. Portions of the site became the first collection of digital art to be acquired by a major museum, San Francisco's Museum of Modern Art. Art sites at other companies survived, but usually in some altered form. In its infancy, Razorfish was best known for hosting digital art on a site called The Blue Dot (an astronaut had declared that the Earth looked like one). Kanarick had taken advantage of a new server push gif animation feature on Netscape to produce, overnight, the first animated site on the Web. His bouncing blue dot attracted scads of attention among Web devotees at a time when the World Wide Web was sparsely populated. Like ada'web, The Blue Dot functioned as a commercial calling card, showcasing the creative profile of the company to would-be clients, and it was explicitly used as art therapy for employees (a routine opportunity, according to the mission handbook, for "creative play" and "experimentation").

Kanarick and Dachis decided to go further and formed an all-media company, Razorfish Studios, or RSUB, to produce content in every format, from television shows to digital cartoons. When Omnicom bought 40 percent of Razorfish in 1996, the advertising giant ruled that RSUB was irrelevant to the corporate operation. Unlike ada'web, however, the outfit had a long afterlife. Hived off into a separate company owned by Kanarick and Dachis, Razorfish Studios acquired several notable media assets: *Bust,* the plucky feminist magazine; *Disinfo,* a "countercultural search engine" devoted to all things conspiratorial, which had been developed for TCI and tossed away by CEO John Malone; Self-Timer, a movie company that coproduced a series of distinctive independent films (*Velvet Goldmine, Being John Malkovitch, American Movie, Girls Town,* and *Our Song*); and the RSUB site itself, mostly featuring digital animation that could be converted into television. The retention of the Razorfish name generated concern among some investors, since the sites featured anti-social, often scatological, material. One infamous animated series, "Central Toilet," was set in a cubicled office with a single exposed toilet in the middle of the workplace. Giving the finger to corporate America in this way might not always be good for business, but the sites were a big boost for recruitment and employee morale. For the eyes of their clients and investors, Kanarick developed the more abstemious Razorfish Reports, a series of brief "white papers" about technological innovation (*Information Visualization and Search Engines, Telecoworking and You, Explaining Broadband*) and occasionally playful exercises (*How to Peel a Chicken*, by Stephen Turbek) prepared by his new Science Department.

Alternative, even subversive, art helped to fashion the profile of companies like Razorfish as a diametrical opposite of Wall Street. In fact, the relationship was more akin to the face-off between classical bohemia and the world of the bourgeois, each needing the other to define its own identity. Bohemia flourished from the 1830s as the seamy offshoot of an emerging bourgeois order that was based on tradition, stability, rationalism, conformity, and formal convention. It was a place, elusive even then, where the unbridled energies of modern individualism could be more fully expressed. Many a young bourgeois, unsatisfied with the social expectations that came with his inheritance, would find his way there, temporarily, to test the waters.[23] For the temporary bohemian, voluntary poverty evoked freedom, to be enjoyed among lower-class residents whose involuntary poverty, by contrast, constrained their freedoms. For artists who stayed longer, the low rents of bohemia would begin as a necessity, but in time they became a virtue of sorts, a conventional passage to recognition and success in the art market.

Almost all of the personality traits attributed to companies like Razorfish and their employees could have been lifted from Henri Murger's portraits of the Water-Drinkers and grisettes who were playing hide-and-seek with their sober Parisian elders one hundred and sixty years earlier: rule breaking, undisciplined, self-dramatizing, sexually free, drug-using, youthfully merry, inadvisably honest, unorthodox in their narcissism, and neo-socialist in their sense of community. By the 1990s, *la vie de bohème* had become part of the standard package of "hip" and "cool" in the consumer marketplace.[24] By the end of the decade, the bohemian-bourgeois family fracas had migrated into the business world and had become central to the civil war advertised as New Economy versus Old Economy. In this briefly fratricidal quarrel, there were many defectors to the rebel side, corporate regulars who cast aside their suits and ties to take "the great leap," as it became known, and join the militias waging insurrection from the guerrilla strongholds of their lofts. In the softer, less militant New Age version, depicted in a hundred company ads of the period, a luminous, boho youth explains the Digital Way to a group of Brooks Brothers–clad executives, gathered together in a wilderness setting. In both scenarios, the corporate bohemia promised not only hedonistic enlightenment but also the potential of vast riches, a far cry from the traditionally penurious condition of the peripheral artist.

Why were artists and their trappings so important to the industrial process of New Economy companies? For one thing, artists had been early adopters of Web design tools like HTML and were indispensable as sources of artisanal knowledge, at least until the digital crafts became a credentialed part of the academic curriculum. In addition, artists were an accustomed source of creativity and independent ideas, assets that became central to the ethos of the fast company, trading on innovation and initiative. By the 1990s, conventional managerial wisdom held that employees were looking for more than money or benefits; they wanted "self-actualization," the quasi-spiritual quality that psychologist Abraham Maslow had placed at the top of his influential hierarchy of human needs.[25] Employees could now treat their own jobs as if they were works of art, expressing their own uniquely cultivated qualities.

Just as relevant, and more lasting, was the work mentality associated with artistic producers. Artists (in the broad sense of the term) come with a training in what could be called sacrificial labor. This means they are predisposed to accept nonmonetary rewards—the gratification of producing art—as partial compensation for their work, thereby discounting the cash price of their labor. Indeed, it is fair to say that the largest subsidy to the arts has always come from arts workers themselves, underselling themselves in anticipation of future career rewards. This disposition was a blessing to a startup economy that demanded of its workforce a legendary outlay of time and energy on the promise of deferred bounties. Employees invested a massive amount of sweat equity in the mostly futile hope that stock options would be realized. Industry bulletin boards were soon chockablock with tales of exploitation (sometimes called geeksploitation) penned by employees who became so complicit with the culture of overwork and burnout that they developed their own insider brand of sick humor about being "net slaves," i.e., it was actually cool to be addicted to overwork. Industrial capitalists used to dream about such a workforce, but their managerial techniques were too rigid to foster it.

In their early book-length exposé of working conditions, titled *Net Slaves*, Bill Lessard and Steve Baldwin sketched a portrait of an industry that benefits from the hagiographical "myth of the 22-year-old codeboy genius subsisting on pizza and soda and going 36 hours at a clip." Employees' quality of life, they concluded, approaches zero as a result, in "the complete absence of a social life, a lousy diet, lack of exercise, chain smoking, repetitive stress disorders, and, last but not least, hemorrhoids." "There's going to be a lot of sick people out there in a few years," they forecast, "and worse, they won't even have any health benefits."[26] Industry insiders often traced this chronic burning of midnight oil back to the ritual of crunch time in Silicon Valley when programmers pulled all-nighters as part of a "death march" to meet a software release date. But the technologists were not alone. The impulse to put in overtime for the sheer pleasure of solving a design problem came naturally to those with an arts background.

The Flexible Ideal

Even more important than this apprenticeship in sacrifice was the flexibility of artists' work patterns. Ever since flexibility was promoted in the late 1970s as a central principle of the postindustrial economy, the number of artists employed in the general labor force, as defined in census data and annual Bureau of Labor Statistics (BLS), has swelled from year to year. This number more than doubled from 1970 to 1990, crossing the threshold of 2 million in 1998. In 1997, artists (defined by the Department of Labor as eleven occupations: artists who work with their hands, authors, actors and directors, designers, dancers, architects, photographers, arts teachers, musicians and composers) were enjoying a growth rate in employment (at 7 percent) that far outstripped the general workforce (1.4 percent) and even that of other professional specialists (3.4 percent).[27]

These are impressive numbers, notwithstanding that estimates of artists' employment and earnings are notoriously unreliable. They reflect the expansion of economic sectors devoted to the commercial and nonprofit trade in culture, with the consequence that more and more people are able to sustain a living from the arts as a primary occupation.[28] Many of these jobs sprang into existence because culture is perceived as value-adding, and thus increasingly offers a return on investment. Culture has become a major stimulant to urban economies, in particular, and a controversial instrument of urban regeneration. Whether for purposes of tourism or to boost property values of marginal neighborhoods or simply to satisfy the consumer tastes of urban professionals, every city of middling size now claims its own artsy district, modeled after Manhattan's SoHo, with bohemian status conferred on the neighborhood's nonconformist residents.

However, there may also be a more general trend that supports the statistics. Artists are more and more in demand because the character of work within the knowledge economy conforms more and more to the way in which artists customarily work. Indeed, the traditional situation of the artist as unattached and adaptable to circumstance is surely now coming into its own as the ideal industrial definition of the flexible knowledge worker.[29] As a result, artists are migrating from their traditional position at the margins of the economy to roles much closer to the center. Consider that by 1999, the trends in job growth had reversed, with professional specialty employment now growing at 5 percent, as companies absorbed many of those trained in the arts, while the growth for artists had dropped to 3.9 percent.

What is the profile of this new kind of worker who behaves and thinks like an artist? It is someone who is comfortable in an ever-changing environment that often demands creative shifts in communication with different kinds of employers, clients, and colleagues; who is attitudinally geared toward work that requires long and often unsocial hours; who dedicates their time and energy to distinct projects rather than to a steady flow of production; who exercises self-management, if not self-employment, in the execution of their work; and who is accustomed to a contingent and casual work environment, without overt supervision or judgment from above.[30]

In the workplaces I observed, employee concentration on the job was variable, often erratic. It was a style of work (which the casual observer could easily misconstrue as goofing off) where stints of driven self-application alternated with periods of vivid socializing and with those intervals of undirected play and dreamy indolence that Henry James once called the "unstrenuous brooding sort of attention" that is required to produce art. The fish were not producing anything that Henry James would have cared to acknowledge as art, but they were doing their work in a way that he might have recognized. Company managers also recognized the benefits of accommodating these spasmodic rhythms. This is how the Creative Mission handbook described it: "What is needed is an occasional, carefully timed disengagement from the intensifying focus that concentration on creative work requires. With efficient project planning in place we can leave room for this sort of distancing. Those responsible for scheduling need to continually facilitate this."

Managerial planning at Razorfish never attained the efficiency recommended by the handbook, and so the creative disengagement of employees was neither carefully timed nor was it built into project schedules. Instead, the fish took their cues from the oxygen of permission that circulated through the office. But the managerial dream of efficient scheduling outlined in the handbook is a potent illustration of how the daily work routine might be adjusted to absorb the fitful rhythms of creative labor: twenty minutes of doodling, followed by ninety minutes of application, a fifty-minute break for kibitzing, focused reapplication before a mobile lunch and visit to a nearby art gallery, and then a full hour of surfing and daydreaming, before the first half of the project is complete (repeat or vary the cycle as required). Nor was this kind of tempo confined to the professional creatives on staff. At no-collar companies, every kind of employee is considered to be creative and is regarded as a potential source of ideas and innovation. In effect, the entire workforce functions like a suggestion box writ large, where the contributions of employees are systematically collected rather than voluntarily offered. In some offices, the walls themselves did the collecting, in the form of interactive whiteboards that converted employee notes and doodles into computer script and data.

Wall Art for Take Your Daughter to Work Day, Razorfish, New York (Photo by the author)

Nor was the workday bounded by what happened in the workplace. Ideas and creativity were as likely to surface at home or in other locations, and so employees were encouraged to work elsewhere as and when the spirit took them. A traditional industrial model derives value from workers where and when the company can control their labor. In the realm of no-collar work, the goal is to extract value from any waking moment of an employee's day. In return for ceding freedom of movement to employees along with control over their work schedule, a no-collar company exercises the right to collect returns from areas of their lives that lie far beyond the physical workplace. A similar principle applied to the use of clients, whose employees were considered an integral part of each project team. In companies with efficient knowledge management systems, clients' ideas and efforts could not only be factored into the product but could also be adopted for use in other projects.

The last, and perhaps most abstract, contribution that art made to job performance had to do with the application to business of skills learned from college contact with the likes of Gustave Courbet and Raymond Williams. The creative disciplines were one thing, but many of the fish who worked in business strategy or project management paid eloquent tribute to the influence of their degrees in art history, literature, communications, and cultural studies. Learning how to look at aesthetic composition, or analyzing the "big picture" behind works of art and culture, provided a formal training in problem-solving, and they had found it was critical to their ability to design business solutions. In many respects, they found themselves reversing the steps they had learned in college. One such business strategist explained: "When you learn about a painting, you learn to deconstruct all the parts that go into it—not just the composition of brushstrokes, iconography, and images but also the social and political history and the artist's biography." In business strategy, she assured me, it's exactly the opposite: "We have to figure out the overall solution that we need to provide and then think about all the parts we need to make up that solution."

With SoHo's galleries and museums on their doorstep, it was natural for the fish to talk this way. Steeltables—the Friday lunchtime slot reserved for guest speakers and seminar presentations—was often devoted to art world matters and sometimes involved field trips to nearby gallery shows. Any number of employees had some kind of after-hours creative sideline—dance, photography, art, theater, DJ-ing. Far from being seen as a competing force for the creative energies of employees, such activities were encouraged as potential sources of value, nourishing the work process. Down on Wall Street, however, it was rather surprising to hear employees ruminate about the relevance of their training in conceptual art to the world of financial services and all the more astonishing to find such an artist at the heart of the New York Stock Exchange (NYSE), responsible for the digital makeover of that acropolis of capitalism.

At the height of the tech boom, Danielle Gustafson, a graduate of one of the nation's most avant-garde art schools—Cal Arts and the Whitney Independent Studio Program—had been hired to repair the Exchange's stodgy reputation of being technologically behind the times. The electronic Nasdaq was still on a roll, and other global exchanges, such as the FTSE in London, had gone paperless, while the NYSE was bound exclusively to floor-based operations. Among other things, Gustafson's brief was to help dispel any lingering suspicions about IT's role in the 1987 stock crash, when programmed trading had caused what traders called a "loss of liquidity."

Stopping short of the Rubicon of online trading, Gustafson had built Web sites with a panoply of market data and news feeds for investors, and with "fifteen servers sitting in Illinois" at her disposal, she had the computing capacity to manage a substantial number of vendors and employees. She described herself as a "change agent within a 208-year-old organization." As for the relevance of her art background, Gustafson was quite comfortable comparing changes in the business world to the evolution of art. Clement Greenberg, she commented, had recognized how artists made radical aesthetic advances out of new technical possibilities; so, too, business, whose "corporate culture had become ossified" was now proving to be "surprisingly creative through the adoption of technology." Compared to the art world, she found "the rules here are more equitable," and work conditions much less exploitative. Gustafson still considered herself part of Silicon Alley, but she felt her job was more secure—"the last tenured job in America"—with better benefits, real vacations, a sane workload, and a work environment where unions were well represented. She worked for a "stable, ethical, non-profit" that saw itself as a public utility, dedicated to "doing capitalism better, by making it more fair and more efficient." The technology she had introduced would allow the NYSE to better guarantee liquidity by ensuring that individual investors got the same information as the big brokers and were able to trade on more equitable terms. The result would be more like the "pure capitalism" that New Economy evangelicals believed was on its way to supplant the corrupt ancien régime.

We took breakfast with Jay Mahoney, the director of the NYSE, and Murray Teitelbaum, its director of education, in the prim clubhouse repose of the oak-paneled dining room, flanked at its entrance by statuary of a bull and a bear, and sparsely populated on the Friday before Labor Day. In this company, Gustafson was clearly regarded as a wunderkind, and Mahoney was as gung-ho about the NYSE's attachment to technology as his genteel, ex officio manner would allow. "We've always been the well-behaved, respectable member of society," he observed, "but Nasdaq has made it more difficult to take the high road." The high-flying dotcoms may have come as a revelation to

Nasdaq arrivistes, but NYSE veterans like Mahoney had seen much higher price-to-earnings ratios, in the mid-1970s, for example, "when oil stocks were off the charts." Mahoney had little doubt that the NYSE was moving toward a paperless floor, though he acknowledged the high anxiety among its members about how their roles would change with further automation of the floor. For those who actually worked at the NYSE, one thing was certain. Advanced technology meant employees "no longer had to linger long to clean up their books. They can be out of the door," he assured me, "by 4:15 P.M." If that were true, it would be a rare privilege, these days, in most workplaces around the country, let alone in New York City.

As we descended to the already teeming trading floor for the opening bell, Gustafson warned that "later in the day, it can be a smelly environment," especially when there is "fear on the floor." "We rarely have an argument, however, and only one or two fistfights ever," Mahoney added, "though the stress produces heart attacks, and an ambulance is on twenty-four-hour call for any employee, anywhere in the city." A bizarre cavernous space, the NYSE trading room boasts a sumptuous, Gilded Age ceiling from which all the flat screen technology (the world's largest installation of the stuff) hangs, suspended, as if it were a film set. Visual skills are intuitive tools here, since savvy trading depends on the mastery of reading the screens.

The Exchange was pushing its new hand-held information devices to floor traders, in hopes of encouraging more technology penetration on the floor, and I spent a couple of hours in the company of John Charlop, a trader who used one and swore by it. I was hard-pressed to keep up with him as he bolted from post to post, his gaze ricocheting between his hand-held Casio e-broker and the screens at each panel of stocks. In addition, he was receiving a data feed from his earpiece and jabbering in his own mouthpiece. Lavishing praise on his hand-held, he declared, "It's second to none in terms of transactions." Not everyone on the floor agreed. "It's like hockey," cracked Ted Weisberg, a trader from a securities firm who was watching me trying to keep pace with Charlop. "The minute you look down and lose eye contact, you're dead meat." Referencing a different sport, his son Jason chipped in, "It's like poker, when you can read someone else's hand." The Weisbergs were old school and swore that the art of reading other brokers' faces was the key to successful trading. Jason claimed he didn't even wear an earpiece, relying on both of his ears to filter real-world information. "How many ways can you peel a potato?" shrugged his father.

In the strife over technology penetration, there was more at stake than resolving "the best price discovery," which was the competitive service offered by the NYSE. Jobs and livelihoods were also on the line in the brokerage business. No one expected the floor's "high verbal interface," as Mahoney put it, to disappear any time soon. But if the NYSE began to get into the business of online trading, lots of people would be losing their jobs. Gustafson affirmed that it wasn't the folks on the floor who would be disintermediated; it was the big brokerage firms that would lose out. This sounded all too familiar. When new technologies are being promoted, they are always on the side of the little guy, yet they have an uncanny way of ending up in the service of the most powerful among us—not unlike the stock market itself.

Solo Flyers and Idea Mutts

Long before the coming of the Internet industry, technology companies had recognized the business value of artists by recruiting creative teams to dream up marketable ideas. For the most part, however, these enzymes of innovation were quarantined off in separate units, like Xerox Parc, or else their ideas were absorbed from college-based smart tanks, like MIT's Media Lab. On a visit to Xerox Parc, outside of Palo Alto, I interviewed a team from Research on Experimental Documents, who, in their former lives, had been architects, engineers, performance artists, graphic designers, communications professors, video artists, and toy designers and were now, as one put it, "hopelessly hybrid mutts." At the Parc, hard science and fine arts were supposed to be genetically spliced into a single buzzing intellect; the refrigerator art was festooned with cyberpunk slogans about "yellow dangling robo-viruses," and the Smart Matter lab projects in development were showcased to me as spectacular innovations in fields like modular robotics and laser-rich microchips. William Shatner, I was told, had been the most recent visitor to the labs, generating much disappointment when he had shown little technical appreciation for the gee-whizzery on show.

The team had recently completed a project on "The Future of Reading," which tried to imagine how novel ways of reading were emerging from the new media genres.[31] In principle, the company had a commercial interest in reading (that is mostly why we make photocopies), and with Xerox stock in the doldrums and acquisition talk in the air, employees were perhaps more willing than usual to venture that their work had a direct impact on corporate research. Traditionally, however, Xerox Parc was where artists and scientists had a mandate to tinker in ways "not normally attractive to product development." Indeed, team members recounted with pride the number of projects that had been shut down on account of their total lack of commercial potential. They had learned how to craft what they called "sheltering narratives" in order to protect their work. Even so, it was a touchy subject. Over the years, researchers at the Parc had invented products such as the laser printer and the Ethernet, which had brought economic benefits to the company. But Xerox also had an infamous reputation for failing to develop, for their own proprietary gain, many of the household-name software ideas and technology processes that had been devised at the Parc (including such innovations as the computer mouse, WYSIWYG editing, and the Graphic User Interface that made Web graphics possible).

Whether or not their research nourished the company's product line, the team members clearly cultivated their outsider status in the Silicon Valley landscape of office park campuses and custom suburban homes. Regardless of their background, they had adopted what a team member described as the "anti–middle class attitude of artists" while working in a "middle-class environment." Did they feel like part of Silicon Valley, the most successful pocket of industry in the second half of the twentieth century? "We share the same traffic," he responded dryly.

By contrast, urban new media companies tried very hard to dissolve these barriers. There was no longer a hothouse space set apart in quarantine for incubating new ideas. Every employee and every department was expected to be involved in the business of innovation. To meet the challenge of this new industrial model, project managers made efforts to develop tools and templates to standardize (insofar as this was possible) the interdisciplinary processing of ideas. Some companies took advantage of the corporate craze for creativity by taking literally the concept of manufacturing ideas. The Brain Store, a Swiss consulting firm, claimed to be able to produce ideas for clients with assembly-line efficiency. "Our idea factory has all of the elements of an industrial process," declared cofounder Markus Mettler. "You can follow an idea from one step to another. . . . We're striving to perfect our system in terms of speed and efficiency." The company also ran an actual store, where customers could buy over-the-counter ideas, at about $20 a pop. According to Mettler, "it's possible to compress the entire idea-generation process into just 15 minutes. While that may not be enough time to develop a new product, it is enough time to name a hamster."[32]

Not every firm responded to the industrial challenge by scaling up or by taking an assembly-line approach to idea generation. Some clung on to the ethos of the small artisanal shop. Funny Garbage, a Silicon Alley original with no more than thirty employees, was the kind of design hothouse envied by the creatives at the large agencies who were concerned that their talents were being industrialized. There was even more ambivalence about individuals who had struck out on their own and who were subsisting in the world of free agents glorified by New Economy evangelicals.

Vivien Selbo, a prime mover behind ada'web and a digital artist in her own right, had resisted the offer of high office within the AOL empire and was now fully self-employed as a Web designer and developer. A "web grrl" original, from the days when women's prominent presence on the Internet scene was in marked contrast to the boystown of Silicon Valley, she worked out of her Lilliputian apartment in Greenwich Village "with a loose team of professionals" that mutated from project to project. The team was usually multinational in location and met only online, where they had to build trust and a common appreciation of each others' work through their email and Instant Messenger personalities. Selbo (also a Whitney graduate) had developed a formidable client list, including the Museum of Modern Art, Carnegie Hall, the Museum of the Moving Image, the Walker Art Museum, the Goethe Institute, and *Grand Street*. As the Web developer of choice for art institutions that wanted someone to work with their artists online, she was widely regarded as a "proof of concept" of the solo operator living by her new design craft.

Selbo had been around new media for long enough to know where her strengths lay:

I don't fit in corporate environments. Even at ada'web, I was the gadfly who fought the employee contract agreement when AOL purchased the company. I brought in lawyers to figure out how we could protect ourselves from what AOL would do to our intellectual property rights. I speak up when I see things I don't like, and in certain corporate environments you don't fit when you behave like that. I read somewhere that people who haven't worked for someone else for more than five years are actually a liability hire. It signals too much independence, which, ironically, is what I laud in people when I hire them myself.

Unlike other solo flyers she knew, who pined, on occasion, to be told exactly what to do, Selbo never tired of home rule. Of course, there were drawbacks, like the soaring cost of health insurance. Selbo got hers through membership in the World Wide Web Artists Consortium (WWAC), the original affinity group for Alley Web developers. The free agent had to absorb the cost of upgrading her technology, software, and skill levels. "There is also the cost," Selbo acknowledged, "of having to plump up your feathers to make yourself look bigger than you are because clients like to have the imprimatur of a larger organization."

As a result, Selbo usually presented herself as a "royal we," through her corporate identity Cavil.com, rather than as an individual freelancer. She resisted the single authorial domain name not just because it denotes the "prima donna kind of artiste presentation" that she shuns but also because it tends to restrict the full range of her skills. To demonstrate how she meets a range of client expectations, Selbo pulled several different business cards from her wallet. Each contained the same information about herself, conveyed in a different style. "Why pretend to have one identity? Sometimes I just size up the client and then figure out which one they need."

À-la-carte Professional Identities

Selbo's à-la-carte identity was a molecular version of the service offerings of large agencies like Razorfish, constantly changing their shape and scope in response to market opportunities. For the time being, it was proving more sustainable than the big houses. As the Alley's first wave of industry leaders faltered—"the end of the Cambrian Era," she quipped—her own business went from strength to strength, to the point at which she experienced "survivor's guilt." From where she sat, as a Renaissance woman of the Web, Silicon Alley's clamorous rise and decline had been "like a smell that entered the room and then left."

Like Selbo, Clem Paulsen, with whom she occasionally worked (though he was getting to be too expensive), had learned multiple digital trades and skills in his years in different corners of the industry. Trained originally as a physical architect, he had taught himself high-end programming and was now employed as an information systems architect. He had seen the specialization of labor march into the industry, replacing the self-learning ethos that both he and Selbo had been weaned on. What did the good old days mean for him? Paulsen displayed no nostalgia for the work environment or company culture of any of the firms that had employed him. What he missed most from his early Alley days was the personal opportunity to apply a range of skills, plying and integrating his knowledge of each in the course of a project. For a brief period in 1997–1998, he did a stint in advertising. When he returned to the Alley, he found he could no longer be a Renaissance man, or as he put it, a "full contact Web developer": "All the head hunters told me that I needed to choose a track." Paulsen found that he had to "interview for a specialty, and the recruiter was going to ask me about that specialty. This change happened very quickly. It may have been that the projects became so complicated that a team needed to be specialized. Suddenly there was a factory, and you had Taylorization." Paulsen had become a father in the interim, and given his new family duties, the streamlining of skills turned out to be a blessing in disguise: "Now it only takes a very tiny portion of my brain." He was excused from having to yearn for the all-round challenge of artisanal craft, though he clearly felt the tug of regret.

By now, Paulsen's lament had become a familiar one. You could find the same story on the lips of the early computer programmers, like this one whom Joan Greenbaum interviewed for her book on the profession:

> "I remember that in the fifties and early sixties I was a 'jack of all trades.' As a programmer I got to deal with the whole process. I would think through a problem, talk to the clients, write my own code, and operate the machine. I loved it—particularly the chance to see something through from beginning to end. . . . In these days we really had control. Management never understood what we were doing, and we really didn't care. It was fun, and what we were doing made us feel important—we felt like we were accomplishing something."[33]

Listening to Paulsen or this much older programmer, it was easy to see how computer skills, from generation to generation, had raised hopes about the restoration of employee control over the work process. By the 1950s, it had become a platitude of the modern industrial workplace that workers no longer enjoyed the self-reliant stature of the free artisan. This ethic had a storied pedigree in the medieval guilds and the Renaissance humanist ideal of the artist-craftsman, making nature anew, and it had survived for centuries in the small artisanal workshop, where trade knowledge was handed down and protected through the tradition of apprenticeship. With the introduction of large-scale machine technologies, the craft workers' tools and skills were wrested away and absorbed into a production system. They lost control over their time and surrendered psychological as well as material ownership of their work in the industrial factory. At the onset of industrialization, artists, with good reason, had begun to romanticize the craft ethos, and for much of the twentieth century it looked as if they would become the exclusive practitioners of the traditions of the free artisan.

The emergence of computer work in the 1950s and '60s revived hopes of restoring those traditions on an industrial basis. In *The Soul of a New Machine,* Tracy Kidder's book about a computer design team at Data General, he compared the engineers to the stonemasons who built Gothic cathedrals: a vital part of themselves ended up in the finished product.[34] Yet the self-government of the computing professions was continually being eroded as work was broken down, over time, into solitary tasks or farmed out to discrete classes of programmers and operatives. The rise of interface technologies in the 1990s brought fresh energy to the hopes. For those who could position themselves to take market advantage of the new digital tools, it seemed financially viable to choose a contingent career over standard employment. For people like Selbo and Paulsen who "wouldn't have really fit in anywhere else," free agency was a livelihood and a style of work where they "seemed to feel completely at home," and indeed, most of the time they were at home, desecrating the sacraments of space that require us to put some physical distance between our domicile and a waged workplace.

For some enthusiasts, their quest for self-employment involved much more than reclaiming the choice of how, where, and when to work. "Free agency forces you to think about who you are and what you want to do with your life," insisted Deborah Risi, a freelance tax consultant in Menlo Park. "Previously, it was only those wonderful, flaky artists who had to deal with this."[35] Samantha Saturn, who set up on her own as a digital branding consultant, regularly worked out of Les Deux Gamins, a bijou café in Greenwich Village, where she parked her laptop and cell phone. "It makes me feel like I'm in Paris" she confessed, "like Hemingway at Les Deux Magots."[36] For Risi and Saturn, the existential charisma of the artist's profile was an additional reason for deserting corporations that had treated employees like disposable commodities. From the perspective of corporate managers—freed from the need to offer health insurance, paid vacations, sick leave, personal days, pension plans, social security contributions, stock options, quarterly bonuses, infrastructure overheads, or performance reviews—any crusade to heroicize freelancing was a welcome boost to company efforts to extend their policies of subcontracting and outsourcing.

The 1990s saw no end of such heroics. "When nobody has security," declared ex-Gore scriptwriter Daniel Pink, author of a bracing manifesto for what he has called the Free Agent Nation, "everybody deserves freedom." Like John Perry Barlow's "Declaration of the Independence of Cyberspace," Pink's was a credo couched in the prose of revolutionary patriotism: "When in the course of economic events, it becomes manifest that traditional work arrangements stifle innovation, reward timidity, devolve into nothingness, and offer at best a perilous prosperity, it becomes necessary for citizens of conscience and talent to break free from that decaying tradition and declare their independence."[37] Pink and his adherents claimed that this liberated population was growing by leaps and bounds and that it comprised as many as 33 million free agents in the United States.[38] What better proof could there be of the resurgence of native self-reliance and the loosening of corporate bureaucracy's stranglehold on homegrown ingenuity and initiative?

Yet a closer look at the statistics told a different story from the breezy picture that Pink presented. The two decades between 1973 and 1993 had shown a steady decline in full-time jobs and a rise in part-time employment, resulting primarily from *involuntary* contingent work and mostly concentrated in temporary help employment.[39] By 1999, for example, there were 5.6 million workers with contingent jobs (with no "explicit or implicit contract for long-term employment"). Most were young and female, predominantly concentrated in

I am the president of me, inc.

The Individualization of Work (New York University, Advertising for School of Continuing and Professional Studies)

low-wage temping, disproportionately Black and Hispanic, and 53 percent of them would have preferred a job that was permanent.

The BLS category of "workers with alternative arrangements" includes independent contractors, as well as on-call workers, day laborers, temporary help agency workers, and workers provided by contract firms. In 1999, there were 8.2 million independent contractors (or 6.3 percent of the workforce), and they were concentrated in managerial, professional, sales occupations, and in the construction and services industries. Disproportionately white (90.6 percent) and male (66.2 percent), they were more likely to prefer their employment arrangements than the other workers in this category, such as on-call workers (2 million) and temporary workers (1.1 million).[40] Among those 8 million were the free agents whose rosy circumstances were most likely to be profiled by New Economy boosters.

More notably, the five-year span between 1994 and 1999—when the New Economy was booming and when the Free Agent Nation was most fervently promoted—was the first time since the 1960s that the number of workers who classified themselves as self-employed showed a clear decline. In fact, virtually all the categories of nonstandard employment—including part-timers and independent contractors—showed a decrease over this period. After almost three decades of rising self-employment, the portion of Americans reporting that they worked for themselves, either on their own or with a few hired employees, dropped from 8.1 percent, at the height of the last recession, in 1992, to 6.7 percent in 1999, the lowest figure since the prerecession year of 1973.[41] By far the majority of the job growth during the height of the New Economy boom took place inside companies, many of them with a payroll of more than 1,000 employees.[42] For those who did remain self-employed, their income rose by almost a third during this same period, showing that clear advantages did exist for the highly skilled independent contractors, whose talents were in great demand, even if their numbers were not actually growing, as Pink and others suggested.

Setting aside the free agent hype, the reasons for these trends seem fairly clear. In a tight labor market, companies have to offer better working conditions, wages, and benefits at all levels of the workforce. In order to attract employees, the New Economy companies offered almost irresistible working conditions (much of the autonomy of the free agent without the sacrifice of benefits and a guaranteed paycheck). With the appearance of these companies, there was a very fine line between self-employment and regular employment. The incentive to remain in the ranks of self-employment weakens during a boom economy. Indeed, the higher figures of earlier recessions suggest that "self-employment is a refuge from unemployment for workers who are not able to find regular employment."[43]

Manuel Castells points out that, compared to other industrialized nations, the United States demonstrates a much lower level of nonstandard employment (defined as flexible work, without social benefits or a long-term contract, conducted away from a centralized location). Indeed, it is the only OECD country with less than 30 percent of its workforce in nonstandard employment. Castells speculates that this is because job stability and worker rights and benefits are less entrenched within the existing sector of U.S. standard employment: "Where there is labor flexibility in the institutions of the country," he writes, "nonstandard forms of employment are not deemed necessary." Thus, the average job tenure in the United States is much lower

(7.4 years) than in other countries (8.3 for the U.K., 10.8 for Germany, 11.3 for Japan). However, he argues that the figures are quite different for regional subeconomies, such as California, where by the criteria of some studies, 67 percent of workers do not hold a traditional job. The flexible employment model is more distinct in the New Economy strongholds, like Silicon Valley, where as many as 80 percent of the new jobs in the late 1990s were nonstandard.[44]

The blurring of work boundaries also made it easier to get caught in between regular and nontraditional arrangements, neither in nor out, twisting in the limbo of the permatemp. In this regard, free agency could be a cruel trap, as thousands of contract workers at large technology companies like Intel, Microsoft, Hewlett-Packard, and IBM discovered in their long and bitter struggle for recognition as company employees. At Microsoft, for example, these were skilled workers (almost 25 percent of the company's workforce) who wanted a foot in the door at the company and who signed up through local personnel agencies for long-term projects in hopes of becoming Microserfs with stock options.[45] As a result, they did not enjoy the market leverage or the autonomy of the free agent, nor were they offered the benefits of full-timers, although many had worked for the company for longer periods and performed more skilled tasks than full-timers.

With the aid of WashTech (Washington Alliance of Technology Workers), a local union affiliate of the Communication Workers of America, the permatemps launched a class action suit against the software giant. In a momentous legal case, the courts decided that for many years Microsoft had misclassified these long-term contractors as temps when they were in fact "common-law" employees of the company and should have been able to participate in employee benefit plans that included a stock-purchase program. The company finally settled in late 2000 and offered compensation to the permatemps. Widespread media coverage of this suit shed light on the dark side of high-tech work and helped counteract the public image of the technology industry as a latter-day Midas, enriching all employees whom it touched. Yet it also raised the prospect that the permatemp could become a fixed feature of the landscape of work if the high-tech industry (which led all others in rates of employment growth in the late 1990s) turned out to be a bellwether sector of the economy as a whole.

A Hip-Hop Haven

I been in this game for years
It made me a animal
There's rules to this shit, I wrote me a manual
A step by step booklet, for you to get
Your game on track, not your dot com pushed back
Rule number one, always play this game for fun
Watching the Matrix while programmin cold fusion dont
make you The One
Cashing a big check dont mean that you catchin wreck
Went and got labeled "1st generation"
look at yourself broke and burned out with frustration.

—JOHN NUBIAN, "10 DOT COM COMMANDMENTS"

AFTER I STARTED AT RAZORFISH, I DECIDED TO SPEND PART OF MY available time inside a content company, partly as a way of comparing workplaces that boasted good jobs. In a city where the advertising, media, and publishing industries were all concentrated, content had a favored place. "Content is king" was the brassy slogan that touted Silicon Alley's regional advantage over the West Coast, and it sounded sweet enough to the city's underemployed writers and artists. Content may have been a soulless description for what they did, but if was taken in an ironic spirit, as many were inclined to do, then it could be suffered gladly. New media was the more provocative term, coined in early WWWAC circles, and it captured the promise of the brave new world of online Web publishing. It took hold long (at least in Internet time) before e-commerce was dreamed of.

At the outset, little thought was given to the commercial sustainability of new media. For most webster free spirits, the heady prospect of bypassing, perhaps even routing, the editorial gatekeepers of old media, was enough to egg them on. The press had been free only for those who owned one. Interactive media, where users had their full say, now had the chance to sweep away the old media model of monopoly ownership and passive consumption. In next to no time, speculators were devising a financial infrastructure for a full-fledged industry. They calculated that it might develop in the same way as the TV broadcasting boom in the postwar years, which was the last time that a major new industry came to town. Or it might be more like cable in the early 1970s. Or it might take an entirely unforeseen path. Even if new media did not fly so very high, it looked like it could create some pretty decent jobs for folks who sorely needed them because they didn't fit in anywhere else.

Marisa Bowe, editor of *Word,* one of the Alley's most virtuoso webzines, called it The Great Slacker Employment Act of 1995: "What else would we have been doing for a living if it hadn't been for this? It was like a lifesaver thrown to us." There were many like Bowe, for whom the opportunity came as if in a providential form: "I had all these interests I couldn't quite define. I didn't know what they were until suddenly I got the job at *Word,* and it was like, snap, everything I had ever done made perfect sense. I could apply it all to this medium." "It was as if we all got this huge grant from the Internet," she mused. "Some people wanted to start companies and get rich. Others like me just wanted to use the five-year grant to experiment with their ideas." How did she and her MBA-averse contemporaries react to the distasteful matter of capital investments in their companies? Bowe recalled that the business side "was almost like pornography; it had that kind of illicit thrill for us." For her peers, like Rufus Griscom, the cofounder of the erotica webzine *Nerve,* there was little distinction. As Griscom recalled, the art of seeking "total mainstream corporate support" for their companies was the next step beyond the classic bohemian principle that "not making money was a symbol of your integrity." After all, the early pre-dotcom 1990s had been a time, in his Ivy League circles at least, when "poverty was an indication that you were more interested in the cerebral than the material world."

In the fall of 1996, the Internet World convention at the New York Coliseum hosted a sideshow called the IndieNet Festival. Ambitiously modeled on the philosophy of the Sundance Film Festival, it was pulled together to showcase the multimedia art and editorial content that had begun to appear on sundry webzines. Tucked away in the back of the exhibition hall, beyond the lavish trade displays of technology and software, was the ragtag grouping of tables and offbeat characters that made up IndieNet. Bowe was in attendance, as were the folks from ada'web and Total New York (picturesquely garbed in Julia Scher's pink policeman hats and "Security by Julia" uniforms), along with the other webzine pioneers that had popped up on the sparsely populated Web landscape: Word, Feed, Urban Desires, gURL, SonicNet, Disinfo, Stim, Bianca's Smut Shack, Cybergrrl, and from the Bay Area, Hotwired, along with Suck. It was obvious that no one had any real money to spend on the presentation of their wares, and besides, anything worth seeing was on a slow-loading screen.

Visitor traffic to the tables was sporadic—a few curious suits, some weekenders who had taken a wrong turn on the convention floor, but mostly early websters who knew, or had noticed, each other online. Their tables were entirely marginal to the bread and butter events at the convention, but this group (which might just as well have included Blue Dot–Razorfish) already formed the nucleus of what came to be known on the Alley as new media. Many of the founders would be lionized in the local and industry press, and their artful efforts were much scrutinized by startups that followed in their path.[1] Some of their companies were acquired and struggled to retain their idealism and indie ways. Others were absorbed into larger media enterprises, while others folded quickly.[2] As they turned into business concerns with staff on payroll, almost all of them bowed to a revenue model based on banner advertising, which was derivative of print and broadcast media but would prove less sustainable in the online world. In the meantime, pornography proved, again and again, to be the only flush passenger on the ship of content.[3]

The Dream Team

For the purposes of this book, I was looking for a firm that was relatively new, where the founders had a plan to harness the idealism of new media for their own, equally idealistic ends, and where employees had found work that meant something more to them than a good paycheck, solid benefits, and a shot at the stock option lottery. I was also looking for a workforce with a broader racial mix than was typical in the Internet industry.[4] On the far west side of downtown Manhattan, where rising rents had pushed many firms in the last wave of Alley startups, I found 360hiphop.com, a company that seemed to fit the bill.

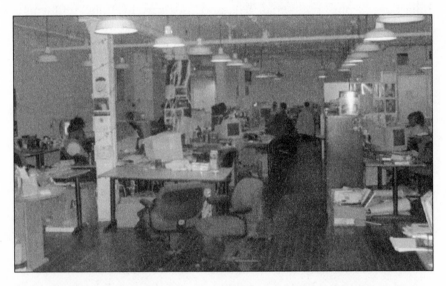

Office Space on 10th Avenue, 360hiphop, November 2000 (Photo by the author)

Because 360 was the digital child of hip hop mogul Russell Simmons, it had been blessed with instant publicity and goodwill in the entertainment industry and among music fans when plans for the site were announced in November 1999. Promoted at the time as "the ultimate destination for all things hip-hop," and backed by entertainment mavens like Jay-Z, Will Smith, Queen Latifah, Leo Arcole, Tyra Banks, and Oprah Winfrey, along with industry giants Sony and Universal, the site was one of the last splashy content plays to hit the Alley when it launched in June 2000. Initially, Simmons had plans for an e-commerce vehicle to sell his Phat Farm products alongside Tommy Hilfiger, Sean John, and Mecca. But this concept for "the best fashion fulfillment house on the Web" mutated rapidly into a plan to build a whizz-bang multimedia site with a content team unmatched in the online world.[5]

By the time of its launch, 360 had been staffed up with a dream team of writers, editors, designers, technologists, and marketers, drawn from all corners of the music, press, and Internet industries. The editorial group was headed by Selwyn Seyfu Hinds, former editor of *The Source*, and Sheena Lester, former editor of *XXL* and *Rap Pages*, both with top drawer reputations in hip-hop journalism. Staff writers, all seasoned notables in their respective fields, were recruited nationally, several of them moving from the West Coast to make good on a rare media career opportunity. They came, at the top of their game, with a wealth of experience at other titles—*Rolling Stone, Vibe, Urb, Bomb, Trace, Vanity Fair, Village Voice, Essence, A Magazine, LA Sentinel, Newsday,* and *WExcel*—and broadcast media channels—NPR, MTV, and CBS. Some had wet their feet at other dot-coms, like Total New York, CD Now, Black Planet, AOL, Platform, Asian Avenue, and UBO. One of the big attractions was the chance to work with each other. As one writer put it, "we're still all cogs in a machine here, but for once, it's all the right cogs."

The company had been conceived at a time when Internet investors were turning their attention to what advertisers call the urban market in hopes of making this influential consumer segment into a lucrative source of online users. The urban market consisted of multiethnic youth (14–25 years), many of whom were actually suburban with "urban aspirational" tastes. Their disposable income had driven global sales in lifestyle consumption for the best part of two decades, and hip-hop was an all-pervasive creed among these young tastemakers and disciples. As an entrepreneur who had made his mark in music (Def Jam), film *(Krush Groove, The Nutty Professor)*, TV (Def Comedy Jam), fashion (Phat Farm), and publishing *(One World)*, Russell Simmons was the homegrown prince of all media in this urban marketplace, and despite the challenge from younger rivals like Sean Puffy Combs, he still enjoyed a sharp advantage in the field. In the Internet world, there was already a profusion of sites aimed at African Americans, some of which had been up and running since 1996 (NetNoir, BlackPlanet, Black-Voices, Africana.com, Afronet, BlackFamilies, Blackwebportal, Black-WorldToday, Ebony.com, Essence.com).[6] For the most part, these sites targeted older, more affluent users and were directed exclusively at black America. The urban market was a good deal more youthful, and since it was cross-cultural and multiethnic (while based primarily on African American taste and experience), it was larger, broader, and more technologically savvy. Market analysts and consultants floated vast dollar figures beneath the noses of investors.

By the time 360hiphop made its mark, it had several competitors who were already in or about to enter the urban new media market: Hookt, Platform, Volume, AKA, and the multisite Urban Box Office. Unlike the dotcom operations that sold things like pet food online, there was a lot more riding on the durability of these urban companies than investors' cash. Survival was also a matter of racial pride among user communities well versed in the long struggle to build independent black-owned companies and institutions. This effort had run into its share of resistance in the world of old media and now faced new hurdles in the Internet industry. A series of much-touted Commerce Department reports had introduced the concept of the "digital divide," suggesting that African Americans were underwired, with only 20 percent of their households online, as compared to 40 percent among whites. This concept quickly became a fixture in the public mind, and it helped to deter investment prospects in black media startups.[7]

Early online black entrepreneurs were all too aware of the challenge they faced with funders. McLean Greaves, who founded Café Los Negroes, the first "virtual hangout" for Gen X Blacks and Latinos, in 1996, lamented the obstacles he encountered in establishing a proof of concept for investors who always expected higher standards from black-owned businesses. "Being a black firm in a fledgling industry," he assumed from the outset, would be doubly difficult. "Unlike our white counterparts, entrepreneurial and technology skills are not widespread in the black community. Plus we haven't been middle-class long enough to have a tradition of high-risk entrepreneurialism." Before he threw in the towel, Greaves had been operating out of what he called a "high-crime underclass neighborhood": "There was no way someone would have thrown a seven-figure check to some dread-locked computer headz in a wretched Bed-Stuy Brooklyn neighbor-hood."[8] By the time of the Internet gold rush in 1999, these obstacles had all but evaporated, and in the case of 360hiphop, Simmons's gilt-edged name dispelled any remaining doubts.

One factor that helped was a series of statistical challenges to the con-cept of the digital divide. Consulting firms like Forrester Research is-sued follow-up reports to the Commerce Department studies that took account of the widespread Internet use by minorities at work or in li-braries. One 1999 study estimated a sharp increase (more than a million, or 10 percent) in the number of African American households that would go online over the next year, while others predicted even higher numbers.[9] Bullish forecasts like these helped to drive investment into new African American sites like BET Interactive, Black Entertainment Television's startup, which announced backing from Microsoft, USA Networks, News Corp., and AT&T's Liberty Digital in August 1999. Robert Johnson, the CEO of BET, reasoned publicly that African Amer-icans needed engaging content in order to draw them online and promised that BET.com would provide the goods. But it was the urban market (estimated at more than 18 million users) that proved the biggest draw. Berry Gordy's Motown empire had created a mainstream pop market—"The Sound of Young America"—for black artists in the 1960s and 1970s. The urban market of the 1980s and 1990s, where Simmons operated as a prime catalyst and broker, was different. It commanded a crossover audience of all races, and it became a dominant youth market without catering to mainstream taste and morality as Motown had done.[10] On Silicon Alley, this urban demographic was used to draw the kind of investors who were still convinced that the potential Internet au-dience among African Americans was too small to care about.

From a technological point of view, 360hiphop was a natural step for its founder. Russell Simmons was the first person I had seen using a mobile phone. The sight and sound of him and his cell, conducting business in the street and in his corner booth at the Time Café, was quite common for downtown Manhattanites in the early 1990s. Part of his public profile was his early adoption of the latest tech gadgets (most recently, the two-way pager), and so a Web site enterprise was entirely in synch with his business personality. In addition, a multimedia site with e-commerce features had the potential to link all of his commercial interests and properties. As he put it, in the original press release, "360hiphop will give us a chance to leverage all my relationships and all my ventures in one place." In that same announcement, Donald Trump, "Russell's close personal friend," was given the last word: "Russell knows the market and he sees the future, and that's the ultimate businessperson."

What Time Is It?

Aside from the commercial promise of the venture, it was clear early on that the site was going to be a vehicle for a new Simmons persona—Citizen Russell. In an election year, Simmons was poised to make a dent on the political scene, and those around him, including his new editorial team at 360, were egging him on. He was coming to politics late, but he came on strong. In May, the company announced a Rap the Vote 2000 initiative, joining the long successful Rock the Vote in a campaign aimed at getting young people registered and into the voting booths in the November election. Rap the Vote ("Register. Vote. Represent.") became an integral part of 360's own advertising campaign.

Rap the Vote, 2000

The joint campaign was planned to focus on the widespread resentment and anger over the rising incidence of police brutality and racial profiling. Attention to these highly publicized injustices would surely rouse prospective voters to register, in addition to drawing them to the site, proving, among other things, that hip-hop online could have a reach well beyond its proven capacity to generate music and lifestyle revenue. As Simmons himself saw it, "we're beginning the process of activating the huge potential of the hip hop generation as a political force."[11] In time, 360 helped promote political events that Simmons backed, including Al Sharpton's anti–police profiling protests and Louis Farrakhan's Million Family March in October 2000. Online political forums with Simmons and rappers at the Democratic convention and election PSAs featuring LL Cool J, Mary J. Blige, Rosie Perez, and Sean "Puffy" Combs were carried on the site. Nor did Simmons flinch from confrontation with the powers that be. Where most prominent New York City businessmen would have taken a pass, he approved an extensive ad poster campaign for 360 that took on Mayor Giuliani's aggressive urban policies. A street shot of the shifty-eyed prosecutor in his pre-mayoral days was captioned, I Am Not Hip Hop.

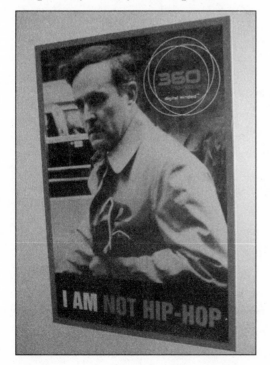

**The Mayor Is Not Hip Hop
(Photo by the author)**

Some employees saw Simmons's use of the site to boost his election year persona as frankly opportunistic but viewed its consequences for them as mostly benign. They estimated, correctly, that his numerous business commitments would prevent him from micromanaging the company. It was widely known that his management style, once he had handpicked his lieutenants, was hands-off, and 360 would prove to be no exception, especially after the election buzz subsided. Others saw a genuine political awakening, prompted partly by his close involvement with the site and the editorial team and partly by the recent birth of his first child. "Having a child makes you recognize mortality," observed a 360 technologist who had known Simmons for several years, "and then the next step is that it angers you toward the world. All the injustice which pissed you off and which you had to learn to numb yourself to, rips open your nerves again when you realize your child is going to have to go through the same things you went through."

Whatever the impetus behind the launching of Citizen Russell, the 360 team took the activist ball and ran with it. Most of them had been drawn to 360 by the chance to parlay their political, as well as their cultural, passions into a decent, creative job. However varied their respective careers, none had enjoyed the privilege of bringing the full range of their personal convictions into a commercial workplace. At 360, the permission to do so promised to be a key part of the job rather than a specialized option or perk. Even the technologists, many of them recruited on reduced salaries from alpha Wall Street firms like Lehman Brothers or Goldman Sachs, were attracted by this ideal. "In this kind of business," explained Jackson Beale, who had put in five years at Morgan Stanley before signing up, "you can find computer headz and you can find hip-hop headz, but very few people who are both at the same time. And we're all right here at 360."

Beale was talking about something much larger than a fan's taste for music. Since most employees were in their late twenties to early thirties, their youth had been touched by the credo of classical hip-hop, and so the idea behind the company was an exercise of faith as much as anything else. In fact, Beale himself described it as a "faith-based organization that became a business." In the months of close-knit teamwork that they spent as a startup team, the "threesixties" came to see the site as a potential fulfillment of hip-hop's ambitions, as well as their own. If it succeeded, then 360 would be much more than hip-hop's premier forum (just as Chuck D once called rap the "black CNN"); it would be a test of what the hip-hop generation could create, given the new technological opportunities, and what kind of political consciousness it could rekindle among the consumer brand–obsessed youth of today. Mostly black, Asian, and white, and as culture savvy as you could wish for, the threesixties were prime candidates for the hip-hop generation's poster children. Chief among their qualifications was that they believed they understood the connection among media, culture, and politics much better than their parents' civil rights generation. At one point in their lives—when Public Enemy, X-Clan, EPMD, Brand Nubian, Eric B. and Rakim, KRS-1, and the Native Tongues crews were in their heyday—hip-hop had promised to make good on that connection. Now that hip-hop was hooked on the fast loot and the high life, the threesixties felt they had been placed on a mission to restore the faith.

The fervor of the golden children of Razorfish had been all about changing the business world through a new medium. At 360, the evangelizing was about using the new medium to realize changes in the world that hip-hop had heralded but only half-delivered. Of course, this was a lot to ask of a mere Web site, but these were heady times, and almost anything seemed possible to those who signed up. Evangelism calls forth a bold new future, but it appeals to the unfulfilled promises of the past to do so. Most of the threesixties I interviewed knew their bread was being buttered by the musical tastes of sixteen- to twenty-year-olds, channeled through the packaged doings of industry stars like Jay-Z, Nelly, Jay-Lo, Sisqo, and DMX. But their own idealism had been forged in the hip-hop flowering of the late 1980s, before the music industry figured out which would be the most bankable formulas among rap's many directions and genres. Golden Age hip-hop—before the platinum hits and g-man profiles of NWA and Dr. Dre became industry templates—was their source, and they often referred to it, with full-bore nostalgia, as "pure and uncorrupted." In his own, book-length memoir, Selwyn Hinds describes "the revolution" promised by that period as "stillborn" and acknowledges that "our yearning for Public Enemy's message" has less to do with the parlous state of contemporary hip-hop and everything to do with the "dearth in our everyday political life."[12] Nonetheless, many of the threesixties believed that the interactive technology at their fingertips might spark a renaissance of that original spirit, which had been technologically ingenious and makeshift and had once given voice to the dispossessed and disenfranchised, offering youth of color a guide to making their own way through the world. Simmons was a trusted face from the old school, and so his figurehead presence comforted those who had moved themselves and their families from far away to join the 360 team.

Hinds's editorial track record and career as an ace journalist was also a big pull. He helped convince potential recruits that 360 would do things that were simply not possible in hip-hop journalism, even at a magazine of record like *The Source.* From the outset, he recalled, the goal was to "create a spectrum of thought and journalism and conversation that really didn't exist anywhere else." Publications that relied on the cooperation of record companies were obliged to churn out (usually favorable) treatment of the current industry stars. No one had been able to offer the 360-degree coverage that hip-hop deserved. The plan for 360 was more enterprising by far. After months of trading ideas and refining design concepts, the team carved out a Web site plan for distinct departments assigned to Music (reviews, artist features, news), Culture (DJs, MCs, graffiti), Politics (national and world affairs), and Lifestyle (fashion, movies, TV sports, sex, gossip). For subscribers, a "community" I-Zone was designed to host interactive MC battles, online chats with rap celebrities, and bulletin boards.

The site would attract eyeballs with catchy A-list celebrity features (chat time with Eve or Snoop about their latest release) or world premieres (listen to a sneak preview of Jay-Z's new album), while the other sections would expand the industry staples with in-depth journalism. "If you only wanted commercial stuff, like DMX or Red Man, you would find that in the Music section," explained an associate editor. "If you were a graffiti head and didn't necessarily listen to a lot of hip-hop, you would find what you needed in the Culture section. If you were a beat digger, who only listened to old records and knew all the breaks and which artists used which samples, you would find that covered in Culture. If you were the kind of political activist who used hip-hop as your firebrand, you'd find that in the Politics section." Consequently, a chat room date with Lil Bow-Wow attracted thousands of his girl fans, making it commercially possible to host a live discussion between Al Sharpton and Talib Kweli, which drew less than a hundred politically-minded users.

This recipe was immensely appealing to creatives who had freelanced or labored full-time in the groves of music industry publications. It even drew political journalists and organizers from the nonprofit world, like Jeff Chang, who hailed from very progressive Bay Area organizations. He had recently helped found the radical magazine *Colorlines*, where he was enjoying what he thought of as his dream job. Chang made the leap to 360 because he saw a rare opportunity to combine his politics with the potential of the new medium. Young people, he estimated, had a chance of being politically mobilized through the Web if their musical and cultural passions were courted as part of the mix. Just as hip-hop had a shot, between 1986 and 1992, at exploring a brand-new medium of expression, 360 would have an "open window for a couple of years," he figured, before content was squeezed into a predictable commercial template. Indeed, a popular analogy around the 360 office was with the early, turbulent years of *Vibe* magazine, before it became a purveyor of upbeat celebrity fare. But for Chang and others, 360 was on a much larger mission than *Vibe*. In their most ambitious moments, they aimed to break the chokehold on information and expression administered by the music industry, the journalism industry, and the opinion industry.

Launching a Titanic

For all of its aspirations to break out of the mold, the 360 mentality was hardly industry-shy. Simmons signed partner agreements with the likes of Jay-Z's Roc-a-Fella Records. In return for Web development services, 360 enjoyed access to that company's artists and first rights to air their new releases. Offering chat room contact with other moneyspinners like Missy Elliott was a core aspect of the business plan. Despite these commercial leanings, however, the site often gave prominence to the kind of features that most industry regulars would see as irrelevant to the business of selling records. These included lengthy pieces on AIDS prison activism, neighborhood gentrification, samba/hip-hop fusion in the favelas of Brazil, the legacy of Tiananmen

Square, South Asian activism in the United States, anti-immigrant hysteria in Britain, the career of Daddy U Roy, veteran Jamaican toaster, and the mysterious death in 1989 of Paul C, an influential rap producer. At the height of 360's venture into investigative journalism, a team in Florida posted original reporting on the racial pattern of voting irregularities in the 2000 presidential election. These bulletins from the pork-and-beans projects in Liberty City about uncounted ballots generated stories that the corporate media initially missed in its focus on West Palm Beach. As part of its extensive video coverage, the 360 team also put in time at the party conventions, drawing hip-hop stars into the campaign debate.

By far the most original project was an interactive piece called *41 Shots*, which took six weeks to produce and ran for a month on the site. A reflective montage about the Amadou Diallo shooting by NYPD officers, the project featured forty-one interviews with an assortment of figures: rappers, kids on the street, parents of the victims of police brutality, religious leaders, police officers, Wall Street employees. The user scrolled over a bloody wall and clicked on each of the forty-one bullet holes on the wall to hear an interview. In industry lingo, *41 Shots* was a pull rather than a push piece. There was no narrative to push. Instead, the user pulled a narrative together out of the perspectives, often in conflict with one another, that were made available on the site. The Brooklyn Museum of Art was offered the piece for its summer 2000 exhibition on hip-hop. It was rejected because it was judged to be peripheral to the culture of hip-hop—exactly the kind of assumption that 360hiphop had been founded to counter.

41 Shots took a legendary amount of time and energy to compile, and the technical problem of hosting it on the Web site was a formidable one. Running the application on a standard dial-up proved just as arduous. In fact, the 360 team landed themselves a Web site overloaded with features and applications that took an eternity to download. Video, audio, and cartoon animations added to the bandwidth problem for a standard modem user with no high-speed Internet connection. To build the site, the company had hired Kioken, a Web developer with a reputation for flashy, top-heavy sites that impressed the neophyte but were a headache to use and maintain. Java, Flash, and DHTML were crucial ingredients behind the main navigation. Access to the site's full range of content also required applications like Shock-wave, QuickTime, Real Player, and IPIX. The result was technical overkill. As Hinds acknowledged, "we just wished the audience further along the curve." Broadband of this caliber would take years to come into being, for the general public at least

Among other things, the technical challenge of putting all the pieces together meant the site was not ready to launch on the announced date. During the week of June 20, Simmons had done the media rounds—CNN, Hot 97, the Howard Stern Show—and flyer posters had been busy around town. News crews from ABC and CNN were present in the office to film the launch, and bottles of champagne were waiting to be quaffed, but in the end, the technicians had to run a demo CD-ROM instead of the real thing. Hip-hop fans who went online that night in search of 360 got nothing but "server error" or "this page is not available" or at best, an intro clip in Flash with an LL Cool J song as backing. The next day, when the site was finally launched, many users found a homepage that took up to ten minutes to load or crashed, as a result of their limited bandwidth.

For many of the creatives, who believed that 360 had one shot and that they had blown it, this was reason enough for the less-than-heavy volume of site traffic in the months that followed. Trying to recapture an invited audience that had showed up and been turned away was an uphill battle on the Web. Typically, the technologists were less apocalyptic: "It felt like we had built this house," Beale recalled, "and all of a sudden the floors started to give, and now it wasn't our dream house any more, so we had to go about fixing it, as any builder would." Kioken, the design shop responsible for the site's architecture, took a hit, while finger-pointing inside the company bred the first wave of serious internal friction. The homepage was redesigned for quicker access, but navigating the rest of the site was always a slow and unwieldy experience.

Despite the technical bottlenecks, content poured onto the site from each of the four departments. Fresh news went up at noon, and the site hosted three or four big new stories a day. In the first few months, traffic built steadily but quickly reached a plateau (around 160,000 unique views per month), after which metrics were no longer readily available to employees. In the meantime, a wave of new hiring filled the office to its physical limit, prompting affectionate insider jokes that it now resembled the slave ship Amistad. The outlay on travel to events and associated expenses soared, and the company, which had had substantial capital on hand at the outset, was alleged to be burning through as much as $1 million every month. For journalists accustomed to covering their rent from story to story, this kind of spending was prodigious. Even so, the illusion of working for a scrappy independent outfit with alternative, street credibility to spare was lucidly preserved among the employee ranks. The combination of working for Simmons and burning up the budget of a multimillion dollar company did not feel exactly like working for the Man.

By the fall of 2000, it was clear that 360 was not going to survive long on its own, nor had it built itself into a position to secure the best acquisition terms. The traffic demanded by advertisers had thinned out, and the bottom had fallen out of the capital markets, gutting any IPO prospects. Content companies in every corner of the Web were faltering, and the company's other urban competitors were hurting badly. In early October, Simmons reached an agreement to sell 360 to BET. From a business standpoint, the acquisition made sense. BET was buying out a competitor and acquiring a brand name with lots of exposure. Since its launch in February 2000, BET.com had become the most heavily used African American site on the Web. Adding the multiethnic edge of 360 meant that Robert Johnson's media empire was purchasing a coolness factor it had long been criticized for lacking. In the meantime, the 360 staff would bring much-needed skills and expertise to BET's interactive group. For the threesixties who were retained, the acquisition offered some prospect of job security. It also gave the company access to national distribution through a cable company that reached an audience of 40 to 60 million. As a result, 360 was still standing, as a proof of concept, albeit a shaky one, when all the other urban portals closed down within a matter of months.

Yet the acquisition was a direct hit to the esprit de corps, and not just because 360's independence and self-intent had been flattened. Of all the potential partners that had been thought viable (*Vibe, Hookt, The Source,* and UBO were others), BET had the most conservative corporate culture. The stiff, middle-class character of its brand was entirely at odds with the maverick ways of 360. Where the threesixties enjoyed a loose, improvised office culture, BET's internal organization was tight as a snare drum. The immediate effect on threesixties was what one writer described as an "immune system reaction." In the fall of 2000, this was not an uncommon spectacle in the Internet industry. A wave of mergers and acquisitions brought the strife between no-collar and button-down within the same company walls. Dotcommers, whose firms had been snapped up by Old Economy companies, were everywhere rattling the cages of the more conventional work environments they were now compelled to occupy. In this case there was a racial element to the friction, between the strictly African American ethos of BET and the multiethnic cast at 360.

As with hip-hop in general, 360 had an African American core, exercising the most cultural authority, but its broad mix of employees also included California Asians, ethnic whites, and South Asians, though few Latinos. The acquisition brought layoffs, and over 30 percent of the 360 staff, including the video unit and the departments that reported on lifestyle and sports, had been axed. With the departure, in particular, of the lifestyle group, the workplace culture felt significantly "less black" to the non-African Americans, by which they meant "black" in the sassy sense that appealed in the urban market. The BET folks who were now in charge stood for a different kind of black—well-groomed, disciplined, and playing by the rules. Robert Johnson's organization men and women had been weaned on the respectable values of a suburbanized black middle class. It looked as if they would be hard-pressed to manage a workplace where an inspirational slogan, posted on every wall at 360, announced, "We Ain't Playing Wit These Fools!!!"

Jamie Green, a Web developer who had jumped ship from the failing UBO, had the same attitude toward BET as the Rudy Giuliani poster caption: "BET is definitely not hip-hop. The whole aesthetic is different; it's almost all about the bottom line and toeing the line. We've basically swung from one end of the spectrum to the other, and I don't think 360 folks can function at all in a nonaesthetic kind of environment." Green had enjoyed a close link with Simmons, described him as "a creative monster," and recalled the mogul's own ambivalence about making the decision to go with BET. "He really loved 360. We had all the vitality, the spunk, and the independence that he loves so much. And he is a BET hater, on account of the kind of programming they have served up to African Americans for the past twenty years.

For us, and for Russell, BET always represented the worst kind of mediocre schlock. He's a little embarrassed to be associated with it. So, up to the very last moment, he was trying to get out of the deal and go with someone else. A couple of other companies were interested, but they wanted to lay everyone off, basically, so we went with the deal that would keep the most people and keep the company alive."

Among employees who were retained, there was much regret for a mission cut short. The acquisition came just at the point when the funds allocated for marketing and distribution were due to kick in and establish a sound commercial footing for the site. But the sense of relief was greater. Although the loose managerial structure of 360 had been savored by all, those who wanted their jobs safeguarded by fiscal prudence welcomed the prospect of the company falling under the firm hand of an MBA. After all, 360 had been run by Hinds, who was an Ivy League intellectual weaned on alternative journalism, whereas Scott Mills, the COO of BET.com was a product of the Wharton School of Business and had a background in investment banking. Among those who cared more about the mission than their job security, there were was a good deal of anxiety about 360's creative work going unacknowledged. As part of the reorg, BET would almost certainly take credit for their efforts. Over the next two months, BET.com traffic did indeed rise to an all-time peak of 1.1 million unique hits (from 287,000 before the acquisition). Some threesixties were convinced the spike was a result of their ideas, though it is likely that increased visibility on the cable network was mostly responsible. In any event, 360's creatives and techies were now supplying both sites, and some of them felt as if they were servicing the enemy. For them, BET had the profile of being "neither black nor entertainment," and this sorry reputation was the chief reason why urban competitors like 360 had been cheered on in the first place.

At the time of the merger, BET managers had promised a renewal of focus for the hip-hop site, but the continued market slump was impacting their own budgets and prospects. Chastened by the loss of home rule, the threesixties—downsized, reined in, and confined to quarters—would soon have harder medicine to swallow. Within six weeks, BET was sold to media colossus Viacom, and 360 had become a slightly dazed stepchild, handed down by one corporate step-parent to another.

BET may not have been a popular choice for the threesixties, but at least it was black-owned, and possession was key to preserving a black infrastructure in the media world.[13] Even after twenty years of fervent anti-unionism (which won BET a place on the AFL-CIO boycott list) and routine disdain for edgy black talent, Robert Johnson, black America's most successful media entrepreneur, still enjoyed some respect for retaining control of the company. In November, that regard evaporated when Johnson sold the company to the faceless media Goliath. BET was not alone. Virtually all the black-owned Internet companies had been taken over by large corporations like AOL-Time Warner (africana.com; netnoir.com), Cox Communications (blackfamilies.com), HBO (cybersoul.com), and Tribune Broadcasting (blackvoices.com), adding to the recent spate of high-profile buyouts in radio—Clear Channel (U.S. Radio)—and print—*Life (Essence)*.[14] With the BET buyout, majority-owned companies were one giant step closer to regaining their monopoly on mass media depictions of minorities. As for Johnson himself, he announced in an interview with black journalists that the days of "100% black-owned anything" are over.[15] A former Friend of Bill [Clinton] and corporate supporter, however lukewarm, of civil rights, he would earn further infamy among African Americans by offering his enthusiastic participation in the new Bush administration's efforts to repeal the estate tax and privatize social security.

Keeping the Faith

By the time I was making regular visits to the 360 offices on 10th Avenue, the Viacom takeover had yet to take full effect. The staff had thinned a little, and the airwaves were less charged. Even so, it was still a busy sonic zone, with musical flare-ups from all genres—soul, jazz, R&B, techno, and rap—competing in every corner of the long and mostly sunless loft space. Sound clash was a core office principle, assisted by the Napster downloading craze, then at its height.[16] It was a place where the drama of each day's work was set to multiple soundtracks. The visual landscape in the office was almost as multilayered as the sound, with computer screens at eye level, a collage of posters, cartoons, and glossy magazine cut-outs on the walls, and TV monitors mounted even higher up. With such a steady and varied supply of aural and visual stimulation, the media blitz in the office seemed like a match for the ambitions of the 360 site itself. Nor was the mix of loyalties any less extreme. Political icons shared the wall space with celebrity pinups above many of the workstations. Pictures of Mumia kept company with Mos Def and Macy Gray, while Huey and Riley Freeman, from the Boondocks cartoon strips, were omnipresent. Just as at Razorfish, there were no dotcom office gimmicks.

Not surprisingly, 360's office culture reflected the spirit of a hybrid workplace. It had lifted elements from the music industry, as well as from the work culture of print and TV journalism, and had grafted them onto the New Economy blueprint of workstations huddled, within easy earshot, around a heavily trafficked central corridor. Internal and external communication occurred by any means possible: Instant Messenger, Eudora, cell phones, beepers, and the intra-office holler. Over at Razorfish, the BlackBerry reigned unchallenged. Here, at 360, all employees were issued Motorola's two-way pager, the favorite gadget of the media, entertainment, and sports celebrity world. Hip-hop had broken in the two-way as a popular technology, and its use in the office was continuous with its appearance in the lyrics of the moment. Postures were wracked by the awkward two-thumbed effort to send messages over the dinky keys and screens of these pagers. So pervasive was their use that the pagers had to be banned from all meetings. Several technologists I interviewed were already in revolt against the overwired world they had helped to build. The glut of communication tools had become too invasive for them, and they were leading the charge to restore the intense face-to-face interaction of the startup days.

In the several months before the June site launch, the office had indeed been a teeming war room, hosting a continuous debate about the shape and purpose of the site. Hinds, who was big on collective process, led the group in discussion and voting and ended meetings with motivational prayers. Employees took shifts at sleeping in a nearby hotel. By the time of the acquisition, face-to-face meetings were occurring much less regularly than they were scheduled, and when they did take place, they served several purposes. In my experience of these meetings, 30 percent of the time was spent kibitzing, 25 percent was for airing grievances and complaints (mostly against BET), 20 percent was for sharing information and insider taste, while constructive planning was accomplished in the remaining 25 percent of the time. At Razorfish, employees who were unfamiliar with the reasons for my attendance at meetings joked about my being an industry spy. At 360, they teased me about being an efficiency expert.

The office layout was open and had been designed to cluster each department in a designated area, but the plan allowed for easy circulation between employees in content, technology, management, and business. The content people, in particular, insisted that they needed the constant stimulant of interaction to spark ideas and generate leads. Stories were just as likely to emerge from random conversations on the floor as from rumors overheard at an industry party or circulated on the Net. "I'm much more prone," explained writer Jill Nguyen, "to gathering ideas from casual encounters, from hearing or overhearing something my colleagues say. Here I'm in an open space with a lot of smart people, and a lot of conversations, ideas, and sounds are going to fire up, lots of images are going to flicker, and I try to process them all. That's what I do, that's my job, that's how I come up with stuff." However, when it came to writing, especially a sustained piece or a feature, Nguyen, like most writers, stayed at home in an environment without distractions. Everyone in the office used headphones when they needed to shut out the din and jangle or when the musical selection of some neighbor proved offensive.

The far end of the loft, by a wall of dingy windows, was occupied by the management team. They came and went in full view of the workforce. The proximity of their workstations, which bled into the rest of the workspace, sent a clear signal about democracy within 360, but the visibility of company leaders was also a liability. Any absences, prolonged or not, from their desks were noted, and duly interpreted, by employees. Employee skepticism about the ability of their managers grew steadily after the fall acquisitions. Like Razorfish, 360 was headed by a charismatic duo whose talents complemented one another: Selwyn Hinds, as Chief Creative Officer, and his college chum, Mark Hines, as Senior Vice President of Creative Technology. Hinds and Hines were ideas people, and their dearth of business experience was floated as a general cause for regret after the acquisitions.

Yet 360, like many other dotcoms built to flip, had not been designed to generate profits. IPO fever was in the air when it was founded, and an incubator helped to shape the company into a format optimized for a gainful acquisition. After the BET takeover, managerial strategy was aimed at saving jobs rather than at expanding a revenue stream that didn't really exist. Hinds, in addition, took some internal knocks, especially from the technologists, for running 360 as if it were an online magazine rather than what they regarded as a genuinely interactive medium. Yet the conditions for the latter, as many content companies learned, proved premature and would have to wait several years before ripening. Opening that interactive door was a dizzy step, which is why every New Economy employee felt the need to think about an exit strategy. The 360 office even had a inadvertent feature to remind employees of the risk. Pinned to the fire exit door, which was used frequently by smokers, a notice outlining "Plan B" captured the dark humor of work in a startup economy:

1. Open door
2. Climb stairs to roof
3. Proceed to edge of roof facing street
4. Pause, and reflect
5. Hurl self—headfirst—off building
6. Repeat as necessary

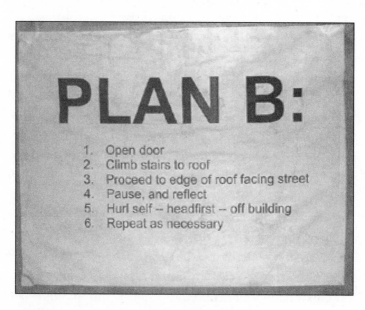

Exit Strategy (Photo by the author)

Hinds, Hines, and several other threesixties had attended Princeton University in the late 1980s (where I had taught some of them at that time), and the tight male bond of this group gave some substance to the cliché of the company family. In addition, real families were often present. The office walls were liberally adorned with stick-figure pictures drawn by the young children of employees. At Razorfish, where employees were overwhelmingly childless, crayon wall drawings were sketched by adult employees in response to an informal policy that encouraged forms of art therapy. At 360, the pictures were not simply a way to personalize employees' workspaces, a common practice in the American office environment; they were an active contribution by the children who were a regular, almost daily, presence in the office, following an example set by Sheena Lester, the executive editor. Lester's example also carried weight in other aspects of the office culture. In the world of hip-hop, where male rituals and misogyny were a given, her regard for women's expression and security was felt in the workplace wherever it was needed. This made a huge difference to women employees, especially those who had survived routine sexual harassment in the industry or at music labels and magazines they had worked for previously. Online content and office politics bore the stamp of her convictions in ways that were subtle but telling, and they would become even more pronounced when she took charge after the departure of Hinds and Hines in March 2001.

Managers like Lester and Hinds set bold examples, but the spirit of tolerance in the workplace was also a group effort. Many threesixties came with sour memories of previous places of employment, whether from race, gender, or lifestyle discrimination, poor working conditions and pay, or the cumulative experience of stifled initiative. They had warmed to the prospect of creating a utopian kind of workplace. Not only was 360 a chance to realize the full potential of hip-hop, but it would also be an opportunity to build an ideal work environment. What could hip-hop itself offer to make the workplace as good as it gets? In its twenty-year span, hip-hop had been many things—an entertainment medium, a community builder, a vehicle for civil rights and protest, a commercial gold mine, a lifestyle guide. Hip-hop attitude had been woven into everything else, so why not work itself? Surely a company might benefit in some way from the result.

Paid in Full

Certainly, there were hip-hop traits that would lend themselves to the workplace culture. The loyalty of its fans to the name and genre of hip-hop could easily translate into bonded camaraderie on the job. It could also feed into loyalty to the company's internal branding. As one writer put it, "we are so used to defending hip-hop to outsiders that we often take a pass on internal critique and opt for unity instead." So, too, the competitive spirit of hip-hop—where emcees battle with words for dominance of the field—might serve employees well when they went up against their rivals in the online urban market. Responding to ritual insults and challenges was part of the dynamic of hip-hop, and sure enough, sites like Crispus Attacks' Urban Exposé were soon bulging with vitriol and crossfire, much of it posted anonymously by employees at new media contenders. Morale was sorely tried by the more scurrilous rumors in circulation.

As for creative techniques, the experimental smarts of hip-hop producers offered a skills model that an interactive company, grappling with a brand-new tech medium, might find useful. Jackson Beale was not alone when he imagined his own skills at the computer console as analogous to the "art of the turntable." Hines, as head of creative technology, proved that the influence was a two-way process in his after-hours work at Poison Ivy, the music production company that he and Hinds had started while at Princeton. Hines had pared the studio down into a mobile unit, little more than a laptop plus a few peripherals, allowing for music to be made or recorded on a train or in the street. This concept became central to Schematics Media, the company that he and Hinds founded after they left 360.

Hip-hop's staple dialogue—a motormouth vocal played off against a rich synthetic vehicle of prerecorded sounds and beats—was not so different in principle from the interplay between 360's wordsmiths and technologists. Rappers, too, had steadily built their talent around a formula for transforming stray, and often mundane, phrases and observations into rich spoken poetry. Again, this was a valuable model for a creative company looking to capitalize on the daily chat of employees and site users, not to mention the torrent of information that washed through the fully wired workplace. 360 even had its own "resident" rapper, Prodigy, from Mobb Deep, who was a close friend of an employee and spent so much time in the office playing with the computers and listening to music that he was often referred to as "on staff." It was alleged that the famous emcee, who had recently launched a solo career, found the 360 environment to be a therapeutic aid for his music.

Naturally, it made business sense for a media company to honor, within the workplace itself, the aesthetic that its employees covered. A work environment with a hip-hop feel might well extract the right kind of productivity from those who built and hosted "the ultimate hip-hop destination." Certainly, there were some threesixties who felt they were *practicing* hip-hop in some way rather than merely working to broker its career. But in at least one crucial respect, they really were a part of hip-hop, because they had been recruited as part of the merchandise. After all, 360 was a company that had been groomed to be a hit. It was itself a hip-hop product, like other acts or brands that Simmons had produced, and it was being promoted in order to be sold to another company, if not on the public market. Other startups that had been prepped by incubators were in the same boat, especially those that window-dressed their creative personnel to help sell the company. 360 had one foot in a music industry that developed talent for the performance market, and so it was not such a great leap to recognize that its own dream team were creative assets that had been cultivated to attract investors.

How did this affect the work mentality of employees? First and foremost, they had to process the fact that they were working for a company that did not have to make money and, in any case, had no prospect of doing so. Several threesixties had worked previously for profitless dotcoms, and they were somewhat familiar with how this concept translated in the workplace. Others had toiled at nonprofits and knew all about fiscal unreality from another angle. None had been in a position akin to that of talent in a creative industry, where fame and wealth could descend suddenly on those groomed to expect success from a hit rather than from the cumulative result of their labor. The writers were accustomed to reporting on talent but had no experience of being treated as an asset primed to break out in anything like the same way. Yet the spendthrift operating budgets they initially enjoyed had more in common with industry splurges for artists. Their loose schedules and the nonconformist ways of the office were more in synch with the daily cadence of someone like Prodigy than that of a technical writer on tight deadlines. At Razorfish, employees performed as if they were artists. At 360, they were more like the talent.

What lay behind this difference between the two profiles? 360 had sprung from the forehead of the music industry, just above the dollar signs for eyes. It may have been designed as an alternative to business as usual, but its employees had few illusions about the cash nexus that anchored their jobs. By contrast, Razorfish grew out of the webby vanguard of the art world, and its boho origins helped sustain the whim of employees that the company's capital was funny money and that its trade was a thing apart from corporate America. The fish were feeding off the legacy of historically white bohemia, whose citizens had always been secure enough to cast aside the privileges of their race and class and make their lives into something resembling a work of art, at a safe distance from the marketplace of commerce. By contrast, this kind of bohemian option was always less likely for artists of color and much less meaningful as an act of self-invention. Voluntary poverty is not generally regarded as a heroic or romantic choice within communities that are already socially isolated and starved of resources.

The most striking examples of this contrast were musical ones. When white musicians adopted the style and sensibility of African American blues in the 1960s, they believed they were challenging the saccharine diet of the commercial pop industry and striking a blow on behalf of civil rights into the bargain. The wizened Delta blues players they idolized as impoverished but authentic souls had long struggled to be recognized as commercial artists who could turn their skills into a meal ticket. Whenever a black bohemia had emerged, as in the case of the bebop jazz enclave, it was almost instantly converted into super-bohemian capital by white emulators like the Beats, hepcats, and street-corner juveniles of the 1950s. When hip-hop made its mercurial rise from the ghetto debris of urban renewal, black music finally became a decent livelihood with a well-paying wage for those who rose above the competition. After an eternity of black musicians being underpaid and robbed blind of their rights and royalties, the goal of getting "paid in full" was more clearly stated as part of the rapper's musical agenda, and it became more important than "keeping it real." Material success for black artists was also more closely tied to status. This blunt focus on just compensation contrasts with the predominantly cultural prestige that white artists look to extract from the thin wages of bohemia.

The new materialism within rap, which glorified BMWs, trophy women, and ropes of gold chain and other "bling bling" accessories, had fashioned a necessity—getting paid—into an opulent fantasy world of conspicuous consumption. The upwardly mobile excesses of rap's star players, lovingly visualized in a hundred music videos, fed off the same go-go climate as the excesses of dotcom entrepreneurs, but they drew on different sources, different histories. These excesses meant something different to those who envied them as just desserts or denounced them as immoral indulgences. Like the rise of black luxury consumption, the New Economy's industrialization of black bohemia did not follow quite the same route as its white equivalent. One of the best ways to gauge this was to move between the Razorfish and the 360 workplaces.

Among 360 employees, solidly identified with the pre-gangsta era of rap, circa 1989, or with the current hip-hop underground of Mos Def and Talib Kweli, there was little affinity for the new materialism. Nor was there outright disapproval. More typical was the wait-and-see attitude expressed by Sonny James, a writer with a wealth of experience in music journalism:

> I had the good fortune of being impressionable at a time when hip-hop was worth being impressed by. Right now, the music doesn't speak for anything. It speaks the new materialism in a very comfortable fashion, it's static and celebratory, and I believe that's actually redeeming in its own way. You can argue that black capitalism simply reproduces mainstream, white-owned capitalism, but 20, 30, or 40 years ago, these structures did not even exist as a viable parallel. Its existence is now useful. Whether it is actually creating an infrastructure, a knowledge base from which things can be drawn and built outward, that remains to be seen.

As far as the art of the music went, James believed an economic crash was likely to have a positive impact on the creative and political spirit of hip-hop. Hard times were a more fertile environment for renewing a culture that had grown fat and happy with gold-plated images of itself.

Because they saw hip-hop both as a means of livelihood and as a political art form, employees like James were typically ambivalent about aspects of the new materialism. They knew, for example, that their own workplace had been funded by high-profile entertainers, looking for a generous return. The rule of informality that prevailed in the office also owed a lot to the easy-rolling street attitude of hip-hop that had been marketed by the music industry into a worldwide money spinner. Indeed, the loose fit of 360's company culture was as much a part of the business plan as the street credibility of rappers was to a record label's revenue. Even so, there were limits to how baggy the work ethic could be. During the crunch time before the site launch, Simmons had lambasted at least one employee for his chronic tardiness. "You're a dotcommer," he scolded. "You're supposed to be here twenty-four hours a day." It was a genuine moment of tragicomedy and a reminder of the high cost of informality.

When rappers tell stories about work, they almost always focus on the romance or the tragedy of the informal economy. Unlike other genres of popular music, including the blues, rooted in the field holler of agricultural work, there are very few rap lyrics about the jobs that most African Americans do for a living. There is no direct equivalent of Dolly Parton's "Nine to Five," or Tennessee Ernie Ford's "Sixteen Tons," Bruce Springsteen's "Youngstown," or The Clash's "Career Opportunity." With the exception of rhymes about making a living from hip-hop itself—such as Eric B. and Rakim's "Paid in Full" or Boogie Down Production's "Outta Here"—or novelty items—like Canibus's "Shove this Jay-Oh-Bee," with its delicious sample of Johnny Paycheck's anthem—rap tends to recount the tactics by which wealth can be amassed outside of the formal work stream.[17] This makes some sense if you consider the limited employment opportunities for many African Americans since the early 1980s, when hip-hop first emerged from the wreck of urban deindustrialization.

Minorities had long been excluded from the primary labor market, and in African American communities, low-skilled workers had only recently been part of the formal economy. The decline in manufacturing and public sector employment, since the mid-1970s, and the suburbanization of many of the remaining core jobs had a disproportionate impact on urban blacks who had enjoyed standard blue-collar employment. The advent of a high-skills economy, which demanded more formal education and familiarity with computers, took an uneven toll on minority populations with less access to these skills and opportunities.[18] The result was a huge increase in involuntary part-time employment in communities long intimate with the experience of casual labor. It also widened the gap between the displaced— forced to make ends meet in low-wage services or in the irregular, underground, or gray economy of licit and illicit trade—and the skilled middle-class winners, some of whom gravitated to no-collar work, though with more caution than their white counterparts.

Working in the informal economy meant falling outside of the orbit of regulation, and it could lead to disenfranchisement.[19] By contrast, in the no-collar economy, casual and informal were marks of achievement, especially for minorities. The 360 workplace was a kind of crossroads where the casual rhythms and the risks borne by skilled New Economy workers brushed up against hip-hop's artful veneration of the risks that are part of the underground work ethic.

Eric MacIntyre, a Web producer who grew up in the steel belt, pointed out that "informality on the job is definitely a privilege for blacks, historically speaking." He cited the example of his own father who had put in forty years for the same corporation and who worried incessantly about the lack of security promised by his son's occupation. "He may have job security," MacIntyre acknowledged, "but he does not have career security. At one time, he had art scholarships to go to six schools, but he was advised by a guidance counselor to seek work in the steel plant. He gave up art for engineering, because the fear of failure was much greater than the desire to work outside of a rigid structure. I don't have the same fear of failure, nor do I need the well-defined structure and sense of expectations and goals. Of course that's a privilege." He found that the informality at 360 did not boost productivity per se, but it did enhance his own sense of personal contribution: "I need to have that informality to feel I am important, my ideas are important, what I bring to the table is relevant and will be listened to. My ideas may be mocked in public, but they will be mocked in my presence, just as I can feel comfortable mocking other peoples' ideas. It's the kind of informality you get in a family."

One aspect of the informality that all the writers brought up was that they were not obliged to take heed of site traffic metrics. In fact, none of them really knew how many people were visiting the site or reading their content. Again, this was regarded as something of a privilege. Sonny James explained: "The idealist in me says, don't tell me the metrics. Let me do what I do. I do it really well, I know I do it really well, and I don't need the hit number to prove it. In fact, the hit number will probably tell me the opposite, that people want to read the really uninteresting stuff and not the good stuff. I don't want to know that. I need to do my shit in a vacuum." Not too many music journalists could enjoy this kind of indifference to their audience. Indeed, within 360, the content team was often seen as unduly blessed; they were generally loath to acknowledge that they were writing for an interactive medium rather than the magazine of their dreams. As one technologist observed, "it was pretty good for us, so it must have been really great for them."

The disheartening side of this utopia, for the writers, lay in not knowing if anyone was actually reading their articles. Anxiety about not having an audience bit hard into their euphoric reprieve from being constantly judged by their ratings. They may have been cranking out the best journalism in hip-hop, and it may have been going nowhere.

Russell's Last Hurrah

By the end of January 2001, office morale was in the toilet, and the threesixties were soberly anticipating a harsh reorganization under the new Viacom regime. It was time for a motivational visit from Russell Simmons. He chose his entrance during a staff meeting about marketing. Scott Mills, the polished COO of BET Interactive, referred to as Darth Vader by some threesixties, had called the meeting to introduce new plans for making the two entities work together. For two months, the threesixties had been pressing for more "convergence" with BET. At the meeting, Mills assured employees they would indeed be "aggressively leveraging all the BET assets." This would involve a series of tie-ins between *Rap City*, the popular BET television show, and the 360 site. The site would host answers to questions asked of the stars on the show ("If you had to sleep with two people simultaneously, who would you choose?"). A series of exclusive downloads would be posted, along with outtakes from *Rap City*. Mills also announced plans for coordinating a new round of celebrity chats. Nas, Ghostface Killah, Aliyah, Snoop, Run DMC, Ginuwine, Janet Jackson, Destiny's Child, and others would be appearing both on TV and on the Web site.

Simmons had rolled into the office toward the middle of the presentation and joined the crowd at the back. Now he stepped forward, his Phat Farm sweater rolled halfway up his forearms, to play his role in a one-act corporate drama. "We made a deal with BET to use their resources, and you know they haven't been there enough for us. We need more love," he raised his tone, egging on the threesixties, "and so now it's time to go out and really *exploit* their resources, and believe me, there's a lot to exploit. It's gonna be real. What you have here in this office is real. It's the nucleus of an entertainment company." Simmons paused long enough for his first round of applause and then built on his open disrespect for BET. "There's no BET stigma attached to you; there's nothing on you, nothing to stop you. Use their money. They have so much of it, and they work so slowly that by the time they decide to fire you, you'll be old." Since Simmons held a seat on his board, Mills was hardly unfamiliar with the tenor of his remarks. Unflustered, he would go along with this game, which now turned in his direction. "Scott bought this company, and his ass is on the line," Simmons observed, milking his audience's growing joy at seeing their new boss played in this manner. "So you know he will be fighting for us." Mills had no choice but to agree, again in the industry lingo that contrasted so sharply with Simmons's street style. "The audience for interactivity," he responded, "between BET.com and *106th and Park* [another popular BET show] is already impressive. Once we create a 360 wedge in *Rap City*, we can develop the same cross-platform market." "That's right," retorted Simmons, "but we have to be more creative than that. Let's change the name of *Rap City* to 360hiphop. You can be sure we'll make the show better."

This kind of fighting talk was ambrosia to the threesixties, who had not seen Simmons in the office for several months and were unaware that he was still so sympathetic to their concerns or that he cared enough to do something about it. Elation was visible in all quarters, and now it was their turn. "You are the only people who have the good fortune of knowing you will be here a month from now," Simmons pointed out, referring to the industry shakeout of urban portals. "You have no competitors left, you're alone now, you have a great team and so you have no excuses. This drought will turn out to be good for us. There won't be any kids coming up to compete." As for the solution to moving forward, Simmons gave a standard media pitch—"You'll get respect if you get a hit. There's nothing bad about our site; we just don't have a hit"—and ended with a call to arms. "Let's show BET we can do it better, and let's go to work on it!" A roar of approval from the boys over in the techie quadrant bounced off the walls, and the threesixties went nuts all over the loft. Simmons made his exit on a high note.

The meeting produced a sizeable bounce in office morale and revived some employees' hopes that 360 might have a second chance. Having failed itself to be a hit, it might at least create a hit and live large on the payoff. Too much depended, however, on the execution of BET's plans for convergent programming. Within a few weeks, the excitement had largely subsided, and there was little visible evidence of a follow-through on the plans for cross-promotion. Some employees reasoned that the Simmons tactic had backfired. His native bluster had been a great crowd-pleaser, but he had merely antagonized the BET bosses, who were fortified now in their resolve not to allow 360's star to rise again but rather to utilize its staff as BET service personnel. Whatever the interpersonal psychology or business logic behind these operational decisions, the future of both outfits lay germinating in the much larger entrails of Viacom, and it would soon rise to the surface.

In mid-March, the Viacom reorg finally took effect. Just before the axe fell, Hinds and Hines announced their resignations, leaving to work on startup plans for their own media consultancy. Later in the week, the layoffs kicked in, wiping out the entire staff of the Culture and the Politics departments. Once again, the technologists, essential to both sites, were largely spared, along with the Music department, which would now merge entirely with their BET counterparts. Archival content would henceforth be recycled to maintain the site's silos in these areas. With the gutting of Culture and Politics, both considered superfluous to a revenue stream based entirely on the media selling of lifestyle, the original inspiration for the company's 360-degree approach died. Within the office, and among those fired, the layoffs did not come as a massive surprise. What shook people more was the widespread response from users and acquaintances who were saddened by the news. Employees were astonished at the volume of feedback. It was the first indication in some time that anyone out there really noticed or cared about their doings. Perhaps they really were having an impact after all.

The Ghost Site

There would be lots of opportunity for hindsight in the months before and after the rump staff moved to a more central Viacom building in NoHo. There they joined Viacom's other online properties—MTVi, Sonic Net, VH1, BET, and Nickelodeon.com. Though all the sites worked out of the same vast floor, none of them were sharing much in the way of resources, and in fact they were encouraged to compete with each other in the broad youth market. Sheena Lester was relieved that "the ghosts of the past were shed," and she was busy protecting her people. Some would survive and join BET full-time in March 2002, when the 360hiphop site was retired for good.

Space to Think at Viacom (Photo by the author)

But it was the layoffs that had dissolved what the threesixties often referred to as their dream. Depending on which version you chose, that had been the dream of re-energizing hip-hop's social and political batteries: of changing industry journalism for the better; of harnessing new media to tap the political potential of the hip-hop generation; of making good on the economic power of the urban market to do the same; and of sustaining a progressive workplace in a black-owned company with multiethnic staff. Inevitably, the company's failure promoted misgivings about their faith in hip-hop itself. "Maybe hip-hop really is nothing more than a lifestyle," mused Sonny James. "Maybe it's not part of something larger. Maybe this is as large as it gets." If hip-hop was not capable of providing a 360-degree program for life, belief, and action, then perhaps the company really had overshot its mark.

Others were more attentive to the changes wrought on the industry as a whole. Content, in general, was a way of drawing attention to commercial sites, and so its capacity to capture traffic had been eagerly courted by each successive wave of business models on Silicon Alley. As a result, content came and went, and came and went again, sometimes in the space of several months. But this fickle pattern did little for the long-term prospects of content companies per se. In addition, it was often pointed out that a media brand took several years to build and that most print media take that long to break even. Operating on Internet time was another matter. Unlike print magazines, online content titles were competing for traffic and attention with almost every other commercial site on the Web, and so they were judged, more often than not, by the same, unforgiving traffic standard. In a Web environment, which hosted a colossal glut of totally free content, the challenge of creating good media jobs and making payroll proved too much for most of the contenders. There were very few content sites that were flourishing, with the exception of those like Slashdot, which employed their users' postings of essays, reviews, and links for free, weblogs like Metafilter, or webzines like Salon, which had begun to charge for premium users.

Notably, the medium itself escaped blame. Many threesixties acknowledged that they, or their bosses, had not understood the Internet as well as non-print folks might have done, but they were hard-pressed to point to other niche-based ventures, outside of the pornography game, that had done better. Even among the writers, where you would least expect to find traces of Internet evangelism, the company's decline had not shaken their confidence in the medium. Bitten, but clearly not shy about its future prospects, Alexa Paley, a writer in the Culture department, had this to say about the next coming of the Net: "When people try to knock down a door, it often sticks, so you make the first push to loosen it, and a second push to loosen it more, and then you make the third push to break through. We were part of the second big push, and it crested and fell, but I think we will see it again for a third time. It may not come in the same form as we have now, but it will come again, and it might still change the world."

Optimize Me

"It was much pleasanter at home," thought poor Alice, "when one wasn't always growing larger or smaller, and being ordered about by mice and rabbits."

—Lewis Carroll, *Alice's Adventures in Wonderland*

"When I make a word do a lot of work like that," said Humpty Dumpty, "I always pay it extra."

—Lewis Carroll, *Through the Looking Glass*

"WHAT DOES ALL OF THIS HAVE TO WITH ME? NOTHING THAT YOU'VE said speaks to me and the kind of work I do." His tone was not belligerent, nor was it especially dispirited, but the speaker, with long curly locks, a blue denim shirt and black leather pants, who was seated toward the back of the function room of the Canadian Consulate General, was clearly annoyed. It was a frigid January evening, and he had sat through a long panel discussion on "The Future of Silicon Alley." From the approval displayed by many of those in attendance, he was giving voice to a sizeable constituency within the World Wide Web Artists Consortium (WWWAC), which was hosting the symposium.

What was the point of his complaint to the panel members? No one could say they had spoken out of turn or ineptly. They were Alley

veterans of the sort that the WWWACies commonly respected: Jason
Chervokas, one of the most highly regarded industry journalists and
cofounder of @NY, the longest running daily newsletter in Silicon
Alley; Michael Wolff, *New York* magazine's outspoken new media
columnist and author of *Burn Rate*, which had chronicled his own career as an Alley entrepreneur; and Owen Davis, CEO of Sonata, Inc,
a Web pioneer, and author of *Instant Java Applets*. Nor had the panel
been dull. Chervokas had delivered a realistic diagnosis of the state of
new media in New York, assessing the immediate prospects of various
technologies—broadband, wireless, peer-to-peer—and praising what
Internet companies had done right so far. By contrast, Wolff had offered a spectacularly glum picture. "It's over," he announced. "New
media didn't work, it failed to compete with old media, and a year
from now, no one in this industry will be doing what they are doing
now." Davis had been cherry-picked to represent the middle ground.
Many more companies will go out of business, he predicted with
stunning sobriety, while those who stick close to Web essentials will
survive.

In due course, the differences between Chervokas and Wolff esca-
lated into a quarrel over business models. It was more or less the
same dispute that had animated entrepreneurs and industry watchers
for the past five years. Can advertising support this interactive
medium, and if it won't, what will? During that period of time, investors had hot-tailed it from one business model to another; from
portals to content, then to e-commerce (B2C), and business-to-business (B2B). By January 2001, the tone of the debate was, in part, ret-
rospective. In the words of a wry technologist seated next to me, "the
Internet had run out of money." For his part, Wolff argued that the
Internet industry never was an alternative kind of business, nor
should anyone have treated it as a separate industry. Chervokas maintained that new media was and still is a genuine innovation, and it had
actually proved that advertising, like any other static industry, was becoming obsolete.

By the time the objector in the audience spoke up, the talk about
monetizing content and leveraging assets had been going on for an
hour and a half. In part, he was registering fatigue with the market
chat, but he was also drawing attention to what business punditry rit-

ually ignored—the experience and prospects of skilled workers like himself. The business babble had become incessant. You could have heard the same rap, albeit of a lesser quality, at any industry gathering, in any trade publication, or on any relevant message board. Everyone had heard the industry bore stand up and give his or her take on the future of digital business.

It had become the favorite bar counter rap of the small guy without credentials, inspired by day trading and the breathless, sports-style market coverage of TV channels like CNBC and CNNfn. Innocuous or not, it was the spillover from the steadily rising tide of financialization. Before long, we were being warned, nothing would be judged according to its intrinsic worth; every physical quantity, idea, event, or human attribute would be optimized to capture its share of market value.

Freed up by broad deregulation and bewitched by the woozy sway of New Economy thinking, entire industries had been sucked into the orbit of financialization. The tangible production of goods or services had been downgraded in favor of short-term equity yields and speculative returns.[1] At the groggy height of the stock bubble, even earnings and profits were dismissed as mundane, if not entirely redundant, features of a bygone economy. Money, it was surmised, could be prized free from its physical moorings by the market's increasingly exotic instruments of speculation. As the Zeitgeist company Enron tried to prove, almost anything, including the weather or insurance risk, could be commoditized and conjured into a financial instrument to be traded online. In this kind of environment, a job was more likely to be viewed as an opportunity to cash out than as an obligation to produce anything useful, let alone as a vocation.

The Pope's Warning

In companies where options were standard issue, it had become customary to put a stockwatch application on the desktop screen of all the computers. As a result, employees got used to a daily round of emotional highs and lows that were directly tied to the fluctuations in their company's stock price. This concept had been beta-tested on senior managers in the early 1990s at a time when executive salaries were first pegged to the stock performance of their companies. The application was a constant reminder of their new duty to deliver shareholder value by any means necessary. In publicly traded New Economy companies, the feature was extended to production-level employees, thereby distributing the psychology of risk downward. It was an unusual form of motivation, and it gave rise to a new species of industrial anxiety. Where once the working day had been dictated by the regimen of the factory clock, now it was regulated by the flux of the stock index.

Throughout the 1990s, American workers in general became more and more aware of how market manipulation affected their jobs and financial security. For one thing, it had become common for Wall Street to reward companies (or more accurately, their CEOs) that laid off employees by promptly boosting their stock valuation. In addition, an increasing portion of the general workforce (almost half of all Americans) were persuaded to buy equities and gamble their futures on the stock exchange. The pensions of millions of employees floated on the roiling seas of stock in 401(k) plans; often (in 20 percent of firms) this included an obligatory investment in the stock of their own company, as was the case, notoriously, with Enron. Many others transferred their family savings from government-insured bank deposits to mutual funds. These funds were large institutional investors, and they took an activist lead in the shareholder revolution in the early 1990s. Soon the fund managers were pressuring corporate boards and executives to do everything in their power to capture an ever-higher market yield. Instead of workers controlling their own companies, where they might have applied their own expertise, they were now in the position of indirectly influencing the destiny of companies about which they knew nothing, often with dire consequences for the employees of these firms.[2] Yet there were few immediate alternatives on a landscape governed by financial volatility. With most low- to middle-income wages either stagnant or falling, and with increasing job instability, the only way for most workers to share in the prosperity was to join the game of making speculative market claims on the future.[3]

The stock ticker on the computer screens—a fickle governor of the psychology and mood of the workday—was only the most visible symptom of how deeply the workplace had internalized awareness of the market's daily doings. Stock options, where they were offered, became a form of golden handcuffs, retaining employees in jobs they might otherwise have left. Wall Street's upsides and downsides forged new kinds of mental and emotional shackles that bound employees to their bosses through the daily indexes, inducing a regimen of stress that recognized no boundaries between work and home. Even workers who were well outside the orbit of the finance sector felt the skittish impact of its gyrations on the world all around them.

In a climate where the manipulation of financial holdings was paramount, labor assets, along with other real assets like factories or offices, were impediments to the agility of companies. Ideas, promises, stories, and visions of the future were the preferred vehicles of investment, intangible assets that could be leveraged to unlock higher levels of shareholder value. Creating this value was a process increasingly divorced from production or social concern. Even Pope John Paul II was concerned about this development and had said as much in an address on the topic of financialization to Christian businessmen: "Today it is possible to create great wealth rapidly without any connection to a defined quantity of work. As can be easily understood, it is a delicate situation that requires careful consideration by all." The pontiff called for new ethical codes, oriented toward the common good, to protect the vulnerable.[4]

There was a whiff of the pope's "delicate situation" at the WWWAC panel that January night. The protester in the audience was speaking for the WWWACies who represented the old Internet and who stood for the community ethos of knowledge sharing and Web craft. They were fond of disparaging the MBA Nation of cash-flow strategists who valued corporate privacy and finance valuations above all else and who had recently swelled the ranks of WWWAC. It looked like a familiar scenario. The early adopters claimed the high ground in the name of art and community, while the money people insisted they were creating wealth and preserving jobs. Except for one thing. It was the character of his job—"the kind of work that I do"—that the protester was invoking. He had heard no acknowledgment during the panel discussion of the skills he had learned or the craft he practiced. How was his labor being recognized, if at all, in the capricious world of monetary speculation?

If the craft ethos was alive anywhere, it could be found among the membership of WWWAC, founded in 1995 as a community resource for Web developers. Although the organization's official meetings were sparsely attended, the WWWAC e-list was abuzz with subscribers sharing advice about technical problems encountered in the course of the day's work and offering information about jobs and compensation, even suggestions for stimulants to help stay awake during those all-nighters. The list also functioned as a collective watchdog for evidence of labor exploitation, such as egregiously low wages, extreme outsourcing, or inhumane management tactics. WWWACies were especially adept at picking apart recruitment ads to expose code words—"dynamic young workgroup," "high-pressure, fun-loving environment," or "we work hard and play hard"—designed to draw gullible young inductees into the bondage of seventy-hour workweeks. When industry analysis was offered, it was seldom from a manager's or investor's perspective and usually from the independent's point of view. The techie humor that circulated on the list was often laced with labor consciousness:

> There is a new virus going around called WORK. If you receive any sort of WORK, whether via e-mail, Internet, or simply handed to you by a colleague, do not open it. Those who have opened WORK have found that their social life is deleted and their brain ceases to function properly. If you do encounter WORK via e-mail or are faced with any WORK at all, purge the virus by sending an e-mail to your boss with the words "This is too much for me, I'm going out for a soda. This better not be here when I get back." Send this message to all your friends in your address book. If you do not have anyone in your address book, then the WORK virus has already corrupted your life!

Most pointed, however, were the ongoing discussions about how to preserve well-paid custom work. For those who had spent years in the trenches learning Web skills, it was a ceaseless struggle to stay ahead of software upgrades that threatened to render these skills obsolete. The Web developer's trade was increasingly standardized, as the industry developed programs and idioms to accomplish Internet work with the same degree of efficiency as in the software development sector.

Throughout history, elder artisans had possessed the fullest knowledge of a trade, and they passed it on to youthful apprentices. In the modern technology industries, this order no longer applied. The newest recruits were often the most skilled because they were up to date on the latest technologies. They themselves stood to be superannuated early in their career if they did not keep up or move into middle management.

Todd Drake, the technologist evangelist at Razorfish, was quite aware of this trend: "I'm forty-one in a couple of months, and it's a little spooky, knowing that your value is going down just 'cause you are getting older. When I interviewed at Netscape back in the day, the recruiter told me flat out that 'We want you to work 110 hours a week. Are you ready to do that? Some people work even more.'" He couldn't see himself keeping up that pace, but still gave himself good odds in outlasting the field. "I feel confident that I'll continue to be employable, at the technology level, and that I'll find the discontinuity point quicker than other others. But it's a race. Luckily, I inherited workaholicism from a long line of ancestors."

Structural economics was working against him, however. A "silicon ceiling" had come into being; the older, higher-priced information workers were being filtered out in favor of young blood or overseas labor. Recruiting for "diversity" had become a code word for hiring much cheaper Asian employees on the H1-B visa track (already accounting for 28 percent of U.S. programmers).[5]

There had been some union talk in the early days of WWWAC, and there was no lack of sympathy for unionization efforts in some back-end sectors of the industry. Customer service representatives at Amazon.com had made moves in the direction of organizing to better their conditions and to combat the company's relocation of its call centers overseas or to cheaper regions of the country. The employees of Etown.com, an electronics retail startup in San Francisco, became the first dotcom to schedule a union election in January 2001, and the first industrial action on the part of Net workers occurred in Milan in February 2002, when Virgilio.it employees protested outside the offices of Matrix, its parent company.[6] In February 2001, a closely scrutinized poll conducted by TechRepublic.com, a Web site for IT professionals, showed that 45 percent of those surveyed would favor joining a high-tech union. Yet little headway was made. Anti-union declarations like that of Amazon's Jeff Bezos—"We don't believe in unions, because everybody is an owner"—were typical of managerial sentiment in the technology industry, and they were generally shared among the higher echelons of skilled employees.[7] Independents by inclination, no-collar workers were generally persuaded that unions were no longer applicable or necessary in a flexible workplace staffed by highly mobile employees and governed by short product cycles. They associated the traditional form of industrial union with the world of their parents—the long-term contract and fixed employment of the New Deal workplace. Despite the massive advances, in recent decades, in the unionization of white-collar and professional employees, the idea of common-interest organization held little cachet for employees who had been weaned on the creed of self-reliance.

A more telling reason, perhaps, was that many employees I interviewed regarded unions themselves as large, sluggish bureaucracies. Their hierarchical ways put them in the same sorry camp as corporate organizations. Both were viewed as industrial-age dinosaurs, on their last, unwieldy legs. Even those who had a passing familiarity with labor history found it difficult to imagine how their current landscape of work, with multiple employers, high turnover, and a global labor pool, would sustain a successful organizing campaign (at least as it is defined by the archaic criteria of U.S. labor law) conducted in a workplace where the majority of employees must vote for the union if it is to be accredited. Nor, for that matter, had trade unionists shown much ingenuity in reinventing the kind of union campaign that would be relevant and appropriate for contingent workers of this kind. The exceptions were few and far between.[8]

One union that had made a valiant effort was the Washington Alliance of Technology Workers, which had led the Amazon campaign and the Microsoft permatemps case. In addition, the South Bay Central Labor Council, under its iconoclastic president Amy Dean, had performed wonders for low-wage employees all over Silicon Valley. Its nonprofit temp agency, Working Partnerships USA, now offered temporary workers job training, affordable health coverage, paid sick leave, and paid holidays. Dean, who had been active in the Justice for Janitors movement, proposed a hiring hall for higher-skilled tech workers. Appealing to their self-image as digital artisans, she campaigned for the return of nineteenth-century guilds, which many saw as a more appropriate form of association than an industrial union for craft workers to protect their interests.[9]

Despite the early union talk, WWWAC had chosen to preserve its neutrality rather than develop into a trade guild. WWWACies would take their chances on the open market, reasoning that custom work would always be in demand, even in hard times.[10] Even so, there was a world of difference between the WWWACies' labor concerns and the business priorities reflected in the New York New Media Association (NYNMA), the premier trade association in Silicon Alley. A week after the WWWAC symposium, I attended the NYNMA equivalent, a grandiose gathering that almost filled the two thousand seats of the Cooper Union's Great Hall with well-heeled, middle-aged businesspeople, corresponding in no way to the youthful, bohemian image from New Economy central casting. Contrary to the media fixation on twenty-something whizz kids, the vast majority of businesspeople in this industry were in their forties and fifties.

The NYNMA event honored the release of PriceWaterhouseCoopers' "climate study" of the industry. A survey of the executive level members of NYNMA had shown "strong optimism" about the state of the industry.[11] The association hoped to use this rational exuberance to counter the irrational pessimism that had fueled media accounts of the industry's recent fall from grace. The panel featured a typical cast of star entrepreneurs (Scott Kurnit, founder of About.com; Martin Nisenholtz, CEO of New York Times Digital; Wendy Millard, president of Ziff-Davis Internet; and Jerry Colonna, the Alley's alpha venture capitalist), each primed to offer their twenty-five dollar predictions about the industry's faltering crusade to turn millions of users into paying customers. In next to no time, the panel discussion worked itself into the familiar conference lather of business bravado, spiked with buzzwords and macho sound bites: "This isn't the first Internet winter." "Content is just taking a nap." "Email is *the* killer application." "We have launched an industry that's only 1,750 days old as an ad medium." "People *will* buy virtual representations of assets." "Endemic advertising is the way to go." "Capital is no longer free." "Revenue is no longer a distraction." "In 1991, no one believed in interactive business either." "Michael Eisner has no idea what he's talking about." "CNN was chicken soup; initially, no one bought into it." "Hey, AOL just acquired a content company [i.e., Time Warner]."

As I was leaving, Jerry Colonna (whose soured Alley investments included Inside.com, UBO, and Kozmo) was wondering out loud whether an Internet industry existed or not. Internet technology, he mused, may have been the medium that finally brought entrepreneurs to the city, but it may not be the industry that keeps them there. Colonna knew his audience, and he was ever adept at turning anxiety and uncertainty into strategic enthusiasm. Whereas the WWWACies were agitated about the survival of their jobs and their digital crafts, the people in the Great Hall were there to chew and chafe over the future glory of their investments.

My Mama Was a Tightrope Queen, My Father Rode the Trampoline

Down on Mercer Street, Razorfish was regrouping for the struggle ahead. Dachis's defiant December declaration—"We are a company, not a stock"—was mildewed history after only six weeks. The company's penny stock faced the ignominy of delisting from the Nasdaq if it could not be raised above a dollar, and so the fish were looking at a raft of New Year resolutions along with a major reorganization, each designed to send the right signal to Wall Street. Nonbillable expenses were now verboten and privation was in, billing rates had been sliced in half, and traditional corporate accounting software (SAP) was being introduced at considerable expense to rationalize the cost structure and further centralize power over the global operations. All employees, including the privileged "floating fish" in R&D who did the sexy thinking about pervasive computing and knowledge management, were assigned to billable projects. The company was about to roll out its own "re-brand," designed to communicate that the formerly avant-garde Razorfish was now a reliable corporate citizen—a shift from "we are different" to "we are relevant." Amid all this bustle, the fish had learned enough about Wall Street to know that a corporate reorg on this scale was considered incomplete unless it was accompanied by layoffs. The slick joke around the offices was that decisions about "capacity reduction" had already been made, but "no one had told Jeff."

Despite the low-level grumbling among the fish about becoming "capitalist enablers," the company's market optimization was hardly news. After Razorfish went public, Dachis and Kanarick had made a concerted effort to elevate the company's profile well beyond that of a design shop. Wall Street, it was rightly perceived, did not take artisanal work seriously. It was a sidestreet on the royal road to investor wealth, where the fattest rewards went to image making and market positioning, hence the subsequent tilt of Razorfish toward brand management and full-service consulting. At the same time that Dachis was taking his December stand against Wall Street, largely for the benefit of loyal employees, the company board was hiring a business hotshot as executive vice president. He formally introduced himself to the fish several days later: "I went to Harvard Business School, but don't hold that against me."

On January 19, 2001, the company's sixth birthday, the fish filed into a multiplex in Union Square for a rollout of the new brand and the new company Web site and to hear a rundown of the reorg. The Cohen brothers' Depression spoof, *O Brother Where Art Thou?* was playing in the cinema. As if in synch, an employee with a 1930s sharecropper look—stringy beard, long straggly hair, a banjo, and raggedy denim wear—kicked off the offsite meeting with an old-timey stomping blues: "My mama was a tightrope queen, my father rode the trampoline," he wailed with great gusto, and then the chorus itself was sly: "It's never good enough, well it's good enough for me."

The corporate music that occupied the rest of the meeting was less ambiguous. Razorfish 2.0., we were told, would be all about devotion to client satisfaction, and the company had a new brand proposition— "Engineers of Opportunity"—to suggest how the customer would be best served. The phrase retained the flavor of technological expertise, but the new promise of value delivered was less specific, and less threatening, than the "digital change management" of yore. Return on the client's investment (ROI) would be central to the brand promise and would become a mantra for fish, as in virtually all Internet companies, in the months to come. Reasoning that digital technology still had the magical capacity to magnify its impact, clients would be promised an ROI ratio of ten to one.

As for the internal reorg, it was modeled squarely on the structure used by traditional Big Five consultancies, with a strong emphasis on internal competition among employees. Employee assessment would be directly tied to utilization. The fish would now have to prove their value to the company; even senior management would be client-facing on projects. To dispel any confusion about the new power structure, a Matrix organization chart was rolled out, which clearly defined every employee's place in the chain of reporting. Jack Welch (or Neutron Jack, as GE employees knew him, for his erstwhile fondness for developing the neutron bomb) was given the final word at the meeting. Quoting corporate America's most feared CEO, Dachis declared, "When the rate of change inside an organization is less than the rate of change outside, the end is in sight." In the next six months, the fish would see little else but change, as round after round of restructuring kicked in, even for their CEO.

At the Triggerfish meeting the next morning, the response, at first, was unsparing. "The presentation was insensitive," observed Brian Schor, a native New Yorker, an interface developer, and one of the most community-minded on the team. "It was not a humane, people-centered message. The tone was like a dictate, and there was no finessing of the emotional side of the change or the transition." His neighbor agreed, and others followed suit: something more should have been said about how to protect the culture. But general criticism of the handling of the rollout soon segued into a sustained bout of anxiety about the psychology of survival, summed up by Schor himself: "If I'm not being well utilized," he wondered out loud, "how will I deal with the feeling of being underused?" It was a classic Razorfish question. The share of employees' time devoted to emotional care had only gotten larger as their sense of security diminished. Now the company's new criterion of performance assessment was being filtered through an intensely personal demand for emotional protection. Is there anyone looking out for my feelings? At times like these, it seemed that the ministration of feelings was more important than the tenure of the job itself. Later that day, as I passed an alcove I overheard Schor, almost in tears, confiding to another male colleague: "I feel as if I've been stripped and put on show. What happened to all the caring in this place?"

Part of the answer to Schor's question lay in the flatness of the company's organization. Authority was widely distributed in companies like Razorfish to ensure that innovation flourished and that the firm maximized its options for responding to an uncertain economic landscape.[12] In good times, a flat company offered satisfaction to employees who savored its creative chaos and freedom from lockstep applications of purpose. Self-management was so pervasive that it even extended to the hiring process. One employee, who was brought on to study knowledge management within the organization, jubilantly described his interview as an act of self-recruitment. Yet when layoffs kicked in, flatness meant that no one could be sure about who was making the decisive cuts or taking responsibility for them. The reasoning behind the selection was often inscrutable. Just as a strong culture could be an emotional salve during the fat years and a source of traumatic churning in the face of crises, so, too, an environment of distributed authority could readily morph from a haven of initiative into a vacuum of nonaccountability.

Something similar applied to professional development. No-collar employees generally thrived in informal organizations where promotion came about in unorthodox and often unexpected ways. This kind of environment suited their dislike of bureaucratic conventions like the promotion ladder or seniority privileges. When the organization was under stress, however, lines of professional advancement dried up even more quickly than they would under the predictable regime of the ladder. Most examples of restructuring, and the one at Razorfish was no exception, followed the model adopted under corporate reengineering and downsizing. Layers of middle management were cut away, and the lines of sight between production-level employees and upper managers were more clearly drawn. In an informal organization, then, the elimination of stepped opportunities for promotion had even more of an impact than in a traditional corporate environment. In addition, a strong culture meant that middle managers generally took on the role of emotional caretakers, in addition to that of professional mentoring. Any removal of this layer of guardians was likely to be taken badly by employees, like Schor, who felt in need of their protection.

Reorgs were part of the story demanded by investors, but they were also integral to the preferred profile of the fast company, which was supposed to be in a perpetual state of reinvention and self-renewal. You could say they were a feature of the company culture itself. How then, could they be viewed, as they were by so many fish, as a threat to the culture? It was a good question, even though you would not find a easy answer among the management gurus who had pushed the concept of company culture for over fifteen years.

If culture was normative—if it was a way of planting a company's core values in the emotional soil where employees worked and played—then whatever took root there was likely to last longer than one or two financial quarters. Every company's version of the HP Way would inevitably come into conflict with an abrupt imposition of change. Resistance was guaranteed. Terrence Deal and Allan Kennedy, authors of the canonical *Corporate Cultures*, warned managers about the "cultural barriers to change." Change, they observed, "leaves employees confused, insecure, and often angry. . . . Effecting real and lasting change is time-consuming, costly, difficult, and risky—in short, not always a good idea." "The old culture," they cautioned, "can neutralize and emasculate a proposed change."[13] Changes in the culture would have to be accompanied by strong signals from power holders, and managers would have to ensure that a visible system of rewards and preferences was tied to the new values. But nothing worked more expeditiously for managers than the imminent threat of layoffs.

Employees knew instinctively that there were two categories of change. Change, when it was self-directed, was part and parcel of the no-collar ideal, and in a fast company, it was worn as a badge of pride. However, it was an entirely different matter when change was imposed from above or ordained by investors. That was perceived as corporate business as usual. Under such circumstances, and they had become common in a financialized economy, employees (the ones whom Deal and Kennedy describe as "insecure" and "angry") usually invoked the old culture in order to protect their interests. At Razorfish, employees had good reasons—other than nostalgia—to recall its values. When they complained that the culture was being neglected in the race to return to profitability, they were trying to retain some control over the shape and velocity of the changes. In response, they were being told that the old culture was out of synch with what clients wanted from Razorfish. Surveys conducted for the re-brand had shown that the winning features of the company's past profile—"cooler-than-thou," "bleeding edge," "downtown New York"—were regarded as exclusionary and intimidating to the more conservative clients that were now being courted. "The surveys seemed tailor-made to me," Schor confided. "All they do is confirm the corporate direction of this company." If his views were not those of a minority, then Razorfish was in trouble.

Morale Wall Slogan—Internal Branding, Razorfish, New York (Photo by the author)

In the reshuffle, teams like Triggerfish were slated to dissolve, along with the community forum they offered employees like Schor to air their feelings. As the Triggerfish general manager, Corinna Snyder was a therapeutic sink for much of the foreboding. Of late, the burden of emotional caretaking had taken its toll on her, and several Triggerfish had begun to ask, "Are *you* alright?" More than anyone, Snyder had correctly anticipated the competitive alignment of the reorg and had expressed some misgivings about her own place within it. She foresaw that she would be more directly involved in closing contracts and owning receipts, and she was none too sure about being so intimate with the beast of revenue. "The nonprofit sector," she mused, "is beginning to look good."

Others had begun to compensate for the changes by reorganizing their own lives. Camille Habacker cut down to a three-day week to focus more on her acting and cabaret career. At the same time, she had not been able to pass up the chance of joining the new business development team, entrusted with bringing in fresh clients. After all, being the pitch queen was another kind of performance for her. It also energized her own belief in the credo of reinvention. Habacker believed that the reorg, far from closing down the spontaneity of the old culture, might bring to it a new relevance of purpose. For example, the new pressure to please the client would be an even greater opportunity for the fish to prove their agility and flexibility: "If you need us to work onsite, we'll work onsite. If you need us to be an IT firm, we'll be an IT firm. Etcetera." The capacity of the company to mold itself to the demands of the moment would be highlighted, and the contrast with its sluggish clients—who, she reported, "have been doing things much the same way since 1492"—would be all the sharper.

Shel Kimen, who had played a strategic role in the year of planning behind the reorg, was relieved that she was no longer involved in decision-making at any managerial level. It had begun to involve the kind of self-censoring that was sheer poison to her free spirit. "The rebels are no longer in control," she declared, and she launched herself into a two-week-long bout of inner reflection and dietary detox. She was worried about the corrosive impact of internal competition on company culture and had begun to throw herself more and more into her music. Like Habacker, however, she still held out for the art of performance in business. As long as she could see ingenuity and invention in her job, she would stay on. After all, her great-aunt, as she had recently discovered, was the legendary dancer Loie Fuller, renowned in the fin de siècle for her Serpentine Dance and her prominence in the Art Nouveau movement. Fuller's stage innovations with electric lighting and costume fabric had made her the multimedia maven of her day. For all her avant-garde stagecraft, she had also been a savvy businesswoman, who founded museums, held several patents, and was respected enough in the scientific community to be elected a member of the French Astronomical Society. "We share many common traits," mused Kimen. "She believed most things were possible," and "she made her own reality."

Other hardened veterans were feeling the pinch. Oz Lubling, a wistful technology specialist who had enjoyed full autonomy within the company, was back in the trenches, working on project teams. He had been employee number one, and so many fish saw Lubling as an icon of the pioneer, arts-oriented spirit of the company. Spiritually famished by a Silicon Valley job that was "entirely devoid of culture," he had responded to Kanarick's bouncing blue dot as if it were a signal from paradise and had snapped up the offer to work in a city environment drenched in the arts. An Israeli by birth, he, like other nonnative fish, had little fondness for the American credo that "work is your savior." Lubling had long struggled to quarantine his job from his other interests and hobbies and was now busy dispensing similar advice to younger fish. The recent decline of the company's fortunes had produced what he described as his "premature midlife crisis." His appetite for stimulation had surged once again, and he was pursuing his after-hours passion for photography. For the time being, he welcomed the boundaries of a regular job, primarily because it had a finite edge: "It is something I can step out of."

Now that the company appeared to be reacting primarily to Wall Street, employees like Lubling no longer felt they could influence or shape its direction. The conversation between RAZF (the stock exchange symbol) and the public markets was "self-propelled," he noted, and the fish were just along for the ride. Even the most otherworldly members of the designer group were beginning to grasp the realities of working for a publicly traded company in the age of optimization. At a group meeting in late January, one of them, decked out in the kind of print dress that usually waits until midsummer to make its appearance, found the wherewithal to ask, "When is the next time that the company's revenue gets announced?" She had finally cottoned on to the concept of quarterly statements and had made the cognitive link with layoffs that most of the fish, by now, felt in their bones.

The Day of the Comet

One Friday morning in mid-February, Sophie, the CEO's dog, presented herself at my desk on the fourth floor, and I leaned over to greet her. "Don't even try to engage," advised one of my neighbors. "She likes it best when people humiliate themselves by trying to earn her attention." Today, at least, she was a harbinger of things worse than humiliation. Within the hour, Philip Kaplan's fuckedcompany.com Web site carried the following rumor alert: "At 1:00 P.M. today, approximately 35% of Razorfish's 1,800 person staff will be laid off. If you work there, I think you have about 2 hours to burn those CDs and steal shit."

At this point in time, fuckedcompany was offering a valuable service to industry employees. Many would learn of the fate of their jobs on Kaplan's site before the news was released internally, and he rarely got his information wrong. On this occasion, he was off by a few days, but more or less correct about the numbers. The fish survived a very jittery Friday and pondered their fate over the weekend. Postings flooded the Web site with several hundred comments in response to the rumor. Kaplan's army of camp followers were not noted for their subtlety. Master trawlers of the scabrous frat boy sensibility, the vengeance they brought down on industry managers was as long on rancor as it was short on nuance.[14] Yet even by the standards of this discourse, the sheer volume of vitriol heaped on Dachis, the company, and the fish was extreme.

On Monday, employees were officially informed about a mandatory meeting at 4 P.M., and soon there was a running real-time commentary about the unfolding events on sites like the Razorfish board at Vault.com. Off-duty cops, it was leaked, would be guarding the building, just in case things got out of hand. (Fresh on everyone's minds was the recent slaughter of colleagues by an AK-47-toting employee laid off at Edgewater Technologies, an Internet consultancy in Massachusetts.) After noon, employees' internal access to the Vault and fuckedcompany sites was blocked, a move interpreted as fundamentally alien to the company culture of free speech. Dachis later explained weakly that the URLs had "been shut down as a precautionary measure to limit our exposure during our blackout period after an earnings announcement."

The internal rumor mill about the ax-cutting had hardly been inactive. Ghetto scenarios had been imagined—everyone would be given a color to wear and separated accordingly. By Monday afternoon, employees knew the news would come in the form of a personal phone call from HR advising the condemned to report to the first floor. At 3.15 P.M. the internal network was shut down, and a delicate panic set in as the Triggerfish careened around the office in search of friends, solace, and reliable information. I had never seen the floor so animated. Fish who were in the know had a good sense about who would be laid off, and those who had been tipped off began to pack up their stuff. Right down to the wire, however, the majority, including several veterans, were entirely in the dark. Even after the phones stopped ringing, there was still some doubt. "Maybe they haven't yet decided on me," mused one of my neighbors.

I decided to join the condemned. We ran the gauntlet of sympathy through the office and down to the first floor meeting room, where the general manager informed all present that they had been terminated. There were some anemic attempts at gallows humor from the floor, especially after his announcement that there were openings at other Razorfish offices for those who were looking to relocate. Even after the severance packages were announced, the meeting looked as if it could be drawn out through a lengthy Q&A. The fish, as ever, seemed transfixed by the drama and the spectacle of the moment, as if it were all a performance, inviting evaluation, or a rehearsal for some other meeting. Surely, this wasn't really the end. The angriest man in the room—a Triggerfish technologist—cut through the emotional fog and insisted that we conclude as soon as possible. Six inches of wet snow lay in wait outside, along with a car service to take the ex-fish home or to a far-away bar.

The morning after, the Morale Team were at a loss to know where to begin to raise the spirits of their colleagues. It had been like the Night of the Comet, one of them observed, and the most comforting rhetoric he could come up with was another media metaphor. "It was all a game, really," he quipped, "and folks had simply been voted off the island." The analogy with reality TV seemed fitting, since shows like *Survivor* were widely seen as a reflection of the social Darwinism that was being preached in the 1990s by the full-throated bull marketeers. Talk about digital Darwinism had been common currency for several years (generating book titles like *Digital Darwinism: 7 Breakthrough Business Strategies for Surviving in the Cutthroat Web Economy*), and the concept seemed to be reinforced now by the cruel

triage underway.[15] Yet the comment also made me reflect on the relationship of this layoff wave to earlier generations of layoffs. How did
employees' experience of New Economy layoffs compare with that of
the Rust Belt manufacturing workers who saw their jobs outsourced
in the 1970s or the white-collar organization men and women who
were downsized in the 1980s and 1990s?

Certainly the entrepreneurial temper of the technology industries
had helped create a climate of pitiless competition. As a result, there
were no guarantees, nor even expectations, of security for New Economy workers. Even so, tech executives had long sought to distinguish
themselves from their counterparts at traditional industrial corporations whose zest for downsizing had earned them widespread public
rancor. In fact, many tech companies had pioneered a culture of zero
layoffs, where employees were supposed to be too highly valued to be
discarded.

When cuts were unavoidable, moral leaders like Hewlett-Packard
asked all employees to take a 10 percent pay cut and stay home every
other Friday in order to preserve the company culture and distribute
the pain.[16] If anything, urban interactive companies had upped the
ante. Their employees were their star assets, and their company cultures catered lavishly to employees' sense of well-being. The climate
of personal respect was matched by labor relations that were distinctly
informal by corporate standards.

Casualties of the earlier waves of blue-collar and white-collar layoffs saw them as a stark betrayal of a social contract that was forged
among corporations, government, and the labor movement in the
Cold War period. As part of that formal contract, there were rules and
agreements to protect the rights of management as well as labor, and
so the corporate push to dissolve the contract in the 1970s and 1980s
required the massive legal changes made possible by government
deregulation.[17] The ending of this contract closed the era of corporate
paternalism and welfare capitalism. Employees were now variable
costs, to be cut or added in accord with demand. By contrast, the successful effort to keep unions out of the high-tech sector meant that
the compact between management and tech employees was informal
and provisional from the outset, and it was shaped more by a cultural
understanding about mutual needs than by any formal contract of

work rules. In Old Economy companies, management craved the legal freedom to order layoffs at will. By the New Economy ethos, laying off employees would be alien to core company values, notwithstanding the customary ebb and flow of team workers at the end of a product cycle. The result, when it occurred, was likely to be taken more personally—as a breach of mutual trust rather than a violation of a contract.

By the mid-1990s, job security was less of an expectation in all sectors of the economy. Nor did strong institutional ties or company commitments rank very highly on the list of no-collar priorities, especially in the job-hopping tech sector. Change, risk, individual mobility, and discrete job experiences had marched into the workplace, eroding the prospects of stability, solidarity, or a long-term career.[18] Against this backdrop, layoffs were just one more discontinuity and therefore easier to accept as a natural feature of the new economic landscape. A layoff was no longer the opposite of employment; it was a routine aspect of work in America and was almost understood to be part of a job description.

Since no-collar jobs had eaten away the boundaries between work and leisure, it was no surprise when some New Economy companies sought to break down the distinction between employment and non-employment. When networking giant Cisco laid off 8,500 workers in May 2001, the company proposed to pay one-third of their salary and provide health benefits and stock options if they committed to work one year for a nonprofit that served the homeless or hungry. In the long run, the scheme was cheaper than cutting six-month severance checks. It also allowed the company to boost its philanthropic profile, and it gave Cisco first crack at hiring back skilled employees that had been kept out of the orbit of its competitors.[19] However unorthodox, the Cisco arrangement was characteristic of an industry that had learned to take full advantage of nonstandard labor arrangements. This even extended to the use of free labor offered through the Internet's gift economy. A common acceptance of open standards and shareware meant that companies could benefit overall from the free use of products and technologies developed on someone else's R&D budget or through the voluntary labor of amateur users. One prominent example was the Open Source movement, a model of software development in which the source code was made freely available to the general public for modification, alteration, and redistribution.[20] But the grander example by far was the World Wide Web itself, which, in its entirety, was the public product of trillions of hours of users' free labor, the greatest collective construction job in all of history.

If the confines of New Economy work were less distinct, the character of corporate governance had also altered. The size and scope of layoffs were still being defined by senior managers and were a reminder, to employees still trying to vest their 5,000 company shares, of who really wielded the power. But the decisions themselves were more and more prescribed by investors and market analysts. In some cases, pension and mutual fund managers had seized a large share of governance on corporate boards in their bid to ensure that stock prices were prioritized at all costs. Twenty years earlier, when corporations joined the race to the bottom in pursuit of cheap nonunion labor in developing countries, American workers got a foretaste of how financialization would come to affect their job prospects. Among the reasons offered for corporate flight, global competition was foremost. But CEOs also learned how to refer to the demands of the market as if it were a sentient being, issuing directives that they had little alternative but to obey. By the end of the century, the volatility of the market was no longer an external cause or reason for layoff decisions but an intimate component of the workplace, to be factored into the expectations we had about jobs and the conduct required of employees and managers in the execution of them.

New Economy employees worked for companies that were commonly referred to as a market "play." Indeed, many were regarded as a gambler's prospect of taking home winnings that far outstripped the collective value of their employees' labor. Stockholders could win in the short term even if the companies eventually failed, and especially if they were only built to flip. The only sure thing was that the losers, as in any casino, would outnumber the winners. It was all part of what Treasury Secretary Paul O'Neill described as the "genius of capitalism." He was responding to the implosion of Enron, the company that most strenuously embodied the principle of virtual trade by pioneering the financialization of energy, along with anything else that could be converted into a tradable derivative. Never had a corporate behemoth fallen so suddenly. Yet the impact of Enron's failure, however far-reaching, was much less physical than it was virtual. In the 1970s, when factories were shut down, the destructive impact on the social and economic life of communities lingered for several decades amid the rust of abandoned physical plants. When New Economy companies closed shop, all evidence of their existence could evaporate overnight, or at least after the auction of their computer equipment and Aeron chairs.

Preparing Aeron for the Auction (Photo by the author)

For whatever reasons, the actual process of laying off no-collar employees was expected to be as humane as their permissive workplace had been. In an employee-sensitive environment, a pink slip should not feel like an ordeal of rejection, though it would be fanciful to expect a feel-good experience. Yet many companies in the new media sector were run too ineptly and callously to follow through on the New Age treatment. Smaller, or shadier, Internet companies often axed employees without severance pay or even back pay. Misleading company statements and layoff euphemisms confused and antagonized employees; notification of layoffs was often nonexistent or appeared in the news before workers learned of the firings; and those who had been pink-slipped were escorted from the premises like felons. The operator of a fly-by-night sweatshop would have done things in much the same way.

By contrast, the more reputable companies made an effort to have counseling and therapy available, along with outplacement services and special stock option plans. The degree of sensitivity applied to the layoff process was sometimes as important to employees as the size and scope of their severance packages. Emotional justice seemed to be a priority. Companies were judged on how empathetic they could be in firing employees, since firing was as much a part of the job as hiring had been. In addition, these were celebrity layoffs, closely scrutinized by the same business media that had made darlings of the companies and their employees. As a result, they became a study in contrast to the harsh legacy of corporate downsizers, who had shown little remorse in "squeezing the lemon." GE's Jack Welch, among the most notorious, saw little point in making anyone feel good about layoffs. In retrospect, he reported that "he should have gone faster," but he "couldn't get through the culture."[21]

At places like Razorfish, the burden of deciding who to vote off the island had brought emotional injury to the middle managers who had been asked to make employee assessments. One such manager, who said he had suffered to distraction, explained his criteria of selection to me. Above all, he had chosen to retain "the strongest, who can produce the amount of business we'll need to survive, and of a high enough quality." These had been people with the right "attitude and energy, as well as the craft skills." Obviously, this group did not include the "prima donnas, who often decided, come Friday lunchtime, that certain kinds of work were too dull and tiresome for them." Even so, he had decided to keep some "real troublemakers who were complete pains in the ass" (more than he had let go, in fact) because they had a "useful energy that needed to be independent" of any managerial authority. Aside from the fact that he considered himself to be bit of a troublemaker, the chief reason behind this selection, he confessed, was that without them, "it would have become a boring place, with boring people doing boring work." The alternative method, which he had imagined as a play he would like to write, would have been more democratic. "We could have got everyone together in a room and said, 'Look, we need to reduce the head count by 50 percent in order to survive, and you need to help me do it. So who needs the job most?' That kind of politics of egalitarianism is what people in this industry profess, so why didn't we do it that way?"

Among the surviving fish, criticism of senior management was hardly in short supply, and there was a groundswell of audible opinion that it was time for the founders to step aside. Closer to home, however, were the verdicts on how the layoffs had been conducted. The European offices were judged to have done the best job of humanizing the firings, and the East Coast offices in the United States had been the least sensitive. Without doubt, the worst stories came from Boston. The day after I had visited, many employees got their walking orders in an early morning Saturday phone call to their home from HR. A more unfortunate date could hardly have been chosen, since it was Saint Patrick's Day—a near-sacred holiday in Boston.

Despite these criticisms, there was a more general acceptance among the fish that no one really had control over the company's financial destiny. The market was perceived as an unchallenged authority that was somehow denying the company permission to succeed, and very little could be done about it. There had been no grand betrayal by management, nor had the company been eclipsed by any of its equally beleaguered competitors. In *Falling from Grace,* her study of downward mobility, Katherine Newman found that white-collar employees tended to individualize the blame for being laid off, whereas blue-collar workers blamed the bosses.[22] At Razorfish, I found that blame was much less common than the revelation of self-deception. We fooled ourselves, many of the fish decided, into thinking that the revolution would be painless. "Why do bad things happen to good people?" was a typical phrase around the offices, as if ascribing a degree of blind fate to the discipline of the market.

Naturally, the strategists on staff had a more systematic diagnosis of the firm's economic plight, though it was hardly theology-free. Daisy Mayhew, who had recently joined Razorfish from a stint at a Wall Street brokerage, was convinced that the market was an accurate reflection of public consciousness. "Currently," the young strategist pointed out, "we don't have permission to bring the business transformation environment into being." Where does this permission come from? I asked her. As far as the public goes, she believed that "permission comes from people's readiness to allow themselves to succumb to technology instead of face-to-face human transaction. People aren't ready for that yet." Accordingly, the market had spoken clearly and accurately on that matter. But the market also responded to what she called "brand permission." Companies can win permission for their business "if their brands have done enough work" to position themselves properly. According to this cosmology, corporate brands have a measure of free will in a universe overseen by the market's ultimate, benign authority. Their power to act freely is relative, however, because it often impinges on the will of others. She had heard, for example, that "Sony was developing a retail bank," and had asked herself, "Does Sony have the brand permission to do that? Will a Citibank allow them to do that? You need the permission to play in a given space." Companies like Razorfish had pushed the limits too quickly, but there was no doubt in her mind that "eventually we will get the permission to be able to use technology to connect it all."

The digital revolution had a pivotal role to play in this theological picture. When technology finally connected us all (business-to-consumer, business-to-business, peer-to-peer), Mayhew believed that capitalism would be "more efficient as a system," and the lines of authority and permission would be "more transparent than they had been." In principle, everyone would have instant and equal access to the information they needed to function as free economic agents. In addition, the market would finally be cleansed of its imperfections and periodic dementia. The business cycle of boom and bust to which capitalism was prone would be smoothed out. There would be less risk of speculative bubbles, like the one that hoisted Internet stocks through the roof, less need for the irrational exuberance that fills them with hot air, or the irrational pessimism that grinds them into the dust. It was all a matter of consent, approval, and trust, and these would come in due time, when the world was ready to give permission. Everything that can be digital sooner or later would be.

For the time being, of course, that moment was deferred. Mayhew's dream of a New Economy that would supplant the neurotic ways of brick-and-mortar markets would have to wait. Her account reminded me of the theology of the seventeenth-century Deists. Swayed by the empirical sciences and methods of Bacon, Descartes, and Newton, they argued that a rationally ordered universe would displace the mystery-ridden universe of supernaturalist theology. Temporarily set back by the fundamentalist backlash of the Puritan Revolution, they believed that their naturalistic beliefs in Christianity would eventually prevail over the revelational religion of the old order. Then, as now, technological invention was a model for the systematic understanding of Nature as a rational process. Early Deists compared God to a blind watchmaker, who had wound up the universe and left it to run its course. In comparison, theories about the Internet had been almost as ambitious and sometimes more occult. Now the backlash had begun, and for a while, it was common to hear it described as a Puritan reaction against the overindulgence of the unorthodox.

Heartbreak House

After the February layoffs had run their course, Razorfish certainly felt like a different kind of workplace. Mirth and merriment were thin on the ground, and survivor's syndrome kicked in. The back wall of the old Triggerfish floor, which had previously hosted the Keanu Reeves poster from *The Matrix,* was painted over with "Opportunity" in large lettering and in several languages. This was internal branding with what some considered to be a Big Brother touch. Insider humor took a Gothic turn, with a distinctly mortuary tone. The death of Triggerfish and the termination of all nonessential expenses was followed by the gradual closing of European offices. Several more rounds of layoffs followed in the spring and summer, as the company shed weight in an effort to return to profitability.

The management team went through its own changes, giving up their building to move back in with the Mercer Street fish and launching a unified effort to dispel old school nostalgia. A War Room had been created for business development, and "Swat Teams" were staffed up to pitch to selected industry verticals: finance, health, media, and entertainment. For the Morale Team, the equivalent was a "rally," introduced by Kanarick as a way to focus the effort to survive: "This can only happen," he wrote, "if everyone in the company unites under this common purpose, stops thinking about the past, and only looks to the future." Kanarick's rally featured weekly detailed

Engineers of Opportunity—Internal Branding, Razorfish 2.0 (Photo by the author)

accounts of the decisions and doings of the management team and responded directly to internal rumors and concerns. It was well received as a real improvement in management communication, though its attempts to shape morale were widely viewed as top-down culture.

One feature of the rally was an internal site, set up as an employee discussion forum. The site was clearly an effort to draw the fish away from posting on public message boards, such as Vault and fuckedcompany, and to contain the PR damage wrought by employee discontent and rumors. The leaking of internal memos had become a steady stream, and the fish had to be reminded sternly about their confidentiality agreements and the company's electronics communications policies. This was hardly a concern for Razorfish alone. Management in every corner of the corporate world were getting used to seeing their company's dirty laundry hanging out on anonymous message boards. The Web had spawned a world of opportunity for employees to speak back, and hundreds of Web sites sprang up for the benefit of ex-employees to air their grievances.[23] Former and current Intel employees even used the Web site of their organization, FACEIntel (www.faceintel.com), to organize class action lawsuits against the microchip giant.[24]

At Razorfish, the preoccupation with online confidentiality and rumor suppression (non-kosher for the company culture) turned out to be the last gasp of the old guard. The new wave was apparent in the triumph of MBA terminology in most every company forum, with the exception of meetings of the design group, where New Age therapy lingo was a preferred mode of empathy. In project meetings that I attended, the biz buzzwords came thick and fast. If "holistic selling" was linked to "market addressability," and if "churn rate variance" and "data warehousing" were properly leveraged by "unified customer reviews" and effective "opportunity management," then "compelling deliverables" and "market optimization" would surely result. The writer group waged an honorable war on this terminology, but they, more than anyone, knew that language was a medium of power, and power was flowing through an idiom of expertise taught in business schools. Razorfish was no longer cranking out cool Web sites; it was "building strong but nimble cross-platform infrastructures."

The most friendly habitat of the homegrown technical dialect was the new discipline of "usability," or more accurately, a sub-unit of the new discipline of information architecture.[25] One of the firm's brand propositions was "Managers of User Experience," and it described a service that the company increasingly perceived as their competitive advantage over the Big Five's lock on Fortune 1000 businesses. Usability expertise was a product of empirical research on how Web sites were navigated and used by real people. When complemented by profiles of specific user types, it offered clients reassurance that their Web site was fully functional and not simply an extravagant expression of some designer's taste. In a time of reduced budgets, IT managers were heeding the no-nonsense advice of usability gurus like Jakob Neilsen, whose Law of the Internet User Experience decreed that "most users spend more of their time on *other* sites."[26]

Unlike product testing, where research is aimed at potential buyers, or advertising audits, where potential viewers are sampled on their perceptions, Web usability research focuses on the behavior of site users. How easy is it to navigate? How effective is the story or journey offered by the site? How efficiently does a brand attribute come across? Razorfish had its own usability lab, where test users were observed behind a two-way mirror and videotaped for analysis with clients. In addition, users were tested in their own work or home, environments where they would actually be navigating a site. As a result, clients could feel that their sites were not simply eye candy but were backed up by solid research on user experience.

The usability push was helping to win new contracts, but Razorfish was now in a market where every agency struggling to survive in e-consulting was slashing its prices. The company also had a tough time in the business press. The dotcom crash was being blamed for infecting the stock market as a whole, and Razorfish was one of the companies selected as a whipping boy. Dachismo made for easy pickings, and so many of the CEO's former boomtown boasts were recirculated as choice specimens of New Economy arrogance. The cofounders were increasingly a liability to the company. A few days after the May Day party—a subdued, arty affair in the RSUB studios, with avant-garde film and samba dancers—Dachis and Kanarick stepped down from their positions, and Jean-Pierre Maheu, the COO with a bona fide business degree, took over the helm. Within a few weeks, Dachis and Kanarick left the company entirely and sold their remaining stock. Some veterans, including employee number one, Lubling (who went off to study photography), went with them. Others saw their departure as permission for themselves to leave.

Shel Kimen, burned out and disconnected from the organization, was one of them. She was tired of being one of the few fish left active in ministering to the culture. The most recent layoffs had hit her kind of "innovative people" who believed in "a different way of doing business," while those spared seemed to her to be "less attached to the Internet's mythology of democratization." It was a decision she had deferred for several months, however. "Sometime around November," she admitted, "my heart got broken in a weird way, and I found something else to fall in love with, which was the music." She realized that this sounded "creepy." Why on earth should anyone fall in or out of love with a company? It was a question worth asking of the fish in general. In Kimen's case, at least, the warm bond was consistent with her commitment to "total risk and vulnerability" in everything she did.

Weaned on punk and indie rock in Michigan, house music in Chicago, and experimental electronica in San Francisco and New York, Kimen believed her eclectic taste would be a big asset in the music store she planned to open. Characteristically, she would be going into business with virtually no savings and with the frankly un-commercial credo that music "should be a utility and not a commodity." Was she worried about what the loss of job security would bring her way? "I've always convinced myself that I want rewards and security, too," she explained. "I just have a different definition of what that means. Security for me means having a group of people I can depend on and turn to, when the shit goes down. . . . So security is community, and reward is about providing value for that community." These had been ideals she had found at Razorfish, for a while at least. Chances are they might be more durable in the underground music scene.

Corinna Snyder lasted a few months longer. After the February reshuffle, she had been promoted to head the client partner group, where she further developed her consulting skills. By the end of a year that had left her exhausted from responding to the neediness, on all sides, of the organization, she had moved to a more traditional kind of work environment at PriceWaterhouseCoopers. There, in her new Midtown office, she said that she was learning to forget what "I had once thought, that work was the most emotionally satisfying thing in my life."

By July, Camille Habacker had joined the ranks of ex-fish who had gone freelance. In her last months as a pitch queen at Razorfish, she had become "the face of the company." Unfortunately, her would-be clients were not biting, and she was bringing in virtually no revenue. Even so, she was stunned by her inclusion in the June round of lay-offs: "Mathematically, it was a straightforward decision, but philo-sophically I was shocked." In next to no time, she was enjoying a free-lance gig as an information architect and a thirty-hour workweek (at $75 per hour) that involved "no political pressure" and "no emotional investment" in any company's success. The work was satisfying be-cause the problem-solving was a challenge, and her loyalty (important to a Scorpio) was to the project rather than to the company that had contracted her. "I don't know why I didn't do it earlier, this freelance thing. What a genius idea." Four or five years ago, the prospect of freelancing would have terrified her, but her Razorfish stint had made her "accept change as just a normal part of life."

In the period of time I had been interviewing Habacker, she seemed to have accepted that "value" always had a flip side in the business world. Many of the qualities that she and her cohort had once cherished at Razorfish had become liabilities as the company's direction shifted. Now she was learning that the profile she had favored in recruiting others at Razorfish—eccentric, self-motivated, and self-disciplined individuals—was just as likely to be a handicap elsewhere. She had recently met with a corporate recruitment officer who admitted to her that "he got nervous about people who have been freelancing for too long" because it meant "they were nonconformist and likely to be unreliable." Of the ex-fish I surveyed in February 2002, Habacker fell into one of the larger categories—13.8 percent had become freelance consultants like her. Snyder's move to PWC put her in one of the smallest categories—those who joined a large corporation (5.5 percent). Kimen's total career switch also put her in a small category (5.8 percent). Most had taken comparable jobs at firms of a similar size or smaller (34.3 percent), while a surprising number had founded their own startup businesses (11.1 percent).[27] Without the company to fulfill or disappoint their ideals, the ex-fish had the choice of carrying around their evangelism, archiving it in the museum of the New Economy, or returning it to the countercultural source, as Kimen had done. For the time being, Habacker was playing it by ear. "Right now, I'm listening to Three Dog Night," she confessed, "over and over again."

After the Kool-Aid

Love is racing across the tundra on a snowmobile which suddenly flips over, trapping you underneath. At night, the ice weasels come.

—MATT GROENING, *LOVE IS HELL*

DESPITE REPEATED RUMORS OF ITS DEMISE, RAZORFISH WAS STILL afloat when the official recession rumbled in at the end of the summer of 2001. Gone were the days, as one wag put it, when the office was like "a living Gap ad" (or as another, more romantic soul remembered it, "like the glorious café culture of Dresden before the bombing"). Managers were now expecting employees to be on the job at 9 A.M. Thus it was that some fish were already at their desks on the morning of September 11. Heads turned when the doleful drone of American Airlines 11 filled the air over SoHo on its way to the World Trade Center, just sixteen blocks to the south. When the towers fell, all networks went down, and the buzzing world of communications data ceased, almost as if the delayed impact of Y2K had finally kicked in. All along Canal Street, the sirens bawled, and the streets outside thronged with a steady caravan of dazed and dusty refugees, advancing against the southeasterly breeze. Within hours, the downtown portion of Silicon Alley was part of what authorities called the frozen zone, bounded by security perimeters and patrolled by troops and paramilitaries on the ground and by F-16s in the skies overhead.

Two years previously, the Y2K panic had been driven by a raft of catastrophe scenarios. The outcome of the scare had boosted the fortunes of technology companies hired to come up with preemptive solutions. Like other agencies, Razorfish added digital security to its service offerings and even hired a celebrity ex-hacker to anchor its team. His career track had been archetypal. Initiated into phone freakdom at age ten, elected to membership in New York's famed hacker circle, the Masters of Deception, he graduated to a post-arrest stint working for the nation's intelligence agencies ("a very shady, unethical operation," he reported) and thence to Razorfish via a Wall Street trading outfit. Because of his intimacy, over the years, with the potential for destruction, he cherished the fantasy of turning off the machine—an impulse shared by so many technologists I interviewed for this book: "Personally," he confessed, "I dream of a day where technology exists all around me, but I can free myself from it. I can see a point where technology will become the bane of a person's existence, and the purest, most chic, and earthy thing to do will be to avoid it. To be truly disconnected will be a major accomplishment."

In hindsight, his low-tech chic offered a somber insight into the events of September 11 and their aftermath. When the apocalypse finally came, it was not in the advanced form of a hack, digital glitch, or cyberwar. Instead, it involved low-tech tools (box-cutters) and fossil fuel (airplane gasoline), effectively deployed to turn advanced science and technology against their makers. To complete the picture of asymmetry, it appeared to have been masterminded by people living in caves. Nothing in the highly developed guts of the state's intelligence or security infrastructure had detected or anticipated these threats. Carnivore, the controversial monitoring system that allows the FBI to scour the Internet bitstream for intelligence, had drawn a blank, and the electronic spymasters who relied on satellite imaging, remote sensing, and telecom intercepts were caught napping. Notwithstanding its other moral dimensions, the subsequent unleashing of military superweapons on a Central Asian country long wasted and impoverished by war was a near automatic response from a culture addicted to the belief that technology would present a solution to all problems and predicaments.

This addiction to technological solutions had flourished beyond the orbit of its military origins, but it was hardly a thing apart from them. Although the development of computing technology was initially an international process, massive amounts of Department of Defense–funded R&D at U.S. companies and universities gave American producers a substantial lead in commercial markets from the late 1950s through the 1980s.[1] DOD funding of the Arpanet (the Internet's prototype) in select scientific centers followed the same pattern of military contracting. The Internet, after all, was devised as a military communications medium that would function when all others had been disabled by war.[2] It was born and bred in the conflict between two superpowers that sought out the most advanced technology to outperform one another. Western elites had come to believe that microelectronics and information technology played a decisive role in weakening the centralized economies of state communism, thereby sealing their fate. What role would IT now play in a new conflict with an asymmetrical enemy that was presumed to have little interest in the devout cause of technological modernity?

The combination of the turn of the millennium, the recession, and 9/11 converted the 1990s and its New Economy into instant nostalgia. More notably, the decade had begun to resemble a breathing space between two eras of militarization. In this scenario, the entrepreneurial New Economy was not so much an alternative to the mega-corporate Old Economy as it was a bridge between two different kinds of war economy. The "war without end" that President Bush declared against international terrorism was imitating the organizational form of the restructured, flexible economy. Pentagon managers were well on their way to adopting the Fast Company paradigms of innovation, change, and nimble strategy. In this twenty-first-century war, for example, U.S. troops were not mass industrialized army units but decentralized teams of specialized operatives, with self-directed goals and strategies. When frontline cohorts were needed on a large scale, they would be subcontracted from allies whose soldiers' lives came cheap. The fully automated battlefield, with battalions of cyborg soldiers, was an outdated fantasy, as redundant as the workerless factory in an age of flexible specialization. High-skilled labor was needed to program and operate ever smarter technology. Special Forces in the field were off the Matrix organizational chart, and lines of authority were often blurred. The delivery of long-range missile weapons was ordered just in time and designed for precision strikes. The potential range of military activity extended everywhere, dissolving the boundaries between home and "over there," while its new surveillance technologies promised zero privacy to citizens of the world. To cap it all, the goals of war were unspecified and were infinitely adaptable to circumstance.

New Patriots

The impact of 9/11 was so grievous that in almost every workplace, employees pondered the meaning and worth of their occupations. Under the circumstances, it was natural to question the purpose of all work that was nonessential. Nor did it escape notice that these had been attacks on workplaces and had taken the lives of people doing their jobs. In the anthrax scare that followed, the security of workplaces was further imperiled. Over the past two decades, the American workplace had shed its association with job security. At the same time, some employees had come to feel more at home there than they did anywhere else. The no-collar people went even further and took most of their lives to work with them. As a result, they may have been even less prepared than others to contend with the new winds of risk that blew into their lives after 9/11.

For several years, the New Economy songbook had included an ode to embracing fear and a chant against risk aversion. Executives who needed a little retraining in the new leadership qualities could sign up for a corporate weekend boot camp, where crack Israeli commando officers encouraged them to vacate their comfort zone by stepping backwards off a cliff. Razorfish had its own, slightly more progressive version, Catapult, where rappelling and white-water rafting conjoined with seminars in creativity management. With physical carnage on Wall Street and the prospect of anthrax in the mailroom, fear was now attached to palpable threats from people who meant business.

On the other side of fear, the spectacle of the sentimental company loomed large. Large corporations took out full-page ads in the *New York Times* to declare how they felt about the disaster. It was, in part, an advertising opportunity and also a way to restore advertising. Public corporations had long tried to match the personal charisma of nineteenth-century entrepreneurs. Over time, they acquired a personality and (thanks to a perverse Supreme Court interpretation of the 14th Amendment) were treated legally as persons, with rights that could be exercised and violated. Now, in the wake of the catastrophe, companies had feelings, and they expressed them in advertising. CoffeeCup, a small software company, called for swift revenge: "We would like to also say on record that if any country is found responsible for these attacks, we call for that country's complete destruction and annihilation." And again, after several communiqués: "This is our last public statement about the attacks on the U.S. It is now time for all of us to rush to be normal. We cried and we were angry in public over the attacks together. No other company would risk feeling like you, and we are very proud."[3]

As always, Razorfish was a lively sounding board for the anxieties of the moment. Some ex-fish had died in the attacks, and everyone knew names in the roll call of victims. The professional emotions that coursed through the workplace were overridden by a wave of communal self-reflection in the days after the New York office opened for business.[4] All of a sudden, the virtual world had a lesser value in the face of such physical loss and destruction. Nor was there likely to be a silver lining for the company, especially since it had recently shed its expertise in security. Eighteen months earlier, interactive services were at the cutting edge of business. In today's stumbling economy, potential clients were more likely to see Razorfish as a luxury item, unless the company could prove in advance that its services would cut costs. If that were not enough, arbiters of taste like *Vanity Fair* editor Graydon Carter responded to the attacks by proclaiming the "death of irony," hitherto an essential ingredient in the company culture. Down on Mercer Street, some employees were actually expressing relief at the news of irony's demise and were rallying around the flag.

Like so many other urbanites, the fish were faced with a newfound permission to be patriotic; Old Glory was being unfurled throughout the streets and storefronts of downtown Manhattan, and fighting talk was surfacing in the most unlikely quarters. All of this came as a welcome revelation to Aleck Bourbon, the information architect who had been a soul of the party at Triggerfish: "Perhaps there is something in our generation," he wondered, "that has wanted to be able to embrace something like the flag, to genuinely commit to something as simple as patriotism, or religion, or spirituality in a way that is not conflicted or marked with postmodern irony. Irony and cynicism give you the opportunity to be feel superior, but they don't give you anything lasting to hold on to. I see a lot of folks being outwardly cynical, but inwardly wishing they had something." As we spoke, he gestured toward the two or three flags around us that fish had pinned to their work stations and mused on how this new embrace of the mainstream would play inside the Razorfish culture. Having been an unapologetic member of what he called the "subversive counterculture that rejects the dominant culture," he was now considering "what it means to reject America" in a climate where the country thinks only "in black and white." The solution, for him, at least, was to renounce a mentality that "tends to view everything in six shades of gray, because it begets cynicism." For the time being, he was "charmed by the prospect of individuals reconnecting with more simple values like family, community, and respect for people."

Bourbon could have sounded like someone who cut their cloth to fit the moment, but he was not alone in the Razorfish offices, or anywhere else in the city. In the aftermath of the attacks, New Yorkers became openly compassionate in a way they were not ordinarily allowed to be. The empathy toward the city from other parts of the country was unexpectedly spirited. For one thing, the victims had held jobs that were recognizable to the rest of America: the suburban business class and its secretarial staff, in-person service workers, and the public service workers in fire and police departments who were lionized as working-class heroes. By contrast, those New Yorkers who traditionally were less popular with middle America—ultra-liberal New York, ultra-ethnic New York, cosmopolitan New York, queer New York, countercultural New York—were uneasy spectators of this new romance, as they had been of the devastation itself. Used to being viewed, on the national landscape, as pariahs, many were unsure about how best to preserve their distinctive opinions amid the tidal wash of feelings that was being channeled and distilled through the mass media and the White House into patriotic fuel.

Most of the fish, I found, fell into this latter camp. The flags on display in the office were primarily an emotional response, a hopeful (and short-lived) gesture at staving off the helplessness that gripped everyone who lived or worked downtown. Pressed for an analysis of the political situation, many employees held views that were quite at odds with the vengeful saber rattling that would take the country to war. "This moment has been a long time coming," explained a project manager who sat next to Bourbon. "If you sit down and list the grievances of all the people in the world that might attack us—not that it gives them the right to attack—it's easy to see what they might get angry about." "Should we return their anger in the form of missiles?" he asked. "No, we should be rethinking our behavior in other parts of the world. I'm fed up with being seen as an Ugly American."

It was too early to say whether these views were in tune with the mantra that "everything changed" after September 11. While the concerns of the workplace temporarily took a backseat, it turned out that most things, of course, had not changed much at all. Each day, for example, brought fresh news of hefty layoffs, as corporations in every sector cynically took advantage of the crisis to slice their workforce. Within six weeks, more than half a million full-time employees were axed nationally, plus many more part-timers and undocumented workers. In Silicon Alley, a cold front of consolidation was taking its full toll on the Internet industry. Capital funding was thin on the ground, and the recession was nipping at the heels of Web companies still in business. Digital skills were no longer the preserve of interactive service companies; they were more widely spread throughout the business world. Silicon Alley was morphing into a less distinct entity, and its habits, energies, and spirit were being dispersed into other parts of the economy, demonstrating how fluid the landscape of work had become.

Some of Razorfish's rivals had recently gone under (MarchFirst) or had been acquired (Zefer, Organic, Agency). The firm's new CEO, Jean-Pierre Maheu, a solid Frenchman with a family, who had cut his own salary from $400,000 to $300,000, was about to shutter the company's remaining overseas offices. The workforce everywhere had been sliced down to about 300, and the fish were reminded constantly that their continued employment was a personal achievement. The clients were the big corporate names that Razorfish had started chasing a year earlier: Ford, Bechtel, Cisco, Genentech, Fox International, HBO, Glaxo SmithKline, Avaya, Vodafone, McKinsey, Cemex, Verizon, and 3Com.

Last Days on the Fourth Floor (Photo by the author)

Yet there was still a place for the old-time silicon religion. At Fish-Patty, an August 2001 offsite retreat for the Boston and New York offices, a West Coast technology evangelist had flown in to deliver a motivational speech about the new wave of digital change, in the form of the Next Generation Internet Platform (NGIP). This initiative involved "metadata engineering" aimed at producing an efficient knowledge map of all of the data held by an organization. "You guys are all survivors," he reminded his audience, "because you still believe, and because you trust your digital DNA. We are still pioneering this stuff, and we need to get on the Third Wave." More sober by far, Maheu himself spoke of "keeping the faith" and envisaged a time soon when the company would hire and grow again. For the time being, he urged everyone to "listen to markets and listen to clients." How was the company now defined? Razorfish, according to its CEO, was a "global digital solutions provider" offering "project-based consulting services."

Out on the floor, the fish had their own spin on the company's shrinkage. For the past year, each employee had affiliated with one of four networks (Experience, Technology, Value, Strategy), but the insider joke was that there were really only two—the Competency and the Incompetency networks. It was the Competents, for the most

RAZORFISH EAST

FishPatty 2001

RAZORFISH'S 2002 DIRECTION . NEX' GENERATION INTERNET PROJECTS
CLIENT CONVERSATION . WORKSHOPS . NETWORK BREAKOUTS .
GLOFISH AWARDS . TALENT SHOW . MUSIC . FOOD . DRINKS

BOSTON . NEW YORK
INFO: ALEX.SNELL@RAZORFISH.COM

BONY Together
September 7 . 2001

FishPatty, 2001, Razorfish East (Design by Hoover Chung)

part, who had survived the layoffs, and they were working more efficiently than ever before. "Our project discipline now exceeds our
client's discipline," reported an information architect from the old
Triggerfish team, "and we are being stretched across the skills landscape." "We are becoming Renaissance men and women again" was
his wry conclusion. This time around, however, he had learned to protect his time, by working no more than fifty hours a week, and also his
creativity: "I am preserving the creative side of myself from the va-
garies of the market, and from other things I have no control over."

By the end of 2001, the reorganization known as Razorfish 2.0
seemed to be paying off. Now 75 percent of each employee's time was
billable, and the company had returned to pro forma profitability. It
had "come back from the brink," as an article in *Crain's* magazine put
it.[5] In the first quarter of 2002, the company showed real profits again,
and in the months that followed, postings for job openings began to
appear. By July, the fish were once again enjoying performance-based

bonuses. Against all the odds, the company had survived. So, too, most employees were finding their work as intellectually challenging as in the past, if not more so; it was "genre-changing, bolt-from-the-blue, theoretically interesting computing work," as one technology enthusiast put it. "The culture of free exploration and idea sharing for its own sake" was no longer rewarded, but "the memory of permission" lingered, as did the passion for innovating the medium wherever a client project allowed.

The Competents tended to be a little older, with their party days behind them. Gone were most of the strategists who had been rushed in to lead the push toward e-consulting. Folks like Bourbon, who had fought their influence, were happy to see the back of them: "We had a sudden influx of people who wore blue shirts and khaki pants, and who questioned the quality of our work. They assumed they had been brought in to teach us what professionalism really was and make us value the things they valued. Well, it turned out these MBA types were not all that great, their solutions did not help the company, and they had a cancerous impact on the culture. Now we're left with the more creative people, but we no longer have an outlet. We're all beaten down, and our heart is not in it any more."

It was easy to find a match from the other side for Bourbon's thumbnail account. Project manager Lola Brill had been hired along with the MBA wave and had run the gauntlet of scorn from the old guard when she tried to introduce standard tools and templates for coordinating projects: "These people were totally in charge," she recalled, "and they were here in order to be wild and creative and out of the box. They had no interest in being managed efficiently or in helping clients to manage more efficiently, and now they are mostly gone." With a background in experimental film, Brill was not an MBA herself, and so she did not have a particularly high-minded sense of the company's business product: "Basically," she admitted, "we are building a way for people to be able to buy more hamburgers." As far as she was concerned, the struggle for the Razorfish soul had "all boiled down to who was willing to cede or win control over the process of building." In her view, the old guard had lost, fortunately, and those among their number who had stayed on payroll had done so by ceding control. Now it was "the client who called the shots."

Brill and Bourbon held mutually opposed views of the company's recent history, yet each acknowledged the basic dimensions of the internal struggle that had consumed Razorfish and other companies in the Internet service sector. It had been well over a year since hostilities had first broken out. Both Brill and Bourbon felt their side had prevailed, though each viewed the victory as a Pyrrhic one. In reality, there had been no conclusive outcome. The market's disregard for the sector as a whole had provided little support for either side of the case. Nor had the company's new client base eviscerated the creative dash of the old Razorfish. Each project continued to require a different mix of expertise. Some were long on strategy talk, others wanted nuts and bolts infrastructure, and still others wanted a sexy product, for which the company continued to win design awards.

Much had happened since my first Triggerfish meeting, but the spirited debate I had witnessed then—between advocates of "building" and advocates of "consulting"—was still generating some heat. At that meeting, the battle lines had been clear. Were we making tangible things or were we trading intangible services? Over the course of my time at the company, I had seen how important it was to some fish (and to no-collar people in general) that their work retain some connection, however romantic, to the notion of craft manufacture. For employees in this camp, consulting was still regarded as a less noble form of labor, yet they saw that the goal of securing long-term client relationships was more highly valued by company managers and by Wall Street. Had Razorfish ever turned the corner on this question? Despite all the management efforts to persuade them otherwise, some employees continued to believe that they were working for a media or design company and that they were making useful, cultural things. This belief was critical to their professional identity. It bolstered whatever security or sense of control they had within the company ranks, and it immunized them against their ultra-corporate clients.

The Primordial Soup and the Black Art

In reality, Razorfish was a hybrid kind of company, as were most New Economy firms that tried to preserve their options. They did not fit the mold of mature industries or their sub-branches, and they were groomed to respond to the uncertainties of a volatile economy. To their detriment, they had been guided and judged by business models lifted from other industries—media in New York, and technology in Silicon Valley. Neither of these models turned out to be very applicable. Content firms had to conform to the advertising- or subscription-based forms of media marketing, and yet they were also incubated and prepared for the public markets. Integrators like Razorfish had actively pursued the Silicon Valley route of the IPO, yet they were compelled to compete with consulting firms that were private partnerships or with small design shops that retained an independent profile. The result was a bit of a mess, primarily because the business world was not primed to deal with such crossbreeds. According to the lore of traders, Wall Street does not like hybrids. The analysts had treated the firm as an Internet stock, but now it was classified as telecom. Neither designation made much sense to what the company actually did.

Unlike firms in a traditional industry, Razorfish was not tied to any specific product, vendor, platform, or client but responded to variable combinations of all four. Naturally, this agnostic stance proved an impediment to the development of standardized processes for carrying out projects. In the beginning, everything had been new. The fish had been swimming, as Bourbon saw it, in "a primordial soup of roles and skills and talents and activities—a new profession and a new communications medium with no real precedents." "There was a time," he recalled, "when we were doing very important, groundbreaking work, as a company, for the profession at large. There was a lot of internal talk and discussion about roles and processes. It was often painful; it was not pretty; it was something that needed to be done over and over again, not just for the company, but for the discipline, the culture, and the future of the field. Then it all stopped, and all of that talking was seen simply as unproductive work." As the company's need to survive took precedence, the evolution of the process was put on hold, and to Bourbon's mind, the fish remained in the primordial soup, "figuring things out as we go."

Would those conversations have led to a codified process that all the disciplines would respect and obey? Surely that was one of the goals behind the effort to forge a proprietary methodology, or template, that made the most efficient use of knowledge management? Bourbon demurred. "There can be no single template. We are an Internet company, and so we want to apply Internet technology to everything that we do. But I can say with absolute certainty that knowledge management is a human process, and there is no intranet site that can take the place of human decision-making and human ingenuity. The point is not to codify everything, and that's a healthy thing to acknowledge and embrace." Razorfish had indeed built a business development intranet that hosted a mass of proposals and solutions from previous projects, along with documents and papers from the knowledge management group, urging a more efficient use of the company's collective intelligence. Bourbon explained why it was hardly ever used: "We are a company of subversives who don't want to just take a template off the shelf. There's no way you could ever impose a knowledge management system on this company. That's not how we think, how we work, or what we value. It's like the difference between following a recipe and really being able to cook."

In his view, there was even reason to suspect the criteria that usability experts had so far developed as rules for producing good Web sites. Following the recipe and observing standard measures of navigability, typeface consistency, and the like was no guarantee of a quality product.[6] Nor was it possible, he believed, to quantify a good user experience. It was all in the cooking, or in the Web developer's head. There was only so much that could ever be standardized, and digital artisans like Bourbon were at odds with any attempts to prove otherwise. In addition, he believed that knowledge workers, with their nonphysical product, differed from preindustrial craftsman and that their industrial future would not follow the same path that physical manufacture had followed. A Web site was not functional in the same way as a gun or a car. No two people were ever likely to agree about how well a Web site worked or even whether it worked.

Lola Brill, a devotee of templates, saw the matter more from the perspective of custom manufacture: "You don't need to have the exact same car to be able to use the same set of tools. A common set of tools will allow you to work on a truck or on a sports car. In a shop with five workers, this doesn't matter so much; everyone will hear and know a little bit about everything." In a shop of eighty people, she argued, templates and codification made perfect sense: "It's a way of ensuring that you don't make the same mistakes twice." From her point of view, as a project manager, the templates were primarily for monitoring progress. They didn't alter the creative process much, if at all. For her, then, the task of managing the creatives remained "a nightmare." "They are not like code writers or programmers," she declared. "I can ask a designer, 'Is it done?' and they'll say, 'No.' 'Is it almost done?' and they'll say, 'Not even close.' The next day, it's done because they had a burst of inspiration. It can take weeks for them to go from 20 percent done to 30 percent done, and then it goes to 90 percent in a day."

Frustrated as she often was with the quixotic work tempo of the creatives, the codification that Brill had in mind was not the kind that led inevitably to rote standardization and passive worker drones. "Ideally," she mused, "any codifying of the tool set should be to increase the flexibility we need to respond to different projects, clients, and team members." All along, this had been the challenge faced by companies like Razorfish, and meeting it had been slow going. She had expected the company to fold before it got much further along that road, but others would pick up the challenge.

In moments of distraction, Brill told me, she pried old sewing needles from between the floorboards beneath her. These leftovers from the garment workers whose toil and industry directly preceded hers, she said, helped her place her own work "in a historical context." What, she wondered, would her company leave behind? It was a poignant thought, and all the more compelling if you took the elevator, as I sometimes did, to the top floor of the Razorfish building, where the local branch of the Social Security Administration was housed. In reality, this was the Chinatown branch, and at any time of the day, dozens of laid-off garment workers could be found, seated expectantly. Most of them were immigrants from the coastal provinces of China where factories were already cranking out most of the computer parts that Razorfish needed to perform its daily work. By the end of 2001, ads had even begun to appear for Web shops and advanced Web services in China. Modern Translation, a Web site design and localization company in Guandong province, sent me one such solicitation, promoting its "experienced translators and technical specialists" and its offerings—a "full service package or just one of the solutions"—at prices that were beyond competitive.

Of all the disciplines, it was the technologists who saw their own future reflected in the career of the garment industry. Rocky Blint, one of the last techies to be recruited at Razorfish, had put in time at companies all over Silicon Alley and had a sober understanding of how the industry valued his skills. "Supply caught up, our skills became commoditized, and now they can be outsourced, just like any other commodity labor, for one-tenth of our current price." As we spoke, he gestured toward a copy of the magazine *Silicon India*, on a work table nearby. "We bill $175 an hour for Java work that can be done for $25 in India." So far, Razorfish had outsourced only a small portion of its work to a local partner that used Indian programmers, but Blint reckoned it was only a matter of time before the volume increased. "Everything that can be commoditized, will be," he joked, and predicted that "brand intelligence was next in line to be priced down." If it continues, "we will soon be in the same boat as the garment industry."

The garmentos had seen their high-volume production emigrate overseas. The only jobs that could be preserved were in the custom market—quality work that could not be entrusted to low-wage contracting. That is, until a new influx of cheap immigrant labor, combined with loosened labor regulation, allowed the sweatshops to return to Chinatown, Sunset Park, and Williamsburg. In Blint's view, Net workers might well be reduced to similar choices in the near future. Some would continue to be labor aristocrats, seizing on high-end niche opportunities to do custom work. Most of the others would have no choice but to compete with the cheap labor markets of Eastern Europe and South Asia, by taking discounted, chopshop work on the low end. In his speech at the FishPatty gathering, Maheu acknowledged these conditions when he floated his blueprint for a revived company, with a two-tier labor system. New hires would be doing the bulk of the standardized work, leaving the custom tasks to veteran fish.

Blint could see the appeal of the historical analogy with preindustrial craft, but like Bourbon, he believed it had its limits. For a while, his kind had benefited from what he called the "black art of craft," when their skills were arcane and sought after like an alchemist's stone. But technical skills could no longer be hoarded the way they used to be. For centuries, freemasons protected their monopoly on knowledge of their trades through oaths of secrecy and by limiting the labor supply of their skills. In modern times, hackers had created their own stylized version of a secret craft society. In the age of the Internet, however, technical knowledge was much too easily transferred to stay in one place for very long, and there were no craft unions to look out for those whose livelihood was threatened as a result. Blint acknowledged that he was on his own, in a profession that favored the young, and that he was likely to face pitfalls that were deeper and longer than the high-flying rewards had been.

Potemkin Industry?

It was tempting to conclude that the Internet industry was going through a cycle in the course of a decade that the New York garment industry had taken a century to complete. A peculiar intimacy had developed between these two workplaces. Their employees constantly passed each other, without much acknowledgment, on the stairwells or in the elevators of multistory buildings they shared, often at the end of equally long shifts. Like the garment sweatshops that they often displaced, Silicon Alley firms could set up shop and disappear overnight without leaving much of a trace. And like the world of fashion, Silicon Alley hosted a sexy high-end industry that obscured the harsh conditions endured by low-wage HTML, data processing, and microelectronics assembly workers all over the world.[7] There were many other factors, however, that did not fit the parallel at all.

For one thing, there was always some doubt that Silicon Alley hosted an industry, let alone one that was likely to mature. If new media was an industry, it was one that existed to transform other industries. Yet employees habitually referred to "our industry" as if it were an established ecosystem with normative, if fickle, patterns of growth. So, too, most of the entrepreneurs, boosters, and promoters who built Silicon Alley had long-term aims. The Alley had its own newspapers, magazines, trade associations, and lobby groups. In its heyday, hundreds of thousands of people worked there in fairly well-defined professional groupings. Yet there were always influential voices, many of them insiders, who doubted that anything like an industry existed, or could exist, on the basis of the commercial potential of Internet services. There were even more naysayers on the sidelines, who saw only a massive shell game, gussied up to resemble an industry for the purposes of conning the pants off anyone gullible enough to play along. For the doubters, Silicon Alley and Multimedia Gulch, in San Francisco, were the equivalent of Potemkin villages, constructed to impress investors, or Western frontier towns with faux façades that concealed the truth about the gold rush.

Certainly, the Internet stock boom lent itself to whimsical claims and bogus feats of construction. But the employees who toiled there were all too conscious of its industrial reality; they put in their long hours, and they knew a good job when they saw one. The depth of knowledge and the level of skills they developed were on a par with other industries, and their standards of professionalism conformed to the pattern followed by emergent disciplines. If their experience differed, it was because of the velocity of change and reorganization within their workplaces and the toll it took on them as risk-bearing individuals. Constant alterations of strategy, company identity, and work orientation undermined any sense of operating in a stable industrial environment. This fluidity was quite unlike employment in a traditional organization, governed by formal work rules and rituals and by a common understanding of products, markets, and performance criteria. A firm like Razorfish morphed from one form of business organization to another—design shop, Web integrator, digital change manager, e-consultant, digital solution provider—and its service offerings changed accordingly. Similarly, 360hiphop was staffed to make a multimedia impact, but its methods of reaching a market audience were entirely experimental, and as a financial entity, it was built to flip. Even after it was acquired and pared down, its employees were still not very sure about what kind of company it was or had been.

Most New Economy firms were on the same wavelength. If they had clever managers, they were assembled with minimal starch and maximal flex to turn on a dime. In this regard, the analogy with apparel was threadbare. Fashion can be fickle, but demand for clothing is constant, and so there is an immortal dimension to the industry as a whole. By contrast, high technology is governed by the periodic obsolescence of its tools, products, and services. An industrial region like Silicon Valley may have relative long-term stability, but its companies are quite porous, their product development cycles are short, their personnel are highly mobile, and their markets are unpredictable. The urban new media sector was modeled along the same lines, but the conditions under which it developed were even more provisional and likely to alter from quarter to quarter. Each phase of a company's operations was more likely to be transitional than constitutional; each client, partner, or user could have a potential impact on the firm's shape; and each employee could play several roles, both within the organization and in a client-facing capacity.

When the economic downturn deepened, the cheerful line around town was that "the Internet is not going away." On that score, there was no doubt, though the Internet was no longer a mind-expander; it had become an ordinary domestic appliance. Another common truism on employees' lips was that of the swinging pendulum: it will come back around. However useful as a slogan of hope, this was less credible as an economic forecast. In a conventional industry, subject to the ups and downs of the business cycle, the pendulum metaphor may have been applicable. For no-collar people, history, as the Soviet critic Viktor Shklovsky once put it, was more like the knight's move in chess: it took a nonlinear direction. Or it was like the time warp in some episode of *Star Trek* that placed you in an alternate universe, where the environment was slightly modified and the characters, while familiar, were speaking and behaving in different ways. Since you were smart, adaptable, and fearless, you joined the team and quickly learned the new language and the new customs. Places like Silicon Alley captured and fermented the energies, resources, and aspirations of the moment, but they were not built for the ages, not when "Change Your Mind" was tattooed on the brow of the companies that set up shop there.

Candyland Agonistes

In such a volatile environment, local lore about a Golden Age seems all the more necessary. Aleck Bourbon had made a strong case for the good old days, but he could see it was all relative. "As much as it sometimes feels like a morgue, this is still a utopian place. My friends all say 'You work in Candyland. You have the best job in the world.' And I have to agree. Razorfish at its worst is probably better than mostly anywhere else." Lola Brill, who had no time for Bourbon's nostalgia, felt much the same way: "I love it here," she gurgled, "and wish it could go on forever. The mix of people, the community of respected peers, the sense of mutual responsibility, and the trust in individuals doing what they have to do. That's not easy to find."

This was where I had come in, eighteen months earlier, when I read the Vault posting about how good it was for employees at Razorfish. How close had I gotten to the nub of that claim, and what lessons had I learned from the employees I had been following around? Among the features that consistently rated as the people's choice was the absence of chains of command between employees and managers. Almost everyone I interviewed for this book believed that employees had come to exercise a surprisingly large share of control over their work. Authority and responsibility were more evenly distributed, self-management was the norm, and honesty and frankness in interpersonal communication were accepted behavior. The rituals and habits of deference were curtailed, if not entirely suspended, along with those other protocols of rank that serve to remind white-collar workers of their subordinate place in an organization. Many employees experienced the result as a restoration of personal respect and dignity, and it was prized as highly as any measure of monetary compensation. These conditions of autonomy arose from the uncertain operating environment of the industry and from the clout that highly skilled employees wielded over managers who were grateful buyers of their knowledge. But in many New Economy workplaces, the privilege was not restricted to a hotshot cadre; it was extended to all employees and was firmly established in the culture.

From what they had been told or had witnessed, this kind of power sharing was a rare circumstance. Despite her youth, Josie Baxter, who left Razorfish after the first round of layoffs, somehow knew that "this was not the way that capitalism was supposed to be. It was more like those holidays the Romans called Saturnalia where the slaves and servants got to be masters for a day." She was not alone in wondering how management would ever be able to reclaim their authority. Livia Jacobson, a middle manager at rival consultancy Organic, recalled that "the labor relations were entirely inverted from everything else I'd experienced in my professional life. Most of my job was aimed at pleasing my people and keeping them from leaving for a better offer." Nicholas Roope, a veteran new media entrepreneur in London with experience in several companies, explained that "it is absolutely necessary to be as free as possible when you are developing a new medium. The folks at the top know this, but they don't know anything about the medium themselves, so the empowerment has to be spread around." In his experience of management, he said, "once you've given it away, it is so difficult to take back the power and start issuing orders."

Free Agent Nation boosters could go overboard with this apparent repeal of authority. *Fast Company* eulogizers preached worker empowerment in a rhetorical style that was lifted lock, stock, and barrel from the Marxist phrase book. Employees called the shots, and those who lost their jobs were viewed as souls that had been saved. Yet the New Economy was a long way off from the dictatorship of the proletariat. Employee stock option plans offered a stake in company wealth but were rarely linked to genuine forms of employee participation in decisions about policy and work design and almost never to decisions about investments, hiring and firing, and the closure of offices.[8] In this respect, they were a pale shadow of a century's worth of previous attempts, mostly in Europe, at employee self-management, such as the *autogestion* of factory workers in the 1960s and the role played in national governments by worker councils in earlier decades.[9] This gulf between employee empowerment and executive power became more apparent when the layoff season kicked in. Even then, however, it was not uncommon for employees to judge the performance of senior management as if they were working for the employees rather than vice versa.

The origins of Baxter's Saturnalian mentality lay in Silicon Valley engineering culture, and those who hailed from that background had a clear picture of its evolution.[10] According to Imran Ray, a technologist with a Razorfish client in San Francisco, "Bay Area programmers always wielded the power and drove the corporate structure. Companies were valued on the talent of their engineers, and I am eternally grateful that, for once in history, the worker was more valuable than the company itself." At one time, Ray had been interested personally in coordinating that power, by becoming the "Jimmy Hoffa of a programmers' cooperative," until he realized that "we are not the ones being exploited. More often than not, we are doing the exploiting, and it is the companies that should be protected from us, not the other way around, because, unlike with CPAs and doctors, there's no professional certification in this business." Ray, who moved to Northern California in the early 1990s, had made the most of this advantage. In his current position, he had negotiated a $400,000 salary, with five years of job security and three months of severance pay, alongside guarantees that he could be fired only for felony crimes or for refusing to work. In addition, the execution of his job (which he restricted to a forty-hour workweek) left him oodles of time to pursue his true passions of surfing, snowboarding, and mountain biking.

At that moment in time, Ray knew he was surfing an economic wave, but he also believed that his advantage was long term and nearly impregnable. "Managers," he declared, "will never rein us in, because engineers are the natural resource of this industry. You can't have an oil company without oil." Nor did Ray fear technological de-skilling. "Even if they build computer systems with cognitive skills that are smarter than us, which Oracle already has, they will always need us to build the systems. Oracle is more complex than my mind can comprehend, but it's not more complex than a thousand minds like mine. Collectively, the engineers will always be more advanced than the tools."

The contest that Ray was describing—between smart tools and the collective intelligence of employees—was fundamental to industrial history, and it had become even more pronounced in a knowledge economy based on mental labor. For all his pessimism about the ability of capitalists to de-skill and subordinate workers through the introduction of machinery, Marx forecast that capitalism would increasingly depend on what he called the "general intellect" of skilled scientific workers (or the "general productive forces of the social brain") to innovate the technologies it needed to maintain growth and increase productivity.[11] More recent commentators, in the Italian autonomist school, have observed that this reliance on the brainpower and technical skills of employees, combined with the cooperative nature of their knowledge, has complicated the task that employers and managers face in controlling a technoscientific workforce.[12] No-collar workers like Ray knew they were on the frontline of this contest, and they had their own traditions to draw on for ammunition. For one thing, the New Economy workplace was still heavily influenced by the pre-dotcom ideals that are often referred to as the "hacker ethic": open standards, free access to information, and informal networks of cooperation; unregulated speech; the sharing of code and resources; and the decentralization of power and authority.[13] The widespread persistence of these ideals has made it more difficult for corporations to stop employees from taking their knowledge with them or to "enclose" ideas and technologies as their own property, despite the consolidation of Internet real estate in fewer and fewer hands and the devising of intellectual property laws to reinforce their power.[14]

So, too, highly skilled technologists like Ray had managed to hold on to their own individual bargaining hand. His position was difficult to match, yet I found traces of his sense of entitlement, minus the engineer's hubris, among a wide range of employees. Even those whose skills were less tangible, and thus less valuable, than programming know-how enjoyed an appreciable advantage if their employer promoted their intellect as a firm's stock-in-trade. Although market conditions would affect this bargaining power, it was part of the long-term makeup of knowledge-based companies and was not simply a temporary side-effect of the boom. As long as companies were going to trade on innovative ideas and intellectual services, their managers would have to cede some power to brainy, switched-on employees.

The informality of the no-collar workplace and work style was an obvious symbol of these nonstandard arrangements, and so the spread of casual dress and like-minded liberties into Old Economy companies was very closely watched. The traditional managerial class resented the appeal of organizations where privileges could be enjoyed without serving due time in the corporate ranks. But what they feared more was the normalization of Baxter's Saturnalia and the prospect that the granting of autonomy would be taken for granted by employees who had no sense of rank-ordered etiquette or patience for protocol and who had an abiding infatuation with changing things to suit themselves. In reality, the distribution of authority was already happening in a less spectacular fashion. As more and more companies adopted the Web as a business system, decision-making was being slowly decentralized by virtue of the new networking capacity and would eventually be pushed out further to the edges of their organizations. Veteran fish who had seen the technology penetration over seven years swore they could see these changes beginning to occur in the companies of their clients. "You can't put the genie back in the bottle," was a common expression.

Counting the Costs

Because it was guru-driven, in part, New Economy reformism applied to managers as much as to employees. There were many risible examples. Typical of the times was the executive who decided to call himself Vice President of Ignorance because he believed that "what matters is what you don't know."[15] Kyle Shannon, cofounder and CEO of Agency.com, named himself Chief People Officer to advertise his company's priorities and his own accessibility to employees (who addressed him as 3-CPO). In general, no-collar managers were at pains to downplay their importance. As the general manager of the Razorfish office in New York put it to me, "if I got hit by a truck tomorrow, would the business be fine? I believe it would." He and others tried to follow the principle that the hand of management should be light, though not invisible.

Were employees well served by this principle? On the one hand, the freedom to operate without constant or rigid supervision and to exercise personal control over work schedules was seen as a general blessing. Yet self-management, if it was not supported adequately, often meant that employees had no one to protect them, no one to train or assist in the development of their career skills, no one to evaluate their performance, and no one to take responsibility for structural problems within the company. Individuals found themselves taking on burdens that company managers would ordinarily have assumed. The flatter or looser the organization became, the fewer opportunities there existed for promotion and career advancement. Middle management positions were almost always cut as part of a company reorganization, leaving employees, as they saw it, at the mercy of senior management. When it was left untended, the culture of self-management could turn into a recipe for ill will and plummeting morale on a scale much steeper than that experienced in a more hierarchical firm.

Those who were able to survive inside a flexible company craved the kind of manager who would be a trusted mentor with no veto power over their doings, or as the ever vulnerable Brian Schor put it, someone they could treat "like an older brother or sister." Over time, they often learned that they were dealing with a new kind of managerial entity who retained power but did not exercise authority. This applied to "plainclothes," or viral, managers as much as to executive officers. As one Razorfish manager described it: "I try to be a guardrail, a catalyst, or a sounding board, anything that doesn't make me seem like a sergeant." In return, employees were encouraged to levy much of their own work discipline through self-criticism and self-improvement, or else they could look to their peers for guidance in these areas. The result was a *needy organization,* whose members were constantly in search of clarification and assurance. Volunteer stress therapy and morale-making had largely supplanted the fixed arrangement of incentives and rewards administered by senior mentors. From the perspective of employees, liberation management could feel like managers had been liberated from their obligations. One of my Triggerfish neighbors described how she compensated: "I always try to see management as working for me rather than the other way around. Ideally, that's the way it should be."

In times of economic duress, the pressure of the market bore down directly on individuals rather than filtering through layers of the organization.[16] The liberties that were the hallmark of the no-collar workplace could easily turn into mental and economic traps if they were not supported by an infrastructure of accountable managers and professional development options. "I'm free," observed a San Francisco fish, "to follow paths that lead everywhere but a stable career. Free to change my discipline, job title, clothing, and personality, and I'm also free to sleep under a bridge." This last option may have seemed melo-dramatic, but it was inspired by the recent publication of a picture that got worldwide press circulation and was adopted as the unofficial poster image of the dotcom crash. It showed an apparently homeless man standing on a San Francisco street corner, wearing a Razorfish baseball cap. He was holding a hand-written cardboard sign that read, "Will code HTML for food," with "please help" and "God bless you" scrawled in the corners.

The panhandler's plight may have been extreme, but it was a para-ble of the flexible economic times. The liberalization of the workplace had followed much the same path as the liberalization of the econ-omy. Like economic deregulation, corporate de-layering had freed up individual employees (human capital) to manage their own access to market resources, whether within a company or as outside contrac-tors. Like the dismantling of the social safety net, supporting struc-tures within the organization had been dissolved, leaving individuals to assume obligations that the company, or the state, had previously shouldered. Hours spent on the job increased, and the stress load in-tensified. In recompense, the emotional and social bonds of company culture helped to relieve the strain. The workplace provided a ready supply of peer empathy along with helpings of high-octane fun. Cor-porate employees in Cold War organizations had little exposure to this blend of pleasure and danger on the job. It was a new kind of game, and for young guns eager to prove their mettle and test their limits, the rewards were irresistible.

Over time, most of the players could turn into losers, along with all of those declared unfit for the sport for reasons of age, attitude, or un-readiness. As Ulrich Beck has pointed out, there was nothing unusual about societies with winners and losers; what was new, however, was an economy of extreme risk where "the rules of winning and losing become unclear and hard for individuals to grasp . . . no one can tell you what you will have to learn so that you are needed in the fu-ture."[17] The do-it-yourself society came in a package marked "direc-tions not included." In relatively stable economies that had leaned to-ward full, standard employment for well over a century, nothing had prepared workers for such a radical uncertainty about the rules for survival, let alone getting ahead.

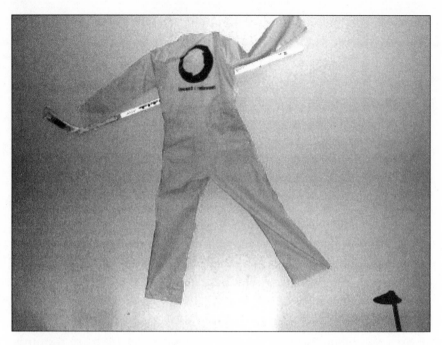

The Internal Museum—Orange Jumpsuit as Art, Razorfish, New York (Photo by the author)

Nor were there any guidelines for those who equate rules with justice. Before she left the firm to move to Sweden, my Triggerfish neighbor told me that she was going there to look for "a just job in a more just economy." She had found a just job at Razorfish, but the firm had not been able to offer sanctuary from the raw economic weather that blew through its rafters. She was hoping for more balance between the two, and she had decided, from her business visits to Scandinavia, that her quest might be better served in a country known for its humane work policies. Our conversation had turned to questions that were quite current among industry-watchers at the time. Was the workplace idyll of the New Economy possible only in boom times? If so, was it a pricey indulgence rather than a reasonable expectation of all employees? She knew that this was a popular perception about the industry and had seen many of her colleagues accept this line of thinking. "It's like saying we can only have good things, like women's rights or human rights, if you are affluent, and then you put a price on these things, or you see them as toys that get handed out only when there's enough to go around." She was none too comfortable with this attitude, and she seemed to think that a gratifying job was more a matter of justice than it was a fringe benefit of the right kind of education or a reward for a lucky throw of the Nasdaq dice.

Hardly anyone in its workforce thought of the New Economy as "just." Its digerati boosters talked the fast talk about a rising tide that would lift all boats, but those who tapped away on its keyboards learned to tailor their habits and expectations to fit a much more volatile scenario. All the same, the workplaces of the New Economy brought ashore some ideals that would qualify as utopian, if that term were not so ragged from overuse. Those ideals were an outgrowth of the hacker ethic, they responded to decades of calls to humanize the workplace, and they coincided with a wave of management reforms. Yet the odds against their survival were always hefty, and not just because they came of age in an economy where gambling and speculating on long odds was becoming a widespread norm. The rough justice of the market was enough of an ordeal, but there was a more sobering cost, and it was much closer to home. When work becomes sufficiently humane, we are likely to do far too much of it, and it usurps an unacceptable portion of our lives. If there is a single argument in this book against the pursuit of the humane workplace, then it rests its case there. Not by any boss's coercive bidding, but through the seductive channel of "work you just couldn't help doing," had the twelve-hour day made its furtive return.

However, this was not the sole experience of the employees who appear in this book, and so I have shared other stories about the mark they have made on the ecology of work. Although they are stories about the here and now, they have usually been improved by a sense of history. For example, no industrial blueprint existed for the application of these employees' digital skills on the job, but managerial efforts to orchestrate new technologies have long posed a threat to the independence of craft labor like theirs. Their tools unlocked the future, yet their efforts to retain control over their work environment and employability echoed with the lessons of many previous chapters in the history of technological de-skilling. In addition to technical mastery, the managers of the New Economy courted employees with a maverick attitude and a nonconformist frame of mind. In order to usher in tomorrow's world, they found they had to fashion a corporate profile out of the seasoned work habits and tempo of the bohemian artist, offering a new lease on life to an old mind-set. Thus, while it bore the logo of the future, the no-collar mentality that I have described in these pages did not spring forth fully formed from the forehead of the digital economy. It drew on several lines of genealogical descent to form a distinct industrial personality before it was absorbed, only half-digested, into the mainstream. This book has documented the adolescent growth of that personality, for the benefit of those who may witness its maturity.

The Advanced Urban Prototype: A Coda

By then, our bad science fiction film from Chapter 2 will need an update. In the new version, the Early Urban Prototype (EUP) whom we met at that point will have been replaced by an advanced model (AUP), devoid of the programming bugs that troubled its performance.

Over by the Fiscal Vat, Kaspar, the mindshare manager at the Brain Dome, will be explaining some of the improvements to a government drone on a routine visit from the Department of Good Intentions. "The new generation of wetware from Fabrodrama has resolved the chronic problems with uneven emotional range; low-level anxiety and blithe spirit are now much easier to regulate. The echoes and flutters in the idea processing units have been zapped. System fatigue," Kaspar grins, "is a thing of the past. Except," he adds, "when we need it to simulate the jaded personality mood of the Arch Creative or the sleep deprivation of the Techno Bravo. Brandcasting is now fully integrated, which, I must say, is a great relief to our sponsors. Best of all, it will soon be possible to include talking stock in our premium product lines. These days," he takes a moment to elaborate, "clients want fully articulate value (FAV) upfront, and they are willing to pay through the nose for it. Our avatarists have been working round the clock to develop basic character traits for the promo appearances on Dow Entertainment. Who would have thought we would finally find a lucrative use for virtual reality!" The drone's frame shakes with mirth, even as it scans the AUPs in the room for an appropriate range of reactions. The result of the scan is near perfect. The Brain Dome, after all, is in the very forefront of modern industry, and its products are central to the lifestyles approved under the agreement between Softer Time and the Global Trade Authority.

Two floors above in the Dada Lab, our nascent rebel, Roxanne, deficiently programmed with an unauthorized learning curve, is hacking her way through the last layer of advertising on the Softer Time firewall. In this endeavor, she is driven solely by technical curiosity. Soon she will break into the Bono Zone and find that there are millions of debt-free people, living beyond the wall. None of these people appear to have commercial security numbers or pollution credit IDs. Some of her own kind are among them, along with many more of the EUPs who defected or were exiled to the Zone before the enhancements kicked in.

Initially skeptical that anyone would choose to forego the benefits of Softer Time, Roxanne is eventually persuaded there is a better way for Sentients and Neos to live, and she finds a way to function on both sides of the wall. On the other side, she will meet, and fall for, Miguel, one of the human prototypes who worked for a first wave Internet company in the late twentieth century. When he speaks of the wanton idealism of that period he sounds like a wistful exile, recalling the lost country of his youth. Miguel is one of the founders of the Zero Payment network, and so he has solid allies and good connectivity in every part of the Zone. They team up and use the network and Roxanne's position at the Brain Dome to shred the firewall. The false utopia of Softer Time is fully exposed to its citizens.

We have all seen this satisfyingly bad movie and can choose, in our mind's eye, between several possible endings. Even the best science fiction tells us much more about our present than about the future. Our imagination takes us out of our routine patterns, but it is no less a creature of our time than the daily grind; its limits are our own, not those of our descendants. As a result, forecasts of the future can always shed light on our current anxieties and desires and clarify them in ways we cannot readily do. Softer Time and Zero Payment are not so easy to separate in our own lives as they are by the firewall in the film. They stand for complex emotions and principles that tug fiercely at each other. For most of us, they are entangled, and no more so than in the workplaces where we toil for a living.

Nor, these days, is it quite so easy to agree on what would be utopian or dystopian about changes pursued for the better. The appetite for utopia is less keen after the blood-drenched twentieth century than it was when Edward Bellamy wrote his genre bestseller, *Looking Backward* (1888), about an American utopia of the year 2000. How did work figure in his future romance of a "universal reign of comfort," where the "modern humane spirit" has triumphed over the barbarism of industry and social inequality? Bellamy envisaged the development of machinery to the point where the number of hours spent on productive work was reduced to a minimum; everyone serves in the "industrial army" for twenty-four years, including women, who are relieved of all housework, and everyone retires at forty-five. As a result, national productivity would be unmatched. In his mixed review of Bellamy's book, William Morris argued that by far the greater "gain to humanity" would be "the reduction of pain in labour to a minimum, so small that it will cease to be a pain." For Morris, "the true incentive to useful and happy labour is and must be pleasure in the work itself," a principle he fleshed out in his own twenty-first-century utopia, *News From Nowhere* (1890).

Bellamy's goal of reducing labor held sway for several decades, but by the time 2000 rolled by, Morris's version of gratifying work was making much more headway—so much so that the standard dystopia no longer depicted mass drudgery and unrelieved alienation under jackboot rule. Dystopia was more likely to resemble a Disneyville of shiny, happy people, taking equal satisfaction in the steady conformity of their labor and leisure. If the advent of the humane workplace (in which pleasure is an incentive) was partly responsible for this shift in content, then it is a good reminder of the suspicion that should accompany every utopian yearning: "Watch what you wish for." Paid employment that is most free from coercion often results in the deepest sacrifice of time and vitality. Nor does pleasure play fair. Gratification is no guarantee of justice, least of all in an economy that feeds on uncertainty and allocates rewards more unequally than it used to do. That is why we should heed Morris's proviso that both his and Bellamy's ideals "can only be dreamed of till men are even more completely equal than Mr. Bellamy's utopia would allow them to be."[18] On that score, we still have a lot of work to do.

NOTES

Chapter 1

1. As Sebastian de Grazia points out, the inclusion of the right to work under the rubric of the rights of man was a direct outgrowth of the early Protestant view that idleness was sinful, even criminal. "If not working is abominable, then men should be protected from the possibility of such indignity; they have a right to work. . . . Thus, what began as the poor man's gaol ended up as the poor man's goal." *Of Time, Work, and Leisure* (Garden City, N.Y.: Anchor Books, 1962), p. 283.

2. Karl Marx, "Estranged Labour," *Economic and Philosophical Manuscripts of 1848*, trans. Richard Dixon et al., *Karl Marx, Frederick Engels: Collected Works*, vol. 4 (New York: International Publishers, 1975), p. 277.

3. Quoted in Daniel T. Rodgers, *The Work Ethic in Industrial America, 1850–1920* (Chicago: University of Chicago Press, 1978), p. 15.

4. See Rodgers' eloquent portrayal of this transition in *The Work Ethic in Industrial America, 1850–1920.*

5. The struggle of employers to rein in craft autonomy was long and bitter, largely because it met with so much organized resistance, first in various forms of mutual support among workers in the nineteenth century and then in sustained opposition to scientific management from 1900 to 1930. David Montgomery documents these movements in *Workers' Control in America: Studies in the History of Work, Technology, and Labor Struggles* (Cambridge: Cambridge University Press, 1979).

6. See Barbara Garson's documentary account of her visit with the Lordstown plant's workers in *All the Livelong Day: The Meaning and Demeaning of Routine Work* (Garden City, N.Y.: Doubleday, 1975). See also Stanley Aronowitz's analysis in *False Promises: The Shaping of American Working-Class Consciousness* (New York: McGraw-Hill, 1973), pp. 21–50; and Bennett Kreman's discussion with workers and unionists in "Search for a Better Way of

Work: Lordstown, Ohio," in *Humanizing the Workplace,* ed. Roy P. Fairfield (Buffalo, N.Y.: Prometheus Books, 1974), pp. 141–150.

7. *Work in America,* Report of a Special Task Force to the Secretary of Health, Education, and Welfare, prepared under the auspices of the W. E. Upjohn Institute for Employment Research (Cambridge: MIT Press, 1973). Similar testimony was recorded in the hearings on Worker Alienation conducted by the Subcommittee on Employment, Manpower and Poverty, of the U.S. Senate's Committee on Labor and Public Welfare (92nd Cong. 2nd Sess., 1972).

8. Studs Terkel, *Working: People Talk About What They Do All Day and How They Feel About What They Do* (New York: Pantheon, 1974), pp. 187–196, xi.

9. Jill Andresky Fraser, *White-Collar Sweatshop: The Deterioration of Work and Its Rewards in Corporate America* (New York: Norton, 2001).

10. Amanda Bennett, *The Death of the Organization Man* (New York: William Morrow, 1990), p. 15.

11. Rosabeth Moss Kanter, *The Change Masters: Innovation for Productivity in the American Corporation* (New York: Simon and Schuster, 1983), p. 367.

12. References to a "new economy" date back to the 1970s, when the term was used to refer to the rise of the service sector. Its association with computer technology has been fairly consistent in the decades since then. In the last five years of the century, the stock boom and a sharp rise in productivity led analysts to support economic predictions that the business cycle was now a thing of the past and that new economic rules were in effect, triggered by the productivity of information technology. The commercialization of the Internet coincided with this period, and the Internet companies that lay in the vanguard of the stock boom became associated primarily with the New Economy. For some analyses of the New Economy, see Doug Henwood, *A New Economy?* (New York: New Press, 2003); Robert Shiller, *Irrational Exuberance* (Princeton: Princeton University Press, 2000); Geert Lovink and Eric Kluitenberg, eds., *Tulipomania Dotcom Reader: A Critique of the New Economy* (Amsterdam: De Balie, 2001).

13. In the mid-1980s, Robert Earl Kelley used the term "gold-collar workers" to describe high-value occupations that depend on brainpower. He argued that the emergence of these occupations had rendered traditional modes of management redundant and that the task of "handling" these workers needed to be rethought if their resources were to be mined profitably. *The Gold-Collar Worker: Harnessing the Brainpower of the New Work Force* (Reading, Mass.: Addison-Wesley, 1985). Richard Florida has more recently argued for the existence (not yet self-conscious) of a "creative class," which he has esti-

mated to account for 38 million members, or 30 percent of the U.S. workforce, and which is now "the dominant class in society." *The Rise of the Creative Class, and How It's Transforming Work, Leisure, Community, and Everyday Life* (New York: Basic Books, 2002). In this book, I use the term no-collar primarily to describe a *work mentality* rather than a specific set of occupations or a professional class sector. Although it is not the sole property of high-tech employees (the no-collar mentality of artists and other creative workers figures in these pages), it has evolved most visibly and influentially in the high-technology industries.

14. The concept of the digital artisan is most closely associated with British media critic Richard Barbrook, who wrote "The Digital Manifesto," along with other influential essays about Internet culture, including "The Hi Tech Gift Economy" and (with Andy Cameron) "The Californian Ideology," <http://www.hrc.wmin.ac.uk>.

15. Daniel Bell, *The Coming of Post-Industrial Society: A Venture in Social Forecasting* (New York: Basic Books, 1976).

16. Although the roots of this idea go back to Saint-Simon, its twentieth-century lineage can be traced from Thorstein Veblen's "A Memorandum on a Practicable Soviet of Technicians," in *The Engineers and the Price System* (New York: B. W. Huebsch, 1921). On the "revolt of the engineers," see William Akin, *Technocracy and the American Dream: The Technocracy Movement, 1900–1941* (Berkeley: University of California Press, 1977); and Henry Elsner, *The Technocrats: Prophets of Automation* (Syracuse: Syracuse University Press, 1967).

17. For the classic account of managerial capitalism, see Alfred Chandler Jr., *The Visible Hand: The Managerial Revolution in American Business* (Cambridge: Harvard University Press, 1977). Those who waged the "shareholder revolution" argued that the impact of the separation of corporations from the immediate control of owners had been detrimental to the pursuit of profit. Managers had focused on long-term stability and growth, rather than profit maximization, in order to perpetuate their own positions within their organizations. They had become disconnected from shareholders and unaccountable to board directors.

18. American Management Association, "Workplace Monitoring and Surveillance: Policies and Practices" (New York, 2001); Barbara Ehrenreich, "Warning: This Is a Rights-Free Workplace," *New York Times Magazine,* March 5, 2000, pp. 88–90.

19. In the early 1980s, Shoshana Zuboff studied workplaces where IT was being introduced. She distinguished between workplaces where managers chose to deploy the new technologies in despotic ways that simply reproduced the patterns of industrial machinery and those where IT's capacity to "infor-

mate" (rather than automate) was used to develop new "intellective skills" in employees. *In the Age of the Smart Machine: The Future of Work and Power* (New York: Basic Books, 1988).

20. Recent biographies of failed companies include Stephan Paternot, with Andrew Essex, *A Very Public Offering: A Rebel's Story of Business Excess, Success, and Reckoning* (New York: John Wiley, 2001); J. David Kuo, *Dot.bomb: My Days and Nights at an Internet Goliath* (New York: Little, Brown, 2001); Brenda Laurel, *The Utopian Entrepreneur* (Cambridge: MIT Press, 2001); Ernst Malmsten, Charles Drazin, and Eric Portanger, *Boo Hoo: A Dot Com Story (New York: Random House, 2001)*; Tom Ashbrook, *The Leap: A Memoir of Love and Madness in the Internet Gold Rush* (New York: Houghton Mifflin, 2000); Gary Rivlin, *The Godfather of Silicon Valley: Ron Conway and the Fall of the Dot-coms* (New York: Random House, 2001). More general accounts of the Internet gold rush include John Cassidy, *Dot.con: The Greatest Story Ever Sold* (New York: HarperCollins, 2002); and Philip Kaplan, *F'd Companies: Spectacular Dot-Com Flameouts* (New York: Simon & Schuster, 2002).

21. Tom Peters, "Brand Called You," *Fast Company* 10 (August 1997): 83.

22. See Christena Nippert-Eng's study of workplaces, in which employees either integrated or segregated their workplace and domestic lives. *Home and Work: Negotiating Boundaries Through Everyday Life* (Chicago: University of Chicago Press, 1996).

Chapter 2

1. These figures are drawn from the *3rd New York New Media Industry Survey,* conducted by PriceWaterhouseCoopers and issued by the New York New Media Association, March 2000.

2. The roll call of Razorfish's acquisitions included Avalanche, New York, January 26, 1998; CHBi, London, May 18, 1998; Plastic, San Francisco, May 18, 1998; Media, Los Angeles, July 27, 1998; Sunbather Ltd., London, October 21, 1998; Spray Network AB, Hamburg/Helsinki/Oslo/Stockholm, January 1999; Electrokinetics, New York, June 11, 1999; Fuel and Tonga, Los Angeles, July 1, 1999; Lee Hunt Associates, New York, December 1, 1999; TS Design, Boston, December 1, 1999; Qb International Holding AB, Stockholm, January 24, 2000; Limages Dangereuses, Rotterdam, May 15, 2000; Intervision, Tokyo, July 1, 2000 (joint venture with Sony affiliate, announced May 17, 2000); MediaLab AB, Munich, August 21, 2000; i-Cube, Cambridge, November 2, 2000.

3. Douglas McGregor, *The Human Side of Enterprise* (New York: McGraw-Hill, 1960).

4. Thomas Peters and Robert Waterman, *In Search of Excellence: Lessons from America's Best-Run Companies* (New York: Harper & Row, 1982), along

with Peters's other books: *Thriving on Chaos: Handbook for a Management Revolution* (New York: HarperPerennial, 1991); *Liberation Management: Necessary Disorganization for the Nanosecond Nineties* (New York: Knopf, 1992); *The Pursuit of Wow: Every Person's Guide to Topsy Turvy Times* (New York: Random House, 1994); and *The Circle of Innovation: You Can't Shrink Your Way to Greatness* (New York: Random House, 1997).

5. In due time, billability would become a gauge of how long you could expect to remain employed within the company.

6. Arlie Russell Hochschild, *The Managed Heart: Commercialization of Human Feeling* (Berkeley: University of California Press, 1983).

7. Casey Hait and Stephen Weiss, *Digital Hustlers: Living Large and Falling Hard in Silicon Alley* (New York: Regan Books, 2001), p. 45.

8. For an incisive study of offshore pink-collar workers, see Carla Freeman, *High Tech and High Heels in the Global Economy: Women, Work, and Pink-Collar Identities in the Caribbean* (Durham, N.C.: Duke University Press, 2000).

9. Peter Drucker, *Landmarks of Tomorrow* (New York: Harper, 1959), and *The Age of Discontinuity: Guidelines to Our Changing Society* (New York: Harper & Row, 1969). However, Drucker credits economist Fritz Machlup with the coinage of the term "knowledge industries." See Machlup's *The Production and Distribution of Knowledge in the United States* (Princeton: Princeton University Press, 1962); Marc Porat, *The Information Economy: Definition and Measurement* (Washington, D.C.: U.S. Dept of Commerce, Office of Telecommunications, 1977). A more theoretical view of the centrality of knowledge work is offered by Daniel Bell in *The Coming of Post-Industrial Society: A Venture in Social Forecasting* (New York: Basic Books, 1973).

10. Manuel Castells, *The Rise of the Network Society* (Oxford: Blackwell, 1996), pp. 259–260. Castells breaks down the work process into three dimensions: the value-making process (which employs commanders, researchers, designers, integrators, operators, and the operated); the relation-making process (which employs networkers and networked and switched-off workers); and the decision-making process (which employs deciders, participants, and executants).

11. Karl Marx, *Capital: A Critique of Political Economy*, vol. 1, trans. Ben Fowkes (New York: Penguin Books, 1976), p. 425.

12. Amy Sue Bix surveys the history of this concept in *Inventing Ourselves Out of Jobs? America's Debate Over Technological Unemployment, 1929–1981* (Baltimore: Johns Hopkins University Press, 2000). For more contemporary diagnoses, see Stanley Aronowitz and William DiFazio, *The Jobless Future: Sci-Tech and the Dogma of Work* (Minneapolis: University of Minnesota Press, 1994); and Jeremy Rifkin, *The End of Work: The Decline of the Global Labor*

Force and the Dawn of the Post-Market Era (New York: G. P. Putnam's Sons, 1995).

13. Quoted from Andrew Pettigrew's case study of English programmers, in Joan M. Greenbaum, *In the Name of Efficiency: Management Theory and Shopfloor Practice in Data-Processing Work* (Philadelphia: Temple University Press, 1979), p. 65.

14. Dick Brandon, "The Economics of Computer Programming," in *On the Management of Computer Programming*, ed. George Weinwurm (Princeton: Auerbach, 1970).

15. Philip Kraft, *Programmers and Managers: The Routinization of Computer Programmers in the United States* (New York: Springer-Verlag, 1977).

16. Annalee Saxenian describes this comparison best in *Regional Advantage: Culture and Competition in Silicon Valley and Route 128* (Cambridge: Harvard University Press, 1994). For other accounts of Silicon Valley, which vary from the breathless to the highly critical, see Everett Rogers and Judith Larson, *Silicon Valley Fever: Growth of High-Technology Culture* (New York: Basic Books, 1984); Dirk Hanson, *The New Alchemists: Silicon Valley and the Microelectronics Revolution* (Boston: Little, Brown, 1982); Steven Levy, *Hackers: Heroes of the Computer Revolution* (Garden City, N.Y.: Doubleday, 1984); David Kaplan, *The Silicon Boys and Their Valley of Dreams* (New York: William Morrow, 1999); Paul Freiberger and Michael Swaine, *Fire in the Valley: The Making of the Personal Computer,* 2nd ed. (New York: McGraw-Hill, 2000); Chong-Moon Lee, ed., *The Silicon Valley Edge: A Habitation for Innovation and Entrepreneurship* (Stanford: Stanford University Press, 2000); Michael Lewis, *The New New Thing: A Silicon Valley Story* (New York: Norton, 2000). Charles Darrah, J. A. English-Lueck, and James Freeman, a team of anthropologists from San Jose State University, have conducted a fifteen-year study of work and family life in Silicon Valley: *Cultures@Silicon Valley* (Stanford: Stanford University Press, 2002). The Web site of their Silicon Valley Cultures Project can be found at <http://www.sjsu.edu/depts/anthropology/svcp/>.

17. Ted Nelson, *Computer Lib/Dream Machine,* revised ed. (Redmond: Tempus, 1987), p. 7.

18. For a full list of the Silicon Valley spin-offs, see <http://www.tbtf.com/siliconia.html>.

19. Paula Borsook, *Cyberselfish: A Critical Romp Through the Terribly Libertarian Culture of High Tech* (New York: Public Affairs, 2000), p. 63.

20. Despite the public perception that these are light manufacturing workplaces, microchip workers suffer industrial illnesses at three times the average for other manufacturing jobs, and studies routinely find significantly increased miscarriage rates and birth defect rates among women working in chemical

handling jobs. The more common and well-documented illnesses include breast, uterine, and stomach cancer, leukemia, asthma, and vision impairment. In many of these jobs, workers are exposed to hundreds of different chemicals and over 700 compounds that can go into the production of a single work station, destined for technological obsolescence in a couple of years. Very little occupational health research exists that analyzes the impact on the human body of combining several of these compounds, and research on reproductive hazards, in particular, has been seen as a women's issue and is therefore underfunded and underreported. The Silicon Valley Toxics Coalition <http://www.svtc.org> has charted the "toxic flight" of the "dirtier" processes of high-tech production to regions with sparse union activity and softer environmental and safety regulations—like the U.S. Southwest or the developing countries of the world. See Dennis Hayes, *Behind the Silicon Curtain: The Seductions of Work in a Lonely Era* (Boston: South End Press, 1989); Robert Howard, *Brave New Workplaces* (New York: Viking, 1985); Lenny Seigel and John Markoff, *The High Cost of High Tech: The Dark Side of the Chip* (New York: Harper & Row, 1985); and Leslie Byster, "The Toxic Chip," *Environmental Action* 27 (Fall 1995): 19–23.

21. For an ethnographic account of work at an assembly plant in Silicon Valley, see Victor Devinatz, *High-Tech Betrayal: Working and Organizing on the Shop Floor* (East Lansing: Michigan State University Press, 1999).

22. See "The Scourge of Silicon Valley," Ed Frauenheim's account of the anti–H-1B crusader Norman Matloff, in *Salon*, October 19, 2000. Matloff's repeated challenges to the industry claims about a "shortage" of IT workers were supported by the Institute of Electrical and Electronic Engineers. In 1998 testimony to the U.S. House Judiciary Committee (Subcommittee on Immigration), he argued that older programmers and coders were systematically being made redundant in their mid–forties and that the H1-B program obscured these statistics. He reported a 17 percent unemployment rate for programmers over age fifty and pointed out that among graduates of college computer science programs, only 19 percent were still in the field twenty years after completing their studies, compared to 52 percent for civil engineering majors. <http://www.house.gov/judiciary/6096.htm>.

23. Ernesto Galarza, *Merchants of Labor: The Mexican Bracero Story, An Account of the Managed Migration of Mexican Farm Workers in California, 1942–1960* (Santa Barbara, Calif.: McNaly and Loftin, 1964).

24. In addition to those by Tom Peters, some influential books that contributed in their own ways to this paradigm of business change included Rosabeth Moss Kanter, *The Change-Masters: Innovation for Productivity in the American Corporation* (New York: Simon & Schuster, 1983), and *When Giants Learn to Dance* (New York: Simon & Schuster, 1989); Gifford and Elizabeth

Pinchot, *The End of Bureaucracy and the Rise of the Intelligent Organization* (San Francisco: Berrett-Koehler, 1993); George Gilder, *Microcosm: The Quantum Revolution in Economics and Technology* (New York: Simon and Schuster, 1989); Peter Senge, *The Fifth Discipline: The Art and Practice of the Learning Organization* (New York: Doubleday, 1990): and Stanley Davis and Christopher Meyer, *Blur: The Speed of Change in the Connected Economy* (Reading, Mass.: Addison-Wesley, 1998).

25. In *One Market Under God*, his acerbic chronicle of this capitalist insurgency, Thomas Frank analyzes the full-blown religious overtones attached to the Market Triumphant of the 1990s, noting how carefully distinctions were drawn between the practical work of entrepreneurs and the miracles wrought by their digital wares in the dogma of the market faithful: "So pervasive did the business-as-God routine become that in 1999 the Merrill Lynch brokerage actually ran commercials seeking to correct an apparent heresy in the new faith. Reminding us that however wonderful computers might be, they had still been constructed by Business Man in his own image, the brokerage admonished us to get our theology straight: we were to 'admire machines' but worship their inventors." *One Market Under God: Extreme Capitalism, Market Populism, and the End of Economic Democracy* (New York: Doubleday, 2000), p. 4.

26. A typical example of management literature that addresses this problem is Peter Weill and Marianne Broadbent's *Leveraging the New Infrastructure: How Market Leaders Capitalize on Information Technology* (Cambridge: Harvard Business Press, 1998), which invites company managers to think of their IT infrastructure in the same way as they consider their investment portfolios, leveraging their assets accordingly.

27. Some of the literature on the productivity paradox includes Henry C. Lucas Jr., *Information Technology and the Productivity Paradox: Assessing the Value of the Investment in IT* (New York: Oxford University Press, 1999); John Thorp, *The Information Paradox: Realizing the Business Benefits of Information Technology* (New York: McGraw-Hill, 1998); Paul A. David and W. Edward Steinmueller, eds., *Information Technology and the Productivity Paradox* (New York: Harwood Academic Publishers, 1999); Leslie Willcocks and Stephanie Lester, eds., *Beyond the IT Productivity Paradox: Assessment Issues* (New York: John Wiley, 1999); Jessica Keyes, *Solving the Productivity Paradox: TQM for Computer Professionals* (New York: McGraw-Hill, 1995).

28. Stephen Oliner and Daniel Sichel, at the Federal Reserve Board, estimated that a full two-thirds of the post-1995 productivity growth was due to the growth of computer investment. "Resurgence of Growth in the Late 1990s: Is IT the Story?" *Journal of Economic Perspectives* 14 (4) (2000): 3–22. In the same issue, dissenting economist Robert Gordon argued that the effects of the business cycle accounted for half of the growth increase and that IT gains

came from the producers of computers, not their consumers. "Does the 'New Economy' Measure Up to the Great Inventions of the Past?" (pp. 49–74). U.S. Department of Labor data, released in August 2001, revealed a revised rate of productivity growth for the period from 1996 through 2000. According to this data, the nonfarm business sector of the economy had shown an annual average rate of productivity growth of 2.5 percent, as opposed to the 2.8 percent previously accepted.

29. David Noble, *The Religion of Technology: The Divinity of Man and the Spirit of Invention* (New York: Knopf, 1997), p. 5. Also see Erik Davis, *Techgnosis: Myth, Magic, and Mysticism in the Age of Information* (New York: Harmony Books,1998).

30. Kevin Kelly, *Out of Control: The New Biology of Machines, Social Systems, and the Economic World* (Reading, Mass.: Addison-Wesley, 1995); and *New Rules for the New Economy: Ten Radical Strategies for a Connected World* (New York: Viking, 1998).

31. For a chronicle of the life and times of a Bay Area programmer, see Ellen Ullman, *Close to the Machine: Technophilia and Its Discontents* (San Francisco: City Lights, 1997). Other documents, fictional or otherwise, of the West Coast tech culture include Douglas Coupland, *Microserfs* (New York: HarperCollins, 1995); Po Bronson, *Nudist on the Late Shift* (New York: Random House, 2000) and *The First $20 Million Is Always the Hardest* (New York: Random House, 1999); and Thomas Scoville, *Silicon Follies: A Dot.comedy* (New York: Pocket Books, 2001).

32. In San Francisco, where the eight-hour day had first been introduced in the 1880s and had become scarce on the 1990s job landscape, a prescient analysis of the New Economy speedup could be found in the pages of *Processed World* (its slogan: Are You Doing the Processing or Being Processed?). This legendary magazine covered the growing pains of white-collar office work in the pre-Internet information economy throughout the 1980s. Its editors were dissident artists and writers who worked as temps in the San Francisco financial district at a time when "information handling" jobs had none of the charisma that would later be associated with the Internet sector. For the office employees who contributed stories, art, and humor to their magazine, the cubicle workplace was profoundly alienating, and computer technology was simply a gizmo for enforcing faster and ever more tedious work. See Chris Carlsson and Mark Leger, eds., *Bad Attitude: The Processed World Anthology* (New York: Verso, 1990).

33. See Naomi Klein's *No Logo: Taking Aim at the Brand Bullies* (London: HarperCollins, 2000) for a provocative account of the brand economy.

34. C. Wright Mills, *White Collar: The American Middle Classes* (New York: Oxford University Press, 1956), p. ix.

35. William H. Whyte Jr., *The Organization Man* (New York: Simon & Schuster, 1956).

36. Thomas Frank, *The Conquest of Cool: Business Culture, Counterculture, and the Rise of Hip Consumerism* (Chicago: University of Chicago Press, 1997). Tom Frank recounts how, in the course of the 1960s, creatives in Madison Avenue's advertising agencies were also encouraged to revolt against the corporate yes-men of the day, break all the rules, and wear wild outfits. The anti-establishment fad began in the Doyle Dane Bernbach agency, which produced the famous Volkswagen anti-car ads, and spread throughout the advertising industry until it was reined in by the 1974 recession. According to Frank, this "creativity revolution" was an effort to coopt the critique of fake consumerism that was fueling the countercultural ferment of the decade. It fizzled out at its source when the energies and values of that critique were absorbed by the mainstream.

37. Juliet Schor, *The Overworked American: The Unexpected Decline of Leisure* (New York: Basic Books, 1991). On the history of the movement for shorter hours, see Benjamin Hunnicutt, *Work Without End: Abandoning Shorter Hours for the Right to Work* (Philadelphia: Temple University Press, 1988).

38. See Michael Maccoby, "The Managerial Work Ethic in America," in *The Work Ethic: A Critical Analysis,* ed. Jack Barbash et al. (Madison, Wis.: Industrial Relations Research Association, 1983), pp. 183–196.

39. Robert Reich, *The Work of Nations: Preparing Ourselves for 21st-Century Capitalism* (New York: Knopf, 1991).

40. Robert Reich, *The Future of Success: Working and Living in the New Economy* (New York: Vintage, 2002), p. 7, 130.

41. Stanley Aronowitz, *The Last Good Job in America: Work and Education in the New Global Technoculture* (Lanham, Md.: Rowman and Littlefield, 2001). Although those who hold academic tenure might well agree with Aronowitz, Joanne Ciulla reminds us that "academics who write about work often mistakenly assume that everyone wants a job like theirs." *The Working Life: The Promise and Betrayal of Modern Work* (New York: Times Books, 2000), p. xiii.

Chapter 3

1. Michael Wolff, *Burn Rate: How I Survived the Gold Rush Years on the Internet* (New York: Simon and Schuster, 1998). *Startup.com,* a much praised 2001 documentary by Chris Hegedus, D. A. Pennebaker, and Jehane Noujaim, focused its cameras on the entrepreneurs who founded govworks.com. The film's treatment of the company almost entirely ignored its employees.

2. Stephen Johnson, *Interface Culture: How New Technology Transforms the Way We Create and Communicate* (San Francisco: HarperCollins, 1997).

3. See Debra Bernhardt and Rachel Bernstein's *Ordinary People, Extraordinary Lives: A Pictorial History of Working People in New York City* (New York: New York University Press, 2000).

4. Just as the "technology industry" spans a vast range of software and hardware products, the "Internet industry" covers a broad spectrum of companies and services, including e-commerce retail, Web design and Web development, content design and distribution, content packaging and marketing, content creation tools, online enabling services, IT consulting, and database and network administration, in addition to many brick-and-mortar firms with large IT departments or online teams of their own.

5. Joshua Freeman, *Working-Class New York: Life and Labor Since World War II* (New York: New Press, 2000), pp. 3–23.

6. There were several projects being developed by the company's department of Physical Design, including a prototype design for a new Web pad, with a cellular connection, that would offer e-mail, calendar, and software capabilities; a proprietary handheld device for the dental industry; and information devices for home and public environments. The common goal of these projects was "true platform convergence."

7. The company's four networks—Strategy, Technology, Experience, and Value—were conceived during the 2000–2001 reorganization called Forlenkla (Swedish for "simplify"). Each network grouped together cognate disciplines. Experience, for example, included writers, visual systems designers, usability analysts, production artists, interface developers, interaction designers, information architects, and audio designers.

8. These estimates are from three annual reports on new media employment, based on surveys conducted by Coopers and Lybrand/PriceWaterhouseCoopers. *New York New Media Industry Survey: Opportunities and Challenges of New York's Emerging Cyber-Industry* (New York New Media Association, 1996, 1997, and 1999). The 2000 survey did not include comparative compensation data. A consultant at PWC, which produced the surveys, informed me that the difficulty of factoring in the value of stock options, which old media employees generally did not enjoy, had made the data redundant. A survey of Silicon Alley professionals, conducted for the Economic Policy Institute, showed them earning an average of $99,000 in 1999, well above the national average. Rosemary Batt et al., *Net Working: Work Patterns and Workforce Policies for the New Media Industry* (Washington, D.C.: Economic Policy Institute, 2001). In September 2000, the *Industry Standard* published the results of its own compensation survey of 2,600 newsletter subscribers. This study found that the median cash compensation—base salary plus bonus or commission—of those Net workers surveyed was $83,000. With women earning about $66,000, the salary gender gap—about 27 percent less than the $91,000 that men received—was in line with the national average computed by the Bureau of Labor Statistics. Though it

did not alleviate the gap, women worked shorter hours in the day—clocking 9.7 hours per day, compared with the 10.3 hours for men—and over the weekend, and also were more likely to be paid for overtime than men. Laura Carr, "Still a Man's World?" *Industry Standard,* December 25, 2000.

9. In *Cyberselfish: A Critical Romp Through the Terribly Libertarian Culture of High Tech* (New York: Public Affairs, 2000), Paula Borsook analyzes Silicon Valley's culture of indifference to the less fortunate.

10. Quoted in Casey Hait and Stephen Weiss, *Digital Hustlers: Living Large and Falling Hard in Silicon Alley* (New York: Regan Books, 2001), pp. 176–177.

11. Designed to parody *fastcompany.com,* Kaplan's site awarded points to users who correctly forecast a company's demise. Through a growing network of industry informants (four or five hundred each day), Kaplan published rumors about layoffs, managerial firings, and shutdowns to come. Much of the scuttlebutt posted to the site in the wake of shutdowns was high-octane, low-flying slander. For some hapless employees, fuckedcompany.com broke the news about the loss of their jobs even before the ax fell. For the desperate trader, the site offered clues about investments going south. Copycat sites quickly followed: fuckedmarketing.com, which mocked the promos and press releases of the doomed, and downside.com's deathwatch, which claims to predict the exact date (months ahead) of a company's appointment with the guillotine, based on an automated analysis of their reported liquid assets and loss rate. Aside from the prurient geek identification with Kaplan's personal taste in the pizza food group and "lesbo porn," his biggest asset was the blunt, unmerciful bluster with which he recorded the scene. For Kaplan's own story, see his book, *F'd Companies: Spectacular Dot Com Flameouts* (New York: Simon & Schuster, 2002).

12. Industry watchers were long familiar with Dachis's record of breathlessly brash comments to the press: "I don't want to be lumped in with the hucksters of the world, because we have the real deal," he told a *New York Times* reporter. "I feel completely and utterly entitled to whatever success comes our way. Not everybody's good, not everybody has the winning idea, not every idea deserves to be funded or to be public. I'm sorry, but there are sheep and there are shepherds, and I fancy myself to be the latter." "Internet Stocks Drive a Rush to Riches for Entrepreneurs in Manhattan's Silicon Alley," *New York Times,* May 31, 1999, B6. Other memorable Dachis pronouncements included the following: "We're the haute cuisine in a premier custom solution shop every time"; and "We have the most complex technology integration skills that exist in the services space. There isn't anybody who has stronger technology skills than we do or the depth and scale to deliver these technology solutions. On top of that we have the most creative individuals on the planet coupled with complex strategists, so you really have a skill set that's above and beyond the caliber of any of the other companies out there."

Chapter 4

1. David Roediger and Philip Foner, *Our Own Time: A History of American Labor and the Working Day* (New York: Verso, 1989).

2. "Neo-Leisure, the Dirty Little Secret Behind the 65-Hour Workweek," *Fast Company*, November 1993, p. 26.

3. Rosemary Blatt, Susan Christopherson, Ned Rightor, and Danielle Van Jaarsveld, *Net Working: Work Patterns and Workforce Policies for the New Media Industry* (Washington, D.C., Economic Policy Institute, 2001), pp. 14ff.

4. The experiments are analyzed in F. J. Roethlisberger and William Dickson, *Management and the Worker: An Account of a Research Program Conducted by the Western Electric Company, Hawthorne Works, Chicago* (Cambridge: Harvard University Press, 1939).

5. Elton Mayo, *The Human Problems of an Industrial Civilization* (Salem, N.H.: MacMillan, Ayer, 1933).

6. Richard Gillespie, *Manufacturing Knowledge: A History of the Hawthorne Experiments* (Cambridge: Cambridge University Press, 1991).

7. William Whyte, *The Organization Man* (New York: Simon and Schuster, 1956), p. 397.

8. Paul J. Andrisan et al., eds., *The Work Ethic: A Critical Analysis* (Madison: Industrial Relations Research Association, 1983), pp. 243–244.

9. Louis Davis and Albert Cherns, eds., *The Quality of Working Life* (New York: Free Press, 1975); and James O'Toole, ed., *Work and the Quality of Life* (Cambridge: MIT Press, 1974).

10. William Ouchi, *Theory Z: How American Business Can Meet the Japanese Challenge* (Reading, Mass.: Addison-Wesley, 1981); Richard Pascale and Anthony Athos, *The Art of Japanese Management* (New York: Simon and Schuster, 1981).

11. Dave Arnott, *Corporate Cults: The Insidious Lure of the All-Consuming Organization* (New York: American Management Association, 1999).

12. John Micklethwait and Adrian Wooldridge, *The Witch Doctors: Making Sense of the Management Gurus* (New York: Times Books, 1996).

13. Joanne Ciulla, *The Working Life: The Promise and Betrayal of Modern Work* (New York: Times Books, 2000), pp. 137–138.

14. Mike Parker, *Inside the Circle: A Union Guide to Quality of Work Life* (Boston: South End Press, 1985). Richard Edwards, *Contested Terrain: The Transformation of the Workplace in the Twentieth Century* (New York: Basic Books, 1979).

15. Barry and Irving Bluestone discuss Saturn and other case studies in arguing that labor-management compacts must move from co-managing the workplace to co-managing the enterprise. *Negotiating the Future: A Labor Perspective on American Business* (New York: Basic Books, 1992). See also

Harley Shaiken, *Work Transformed: Automation and Labor in the Computer Age* (New York: Henry Holt, 1985).

16. Arlie Hochschild, *The Time Bind: When Work Becomes Home and Home Becomes Work* (New York: Metropolitan Books, 1997), p. 46.

17. Ciulla, *The Working Life*, pp. 161–162.

18. Alan Downs, *Corporate Executions: The Ugly Truth about Layoffs* (New York, AMACOM, 1995); David Gordon, *Fat and Mean: The Corporate Squeeze of Working Americans and the Myth of Managerial "Downsizing"* (New York: Free Press, 1996); *The Downsizing of America: A New York Times Special Report* (New York: Times Books, 1996).

19. In his ethnography of a technology company, Gideon Kunda analyzes how company culture was experienced with ambivalence by employees—as both a promise and a threat. *Engineering Culture: Control and Commitment in a High-Tech Corporation* (Philadelphia: Temple University Press, 1992).

20. Lewis Coser, *Greedy Institutions: Patterns of Undivided Commitment* (New York: Free Press, 1974).

21. The concept was developed by two academic psychologists, John Mayer and Peter Salovey. It was popularized by Daniel Goleman, in *Emotional Intelligence* (New York: Bantam Books, 1995) and sold, guru-style, to corporate America through Goleman's consultancy and his EI Consortium.

22. Terrence Deal and Allan Kennedy, *Corporate Culture: The Rites and Rituals of Corporate Life* (Reading, Mass.: Addison-Wesley, 1982), p. 15.

23. Joan Oleck, "Haberdashers Team Up for the Tie," *Business Week,* August 23, 2001. See also Sherry Maysonave, *Casual Power: How to Power Up Your Nonverbal Communication and Dress Down for Success* (New York: Bright Books, 1999); Ilene Amieland Angie Michael, *Business Casual Made Easy* (Scarsdale, N.Y.: Business Casual Publications, 1999); Susan Bixler, Nancy Nix-Rice, *The New Professional Image: From Business Casual to the Ultimate Power Look* (Avon, Mass.: Adams Media Corporation, 1997).

24. Terence Riley, preface to *Workspheres: Design and Contemporary Work Styles,* ed. Paola Antonelli (New York: Museum of Modern Art, 2001).

25. Christopher Budd, "The Office: 1950 to the Present," in *Workspheres,* p. 30.

26. The show, *Workspheres,* was curated by Paola Antonella and ran from February to April 2001.

27. Barbara Garson, *The Electronic Sweatshop: How Computers Are Transforming the Office of the Future into the Factory of the Past* (New York: Simon & Schuster, 1988); and Robert Howard, *Brave New Workplace* (New York: Viking, 1985).

28. Martin Sprouse, ed., *Sabotage in the American Workplace: Anecdotes of Dissatisfaction, Mischief, and Revenge* (San Francisco: Pressure Drop Press, 1992).

29. The most persuasive commentaries include Harry Braverman, *Labor and Monopoly Capital: The Degradation of Work in the Twentieth Century* (New York: Monthly Review Press, 1974); and David Noble, *Forces of Production: A Social History of Industrial Automation* (New York: Oxford University Press, 1986).

30. The Dotcom Issue of *Interiors* (October 2000) lists some of the common features of the dotcom office designed for flexibility: exposed ceilings, chartreuse colors, fifties furniture, jutting, cantilevered surfaces, Aeron chairs (to make the fourteen-hour day tolerable), blob objects and undulating form (nothing too square), game rooms, zen rooms, huts, iMacs, kitchenettes, lexan (a plastic), neon, open plan, pivoting doors, caster rollers, stools, tensile fabric, video walls, and whiteboards.

31. Chris Smith's essays, papers, and speeches are collected in *Creative Britain* (London: Faber & Faber, 1998).

32. Peer, an independent arts charity in East London, collected and curated a dossier of responses to the new policies. Mary Warnock and Mark Wallinger, eds., *Art for All?* (London: Peer, 2000).

Chapter 5

1. David Brooks, *Bobos in Paradise: The New Upper Class and How They Got There* (New York: Touchstone, 2000), p. 43.

2. See Neva Chonin and Dan Levy's three-part series on "Culture Crash," *San Francisco Chronicle*, October 17–19, 2000. See also Evelyn Nieves, "Mission District Fights Case of Dot.Com Fever," *New York Times*, November 5, 2000, p. 27; and Joel Selvin, "No Place to Play Anymore," *San Francisco Chronicle*, October 17, 2000, A8.

3. Albert Shumate, *Rincon Hill and South Park* (Sausalito, Calif.: Windgate Press, 1988). By the early 1990s, South Park resembled a homeless encampment and seemed destined for upscale redevelopment. By the end of the decade, its commercial landlords were asking for rents almost as high as Class A space in the city's downtown Union Square.

4. The cap of 950,000 square feet was imposed in 1986 as a slow-growth measure to stave off the Manhattanization of the city. Proposition L, created as part of a citywide anti-gentrification crusade, would have closed the loophole, but the damage was already extensive. Many key rehearsal spaces for dancers and musicians, along with dozens of galleries, museums, and community centers had already been turned into dotcom offices.

5. Savannah Blackwell, "The Battle for San Francisco," *San Francisco Bay Guardian*, October 18, 2000.

6. Rebecca Solnit and Susan Schwartzenberg, *Hollow City: The Siege of San Francisco and the Crisis of American Urbanism* (New York: Verso, 2000).

7. "Death Notice" circulated by Bryan Lee, of the Stain Gallery.

8. Cushman & Wakefield, *MarketBeat,* Year End—2001 Report (San Francisco, 2001).

9. Hal Cohen, "Invisible Cities: Is the Internet Making Urban Centers Obsolete?" *Industry Standard,* October 2, 2000.

10. Saskia Sassen, *The Global City: New York, London, Tokyo,* 2nd ed. (Princeton: Princeton University Press, 2001).

11. *New York* magazine was the most strident organ for boosting the cause of Silicon Alley, with a succession of cover stories—from its November 13, 1995 issue, which proclaimed "High Tech Boom Town" ("It's 1995, and suddenly New York is Cyber City") to the nostalgia-laden chronicle of the "Early True Believers" in February 2000.

12. In Lower Manhattan, where 60 million square feet of office space stood vacant at the beginning of the 1990s, the "information city" was one of the concepts the Alliance for Downtown New York pushed to revitalize commercial rents in the ailing financial district. Fifty-five Broad Street, formerly the multistory home of junk bond avatar Drexel Burnham, was retrofitted as a cyber showpiece and renamed the Information Technology Center to serve as an anchor for other "plug 'n' go" Internet-ready offices in the immediate vicinity. Renters were offered a lucrative range of tax abatements, rent exemptions, and up to 47 percent energy rate discounts.

13. At the height of the Internet boom in New York, the pursuit of relatively cheap office space had reached 40th Street, as the factories and warehouses in the garment district and the flower district were increasingly being converted for office use. Robert Calem, "Up, Up, and Away (Per Square Foot)," *New York Times,* January 16, 2000, C4. By 2000, the industry had all but exhausted the abundant inexpensive space between Midtown and Wall Street that had created the conditions for Silicon Alley's growth just five years earlier.

14. In figures supplied by the San Francisco office of Grubb and Ellis, a commercial real estate firm, Class A space in SoMa/Multimedia Gulch stood at an asking rate of $30.82 per square foot ($21.86 psf for Class B) by the end of 2001, down from highs of $73.63 ($61.17 psf for Class B) the year before. Since commercial space was not much in demand in the early 1990s, their earliest figures were from 1996, showing a much lower rate of $18.25 per square foot ($13.75 psf for Class B).

15. *New York Ascendant: The Commission on the Year 2000* (New York: Harper & Row, 1988).

16. By the end of 2001, commercial rents in Midtown South had fallen from their boom high of $45.65 per square foot to $38.74 per square foot, but the appreciation from 1995 levels (at $15.24 psf) was considerable. These figures were supplied by the New York office of Cushman and Wakefield, a commer-

cial real estate brokerage. In Boston, Class A commercial space fell 15 percent (less than New York) over the course of 2001. Ross Kerber, "Tech Fallout Lowers Commercial Rents," *Boston Globe,* June 28, 2002.

17. Joel Kotkin, *The New Geography: How the Digital Revolution Is Reshaping the American Landscape* (New York: Random House, 2000).

18. Malcolm Gladwell, "Designs for Working: Why Your Bosses Want to Turn Your Office into Greenwich Village," *New Yorker,* December 8, 2000, pp. 50–67.

19. Sally Whittle, "Keeping the Team Together," *Industry Standard,* April 24, 2000. David Brooks describes the offices of Pitney Bowes Credit Corporation in Connecticut, designed to "resemble a small village, with cobblestone-patterned carpets, faux gas lamps, a town-square-style clock, and street signs at the intersection of the hallways." *Bobos in Paradise,* p. 128.

20. Jane Jacobs, *The Death and Life of Great American Cities* (New York: Basic Books, 1961).

21. Neil Smith, *The New Urban Frontier: Gentrification and the Revanchist City* (New York: Routledge, 1996); Neil Smith and Peter Williams, eds., *Gentrification of the City* (Boston: Allen and Unwin, 1986); Brian Wallis, ed., *If You Lived Here: The City in Art, Theory, and Social Activism,* A Project by Martha Rosler (Seattle: Bay Press, 1991); Christopher Mele, *Selling the Lower East Side: Culture, Real Estate, and Resistance in New York City* (Minneapolis: University of Minnesota Press, 2000); Janet Abu-Lughod, ed., *From Urban Village to East Village* (Oxford: Blackwell, 1994); and Rosalyn Deutsche, *Evictions: Art and Spatial Politics* (Cambridge: MIT Press, 1996).

22. Sharon Zukin, *Loft Living: Culture and Capital in Urban Change* (Baltimore: Johns Hopkins University Press, 1982).

23. See Jerrold Siegel, *Bohemian Paris: Culture, Politics, and the Boundaries of Bourgeois Life, 1830–1930* (New York: Viking, 1986).

24. Ann Powers charts some of this recent history in *Weird Like Us: My Bohemian America* (New York: Simon & Schuster, 2000).

25. Abraham Maslow, *Motivation and Personality* (New York: Harper, 1954).

26. Bill Lessard and Steve Baldwin, NetSlaves: True Tales of Working on the Web (New York: McGraw-Hill, 2000), p. 246. See the Web site of NetSlaves (Horror Stories of Working on the Web) at <www.disobey.com/netslaves>.

27. See Note 78 in the National Endowment of the Arts Research Division Report on "Artist Employment in America," at <www.arts.endow.gov/pub/ResearchNotes.html>.

28. To figure in the BLS survey, "one must be working during the survey week and have described that job/work as one of eleven artist occupations." Respondents are asked to describe the job at which "they worked the most

number of hours in the survey week." Artists working more hours in other jobs outside the arts are classified as employed in those other occupations. By 1999, these amounted to an additional 295,000, for a total of 2,324,000 artists employed in the workforce. NEA Research Division Report on "Artist Employment in America," Note 76, June 2000.

29. Emily Martin analyzes the broader social and cultural contexts of the flexible industrial ideal in *Flexible Bodies: Tracking Immunity in American Culture—From the Days of Polio to the Age of AIDS* (Boston: Beacon Press, 1994).

30. Academic readers will recognize much of their own work mentality in this description. Indeed, their own traditions of sacrificial labor have helped to create a vast tier of contingent teachers in higher education, a sector that more and more resembles the casualized patterns of employment in corporate America. It is no small irony that the heavy hand of administrative management has descended hard upon the arts and education at the very moment it is being lifted from a corporate sector that has declared war on bureaucracy and is busy importing the work mentality of artists and intellectuals.

31. The project team, directed by Anne Balsamo, mounted an exhibition, *New Media, New Literacies*, at the San Jose Tech Museum of Innovation, March 2000.

32. Anna Muoio, "Great Ideas in Aisle 9," *Fast Company* 33 (April 2000): 46.

33. Joan Greenbaum, *In the Name of Efficiency: Management Theory and Shopfloor Practice in Data-Processing Work* (Philadelphia: Temple University Press, 1979), pp. 65–66.

34. Tracy Kidder, *The Soul of a New Machine* (Boston: Little, Brown, 1981), pp. 272–273.

35. Daniel Pink, "Free Agent Nation," *Fast Computer* 12 (December 1997/January 1998): 131.

36. Nina Munk, "The Price of Freedom," *New York Times Magazine*, March 5, 2000, p. 54.

37. Daniel H. Pink and Michael Warsaw, "The (Free-Agent) Declaration of Independence," *Fast Company* 12 (December 1997/January 1998): 152.

38. Daniel H. Pink, *Free Agent Nation: How America's New Independent Workers Are Transforming the Way We Live* (New York: Warner Books, 2001). See also Thomas W. Malone and Robert J. Laubacher, "The Dawn of the E-Lance Economy," *Harvard Business Review*, September 1998.

39. Lawrence Mishel, Jared Bernstein, and John Schmitt, *The State of Working America, 1996–1997* (Armonk, N.Y.: M. E. Sharpe, 1997), pp. 258–273.

40. Eva Jacobs, ed., *Handbook of U.S. Labor Statistics* (Lanham, Md.: Bernan Press, 2000), p. 138.

41. Lawrence Mishel, Jared Bernstein, and John Schmitt, *The State of Working America, 2000–2001* (Ithaca: Cornell University Press, 2001), pp. 245–254.

42. David Leonhardt, "Self-Employment on the Decline," *New York Times,* December 1, 2000.

43. Mishel, Bernstein, and Schmitt, *The State of Working America, 2000–2001*, p. 252.

44. Manuel Castells, *The Rise of the Network Society*, 2nd ed. (Oxford: Blackwell, 2000), pp. 285–289.

45. The Vizcaino case (*Vizcaino v. Microsoft*, 120 F.3d 1006 [9th Cir. 1997], cert. denied, 522 U.S. 1098 [1998]) was often acknowledged as a parable about the dark side of free agency. See Ron Lieber, "The Permatemps Contretemps," *Fast Company* 37 (August 2000): 198.

Chapter 6

1. For one of the most comprehensive, and last, examples of the genre of breathless group profiles, see "Silicon Alley 10003," Vanessa Grigoriadis's cover story on the Alley's "Original True Believers," in *New York Magazine.* March 6, 2000. Casey Hait and Stephen Weiss's *Digital Hustlers* is an oral history, featuring many of these founding figures.

2. SonicNet (Nicholas Butterworth) became part of the MTVi group when it was bought by Viacom. gURL.com (Rebecca Odes) was acquired by dELiA's. Urban Desires (Kyle Shannon, Chan Suh) submerged itself within Agency, Razorfish's chief rival in the Web consulting arena. Total New York (Peter Borthwick) was acquired by AOL. Word (Marisa Bowe) was bought by Zapata and folded in 2000. Feed (Stephen Johnson and Stefanie Syman) merged with Suck (Carl Steadman, Joey Anuff) as Automatic Media and folded in 2001.

3. Late in the day, Jason McCabe Calacanis, founder and editor of *Silicon Alley Reporter,* proposed the porn business model as the answer to all the mistakes made by content companies: "Over the past five years, while we were writing pitches and building demographic surveys, the pornographers were developing their own sophisticated, multi-leveled, and easy-to-use payment systems, including the most popular one, Adult Check, which allowed groups of sites to join the network and share revenues." "Our Second Biggest Mistake: Free Content (or, How Porn Could Save Salon)," *Silicon Alley Daily,* July 12, 2001.

4. According to the *3rd New York New Media Industry Survey* (New York New Media Association/PriceWaterhouseCoopers, March 2000), the average age of Silicon Alley employees was thirty-five, and the majority were male (62 percent) and white (74 percent).

5. Russell Simmons (with Nelson George), *Life and Def: Sex, Drugs, Money, and God* (New York: Crown, 2001), p. 172.

6. A similar wave of enterprise had produced Asian American portals and e-zines like A.Online, AsianAvenue.com, Click2Asia, AsianWired, and GoldSea, as well as Latino sites, like MiGente.com, Latino.com, Quepasa.com, and Loquesea.com.

7. National Telecommunications and Information Administration, U.S. Department of Commerce, "Falling Through the Net II: New Data on the Digital Divide" (Washington, D.C.: 1998) and "Falling Through the Net: Defining the Digital Divide" (Washington, D.C.: 1999).

8. Andrew Ross, "Net-Working: An Interview with McLean Mashingaidze Greaves, in *Technicolor: Race, Technology, and Everyday Life*, ed. Alondra Nelson, Thuy Linh Tu, and Alicia Headlam Hines (New York: NYU Press, 2001), p. 66.

9. By April 1999, Forrester Research ("The Digital Melting Pot") was reporting that 66 percent of Asian Americans households were online, compared to 23 percent of African Americans, 36 percent of Hispanic Americans, and 34 percent of Caucasian Americans. Ekaterina Walsh, the author of the Forrester report, found that Internet use numbers were higher than the federal figures when they included the use of computers and the Internet outside of the home. Blacks and Hispanics, in particular, were more likely to access the Internet at work or in libraries. In February 2001, Neilsen/Net Ratings estimated that between December 1999 and December 2000, the number of wired African Americans in the United States rose by 44 percent to 8.1 million.

10. Simmons, *Life and Def*, p. 4.

11. Ibid., p. 174.

12. Selwyn Seyfu Hinds, *Gunshots in My Cook-up: Bits and Bites of a Hip-Hop Caribbean Life* (New York: Pocket Books, 2002), pp. 4, 76.

13. Hip-hop itself had been a major growth field for black business. Black-owned record companies had a large stake in the musical field, and brands like Cross Colors, Karl Kani, Sean John, and Phat Farm held their own in the hip-hop fashion world. See Juliet Walker, *The History of Black Business in America: Capitalism, Race, Entrepreneurship* (New York: Macmillan Library Reference, Prentice Hall, 1998).

14. The most conspicuous holdout is the Johnson Publishing Corp., which still publishes *Ebony* and *Jet* magazines and remains the largest black-owned media company in the United States.

15. Paul Delany, "Unfocused Future for Minority-Owned Broadcast Outlets" (National Association of Minority Media Executives, February 2001), at <www.namme.org>.

16. For the record, no one, in the heat of the Napster moment, was ex-

pressing any sympathy for the record companies. The majors had misunderstood the Internet and would be embroiled in ham-fisted attempts to suppress and absorb Napsterization for many years to come.

17. The Canibus cut is included in the techie cult movie soundtrack *Office Space* (directed by Mike Judge, of Beavis and Butthead fame), which features the revolt of office workers against their corporate monolith. The soundtrack also features gangsta rap (Geto Boys, Ice Cube) to set off the wannabe gangsta antics of the movie's white protagonists.

18. William Julius Wilson, *When Work Disappears: The World of the New Urban Poor* (New York: Knopf, 1996). One side-effect of the loss of industrial and government jobs was a marked rise in the number of new black businesses, which showed a 26 percent increase in the mid-1990s. By the end of the decade, there were more than one million black businesses in the United States, most of them sole proprietorships. Lee Hubbard, "Getting Your Own: Small Business Ownership Is the Black American Dream," at *Africana.com,* September 4, 2001.

19. Alejandro Portes, Manuel Castells, and Lauren A. Benton, eds., *The Informal Economy: Studies in Advanced and Less Developed Countries* (Baltimore: Johns Hopkins University Press, 1989).

Chapter 7

1. In his chapter on "The Financialization of America" in *Arrogant Capital: Washington, Wall Street, and the Frustration of American Politics* (Boston: Little, Brown, 1994), Kevin Phillips argues that the United States is following the decadent course of earlier financial powerhouses like Spain, Holland, and Britain by becoming a rentier nation of speculators and investors who invest only in overseas production.

2. For the role played by institutional investors, see Michael Useem, *Investor Capitalism: How Money Managers Are Changing the Face of Corporate America* (New York: Basic Books, 1996). On the contradictions between worker ownership and shareholder influence, see Doug Henwood, *Wall Street: How It Works and for Whom* (New York: Verso, 1997), pp. 288–291.

3. Jill Andresky Fraser charts the progress of this plight in her profile of late-twentieth-century office work. *White Collar Sweatshop: The Deterioration of Work and Its Rewards in Corporate America* (New York: Norton, 2001).

4. Pope John Paul II, Address to "Centesimus Annus" Foundation, September 13, 1999.

5. Tom Nadeau has written a colorful tract on the subject of what he calls this "new underclass" of "super-skilled workers who can't get a decent job." *Seven Lean Years: America's New High Tech Underclass* (self-published, 1999).

6. Amazon workers in Seattle affiliated with the Washington Alliance of Technology Workers (WashTech/CWA Local 37083). The United Food and Commercial Workers were active in efforts to organize workers at Amazon's regional distribution centers. Etown folded in February 2001, shortly before the union election could take place and amid a ruckus caused by the employer's illegal interference with the workers' right to organize. Its employees were affiliated with the Northern California Media Workers Guild, a local of Communication Workers of America. Steven Greenhouse, "Dot-Com Is Set for a Union Vote," *New York Times,* January 9, 2001; Katharine Mieszkowski, "The Real Dot-Communists Stand Up," Salon.com (December 8, 2000); Farhad Manjoo, "Unions: Next Dot-Com Revolution?" *Wired News,* December 2, 2000; Troy Wolverton, "Will High-Tech Chaos Finally Give Birth to Unions?" CNET News.com (January 16, 2001). The Virgilio workers' action is documented at <http://web.tiscali.it/tutearancioni/index.html>.

7. During the union dispute, a chapter on Amazon's internal Web site was headlined, "Reasons a Union Is Not Desirable." Steven Greenhouse, "Amazon Fights Union Activity," *New York Times,* November 29, 2000.

8. See WashTech president Mike Blain and organizer Gretchen Wilson's account of "Organizing in the New Economy: The Amazon.com Campaign," *WorkingUSA* 5 (Fall 2001): 32–58. In January 1999, over thirty unions sponsored a Labor Online conference, organized by the Brooklyn College Graduate Center for Worker Education, to chart the labor movement's use of high technology and to examine the future of organizing in the high-tech industry. Union reps showed up in force, but there were very few employees from Silicon Alley. <http://www.laboronline.org>

9. Sean Donahue, "New Dean of American Labor," *Business 2.0,* April 2000; Steven Greenhouse, "The Most Innovative Figure in Silicon Valley?" *New York Times,* November 14, 1999, p. 32.

10. Many WWWACies purchased health, life, and disability insurance packages through the organization in association with Working Today, a nonprofit that ran a Portable Benefit Network. A survey of Silicon Alley employees, conducted by Working Today in 2001, found that 30 percent had no health insurance and that 80 percent had switched between independent work and full-time employment at least once in the previous three years. The report observes that "public policy and the American system of delivering benefits to working people—particularly health insurance—have not kept pace with the changing structure of work." *Mobile Worker, Immobile Benefits* (June 2001) <www.workingtoday.org>.

11. New York New Media Industry Survey, *Climate Study,* January 2001 (PriceWaterhouseCoopers/NYNMA).

12. In their useful analysis of a smaller Silicon Alley consultancy, Monique

Girard and David Stark refer to this kind of organizational form as "heterar-chy." It exhibited minimal hierarchy and maximal heterogeneity, and account-ability was lateral rather than vertical. "Distributing Intelligence and Organiz-ing Diversity in New Media Projects," forthcoming in *Environment and Planning* (2002).

13. Terrence Deal and Allan Kennedy, *Corporate Cultures: The Rites and Rituals of Corporate Life* (Reading, Mass.: Addison-Wesley, 1982), pp. 157–158.

14. In Kaplan's world, employees who had chosen to work at obviously doomed companies were often indicted without remorse, but the choicest deri-sion was reserved for managerial arrogance: "Rumor has it shopnow.com laid off around 117 people—one day after management brought them all to a baseball game" was a typical telegrammatic report, laced with bittersweet scorn. By con-trast, the veteran NetSlaves site ("Horror Stories of Working on the Web," at www.disobey.com/netslaves/) preferred to air employee complaints in their own words and in reasoned narrative form. "We put people out front," explained co-founder Steve Baldwin. "We don't focus on the companies. There's more peda-gogical value in seeing how human beings have reacted to this situation."

15. Evan I. Schwartz, *Digital Darwinism: 7 Breakthrough Business Strate-gies for Surviving in the Cutthroat Web Economy* (New York: Broadway Books, 1999).

16. Robert Tomasko, *Downsizing: Reshaping the Corporation for the Fu-ture* (New York: AMACOM, 1987), p. 192.

17. The classic commentary about the end of the social contract in heavy industry is Barry Bluestone and Bennett Harrison, *Deindustrialization of America: Plant Closings, Community Abandonment, and the Dismantling of Basic Industries* (New York: Basic Books, 1982). See also Mike Davis, *Prison-ers of the American Dream: Politics and Economy in the History of the U.S. Working Class* (London: Verso, 1986); and David Brody, *Workers in Indus-trial America: Essays on the Twentieth-Century Struggle* (New York: Oxford University Press, 1980). For accounts of downsizing, see Charles Heckscher, *White-Collar Blues: Management Loyalties in an Age of Corporate Restruc-turing* (New York: Basic Books, 1995); Alan Downs and Camille Stogner, *Cor-porate Executions: The Ugly Truth About Layoffs—How Corporate Greed Is Shattering Lives, Companies, and Communities* (New York: AMACOM, 1995); and David Gordon, *Fat and Mean: The Corporate Squeezing of Work-ing Americans and the Myth of Managerial Downsizing* (New York: Martin Kessler, 1996).

18. Richard Sennett offers a comprehensive portrait of this mutation in *The Corrosion of Character: The Personal Consequences of Work in the New Cap-italism* (New York: Norton, 1998).

19. John Bourdeau, "Laid–Off Employees Get the Option of Doing Good," *San Jose Mercury News,* May 5, 2001.

20. Tiziana Terranova develops this line of argument in *Network Culture: The Cultural Politics of Cybernetic Communications* (London: Pluto, 2002).

21. Heckscher, *White-Collar Blues,* p. 55.

22. Katherine Newman, *Falling from Grace: The Experience of Downward Mobility in the American Middle Class* (New York: Free Press, 1988).

23. In some cases, as with the much publicized internal policies of Enron, employees, whose identities were electronically traced by managers, were fired for posting messages critical of the company. Alex Berenson, "Enron Fired Workers for Complaining Online," *New York Times,* January 21, 2002.

24. The lawsuits were aimed at recovering unpaid overtime and seeking compensation for fatal and severe health problems incurred by workers in the company's fabs and assembly plants. In *Intel vs. Hamidi,* a critical free speech case in cyberlaw, the company tried to prevent the FACEIntel founder from using email to alert current employees about abusive or discriminatory employment practices and toxic health hazards at the company.

25. Louis Rosenfeld and Peter Morville, *Designing Web Usability: The Information Architecture for the World Wide Web* (Sebastopol, Calif.: O'Reilly, 1998); Jennifer Fleming, Richard Koman, eds. *Web Navigation: Designing the User Experience* (Sebastopol, Calif.: O'Reilly, 1998); and Jared Spool, ed., *Web Site Usability: A Designer's Guide* (San Francisco: Morgan Kaufmann, 1999).

26. Jakob Nielsen, *Designing Web Usability: The Practice of Simplicity* (Indianapolis: New Riders, 1999); Jakob Neilsen, *Usability Engineering* (Boston: Academic Press, 1993); and Jacob Neilsen and Marie Tahir, *Homepage Usability: 50 Websites Deconstructed* (Indianapolis: New Riders, 2001).

27. The survey was conducted on the ex-razorfish listserv, which had 813 subscribers. There were 204 respondents.

Related occupation in smaller company: 17.7%
Related occupation in firm of similar size: 16.6%
Freelance contractor/consultant: 13.8%
Own business or startup: 11.1%
Academic: 8.3%
Nonrelated occupation in firm of same size: 6.6%
Other startup: 6.6%
Total career switch: 5.8%
Employment of any sort in a large corporation: 5.5%
Unemployed: 2.0%

A significant number of respondents said they were working with other ex-fish or had obtained employment through ex-fish contacts.

Chapter 8

1. Kenneth Flamm, *Creating the Computer: Government, Industry, and High Technology* (Washington, D.C.: Brookings Institution, 1988).

2. Katie Hafner and Matthew Lyon, *Where Wizards Stay Up Late: The Origins of the Internet* (New York: Simon and Schuster, 1996); Peter H. Salus, *Casting the Net: From ARPANET and Beyond* (Reading, Mass.: Addison-Wesley, 1995); Ronda Hauben and Michael Hauben, *Netizens: On the History and Impact of Usenet and the Internet* (Los Alamitos, Calf.: IEEE Computer Society, 1997).

3. CoffeeCup's CEO declared: "In this time of conflict of ideals and principles, it should be noted that I as the spokesman and president of an American company have faith in the nations of Islam. In no way do we hold any mistrust or responsibility of [sic] the attacks on the U.S. with the religion of Islam." The CEO's missives attracted enough attention (as intended) to be circulated on several listservs.

4. Razorfish did respond to 9/11 in one virtuoso way. The New York office undertook its largest pro bono effort to date by building a Web site <http://www.aroundgroundzero.net> for a "temporary memorial map," *Around Ground Zero,* produced (under the direction of Laura Kurgan) by the Temporary Memorials Committee of the New York New Visions Coalition for Rebuilding New York. The Web site contains successive versions of the map, documenting the changes undergone by the disaster site.

5. Lisa Fickenscher, "A Close Shave for Razorfish," *Crain's,* December 24, 2001.

6. Jared Spool, one of the most savvy of the usability gurus, acknowledged as much in an interview: "So, which Web site capitalized on usability? None really. We've never seen a site that succeeds more than 50 percent of the time, let alone 60 percent or 70 percent of the time. We don't know what one looks like. We certainly don't know what it takes to build one. Oh, we can pretend we do. But we really don't, because we never have seen one. And what's worse is that the sites that have come closest didn't use what we've been preaching. What does that say about what we know?" "The Usability of Usability," *WebWord.com* (July 25, 2001).

7. Andrew Ross, "Sweated Labor in Cyberspace," *New Labor Forum* 4 (Spring/Summer 1999): 47–56.

8. Joseph Blasi, *Employee Ownership: Revolution or Ripoff?* (Cambridge: Ballinger, 1988).

9. This storied history of autonomy includes the Paris Commune, the workers' and soldiers' soviets of the Russian revolutions of 1905 and 1917, and the failed Hungarian, Italian, and German revolutions of 1918–1920; the autonomous committees of Republican Spain during the Civil War; the long se-

ries of efforts in Warsaw bloc countries to resist central control of production; and the *autogestion* movement in France, Algeria, and Yugoslavia.

10. A number of books that celebrate the industrial culture of Silicon Valley support the proposition that engineers grabbed power from the big financiers. *The New New Thing: A Silicon Valley Story* (New York, Norton, 2000), Michael Lewis's breathless biography of Silicon Graphics and Netscape founder Jim Clark, "the maker of the fastest money ever made legally," comes closest to a seamless weld between wealth worship and "the revolt of the engineers." In Lewis's view, the result was "near the core of the American experience."

11. Karl Marx, *Grundrisse: Foundations of the Critique of Political Economy,* trans. Martin Nicolaus (New York: Random House, 1973), p. 706.

12. Paolo Virno and Michael Hardt, eds., *Radical Thought in Italy: A Potential Politics* (Minneapolis: University of Minnesota Press, 1996); Maurizio Lazzarato, *Immaterial Labor, Mass Intellectuality, New Constitution, Post-Fordism and All That* (London: Red Notes, 1994); Michael Hardt and Antonio Negri, *Empire* (Cambridge: Harvard University Press, 2000); and Nick Dyer-Witheford, *Cyber-Marx: Cycles and Circuits of Struggle in High-Technology Capitalism* (Urbana: University of Illinois Press, 1999).

13. Pekka Himanen and Linus Torwalds, *The Hacker Ethic and the Spirit of the Information Age* (New York: Random House, 2001); Steven Levy, *Hackers: Heroes of the Computer Revolution* (New York: Anchor Press, 1984); Eric S. Raymond, *The Cathedral and the Bazaar: Musings on Linux and Open Source by an Accidental Revolutionary* (New York: O'Reilly, 1999). Also see Richard Stallman's Free Software project, at <www.gnu.org>.

14. Lawrence Lessig, *The Future of Ideas: The Fate of the Commons in a Connected World* (New York: Random House, 2001); Siva Vaidhyanathan, *Copyrights and Copywrongs: The Rise of Intellectual Property and How It Threatens Creativity* (New York: NYU Press, 2001).

15. Thornton May, in a roundtable on "Is Faster Better?" *Fast Company* 13 (February 1998): 132. At the time, May ran Cambridge Technology Partner's Management Lab. When he moved to Guardent Inc., he chose the title of Chief Awareness Officer.

16. Gina Neff, "Risk Relations: The New Uncertainties of Work," *WorkingUSA: The Journal of Labor and Society* 5 (Fall 2001): 59–68.

17. Ulrich Beck, *The Brave New World of Work,* trans. Patrick Camiller (Cambridge: Polity Press, 2000), p. 84.

18. William Morris, review of *Looking Backward,* by Edward Bellamy, *Commonweal,* June 22, 1889.

INDEX